GREAT CAMPAIGNS OF WORLD WAR II

ISLAND BOOKS

List of contributors includes:
Major-General R H Barry
C P Campbell
Paul Carell
Peter Elstob
Major-General Sir Francis de Guingand
Guy Hartcup
Col Robert D Heinl Jr
Lt-Cmdr Peter Kemp
Major K J Macksey
Dudley Pope
Denis Richards
Dr Jürgen Rohwer
R W Thompson

Co-ordinating editor: J B Davies

This edition published in 2002 by
S. WEBB & SON (Distributors) LTD.
Telford Place, Penraeth Road, Menai Bridge
Isle of Anglesey, LL59 5RW

© 2002 Little, Brown and Company (UK)

This book is adapted from
Great Campaigns of World War II
© Little, Brown and Company (UK)

ISBN 1-85605-670-8

Production by Omnipress, Eastbourne
Printed in Singapore

Little, Brown and Company (UK)
Brettenham House
Lancaster Place
London WC2E 7EN

Introduction

This book is divided into four sections which tell the story of some of the most crucial and bitterly fought contests in the history of warfare. Each one of the campaigns was complete in itself, but together they all had a vital bearing on the outcome of the entire war.

The book opens with the *Battle of Britain*. In July 1940, when Göring promised Hitler he would smash the RAF within a month, Britain stood alone against dictatorship. Invasion was imminent. But, thanks to the tireless heroism of the pilots and ground crews of Fighter Command, the precarious superiority of their Spitfires and Hurricanes, and, ultimately, the morale of the entire country, which are all well documented and photographed in this book, that invasion was 'post-poned indefinitely'. By 17 September 1940 the real *Battle of Britain* was over.

The Desert War, seemingly self-contained and remote, was fought in the wastes of North Africa, from September 1940 to May 1943. The book describes in detail the constant see-sawing of activity over a 1,500-mile front, the great clashes of men and machinery, but above all, the great generalship that made this war, and its battles legendary.

While victory in the desert was opening up southern Europe to the Allies, the decision was taken to invade the north. Hitler had boasted to his generals that he was the greatest fortress builder of all time. Buried beneath millions of tons of concrete, behind miles of barbed wire, mines, and guns of every calibre, the 'Atlantic Wall' was the rampart of the Nazis' conquest with the sea as its ditch. Against this mighty bastion the Western Allies pitched their courage, ingenuity, and organizing skill. Operation Overlord, launched on 6 June, 1944 – *D-Day* – was the beginning of the end for Hitler. But the book tells not just the story of that one day, but of the months of careful planning and strategic debate that preceded it.

The Battle of the Pacific introduced the Japanese into the fray and was mainly a struggle between them and the United States. Tacitly encouraged by Hitler, the Japanese began a course of economic and territorial expansion in late 1941. They quickly acquired huge land and sea domains, but in six months had overstepped their ability to defend these vast areas. The book takes the reader through Midway, Guadalcanal, Iwo Jima and Okinawa to the eventual and unforgettable climax – the atom bomb explosions at Hiroshima and Nagasaki – and the sudden end of World War II.

Left: US Marines crouch behind a rock to avoid the blast as a heavy explosive charge blows up a cave connected to a Japanese blockhouse on Iwo Jima in March 1945

Contents

On the road near the town of Carentan, a US doctor is attending to a wounded man who has been hit by sniper in the aftermath of the D-Day landings in France

This extraordinary view is taken from a German Air Gunner's position during an attack on a British plane over southern England

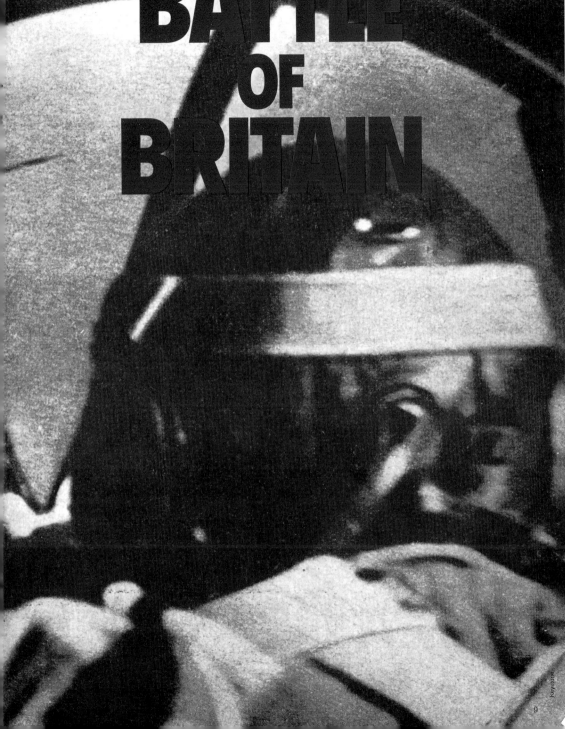

BATTLE OF BRITAIN

Keystone

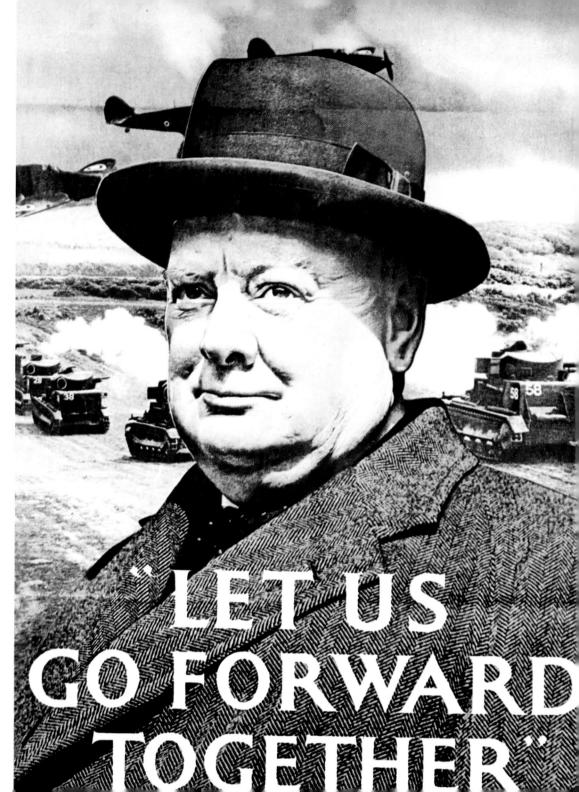

"LET US GO FORWARD TOGETHER"

"The gratitude of every home in our Island, in our Empire, and indeed throughout the world, except in the abodes of the guilty, goes out to the British airmen, who, undaunted by odds, unwearied in their constant challenge and mortal danger, are turning the tide of world war by their prowess and devotion. Never in the field of human conflict was so much owed by so many to so few."

Winston Churchill, 20 August 1940

AIR POWER 1939

After the Armistice in November 1918 the greatly expanded armed forces of the Allies were hastily and clumsily demobilized. Improvised war organizations were dismantled, and the watchwords of the British government were economy and retrenchment. The war had been won, there was no visible threat to Allied security, and Great Britain and France were swept by a wave of anti-war feeling, largely induced by the terrible casualties and intolerable conditions of trench warfare.

In 1925 the League of Nations had set up a Preparatory Commission to explore the ground for a general disarmament conference. Progress in this field is never rapid, and for many years the commission was involved in interminable difficulties and arguments. Eventually a Disarmament Conference was convened in Geneva in 1932, at which proposals for outlawing air bombardment and drastically limiting the loaded weight of military aircraft were discussed. Hoping for success in these negotiations, the British government declined to authorize the design and construction of any effective bomber aircraft. In addition, it had introduced in 1924 what became known as the 'Ten-year Rule', which postulated that there would be no major war for ten years. Unfortunately each successive year was deemed to be the starting point of this tranquil epoch, and so the period always remained at ten years.

The Disarmament Conference finally broke up in May 1934 without achieving any result whatsoever. But meanwhile Hitler had come to power in Germany, and was clearly bent on a massive programme of rearmament. In 1933 the British government at last permitted the issue of Air Staff requirements for a high-performance multi-gun fighter, which in due course produced the Hurricane and Spitfire. It is often asserted that these two aircraft, and especially the Spitfire, were forced on a reluctant Air Ministry by a far-sighted aircraft industry and its capable designers. There is not a word of truth in this. Both aircraft were designed, ordered, and built to Air Ministry specifications.

Even after the collapse of the Disarmament Conference in 1934 the British government was reluctant to rearm. Alone among nations the British seem to think that if they rearm it will bring about an arms race. The result of this curious delusion is that they usually start when the other competitors are half-way round the course. The bomber force was therefore given a very low priority, but development of the fighters was allowed to proceed, though without any undue haste.

In 1935 two British ministers, Mr Anthony Eden and Sir John Simon, visited Germany. They reported that Hitler's rearmament in the air had proceeded much farther and faster than the British government had believed possible. This was because the Germans had made a secret agreement to train the Soviet air force, which enabled them to keep in being a sizeable corps of expert pilots and technicians. The government was alarmed, and ordered quantity production of the Hurricanes and Spitfires before the prototype had even flown— the so-called 'ordering off the drawing-board'.

Lord Trenchard, chief of the Air

Gloster Gladiator II
Gross weight: 4,864 lb. *Span:* 32 ft 3 in.
Length: 27 ft 5 in. *Engine:* 840 hp Bristol Mercury VIII. *Armament:* 4 x ·303 machine-guns.
Crew: 1. *Speed:* 257 mph at 14,600 ft. *Ceiling:* 33,500 ft. *Range:* 444 miles.   The RAF's last front-line biplane fighter, the Gladiator, fought in Norway and France where it inflicted casualties on far superior opponents. During the Battle of Britain only one squadron operated the type over the far north of the Home Islands, but the tough little fighter went on to win greater laurels in the Middle East and the Mediterranean

Staff from 1919 to 1928, had always believed that in air defence the bomber was as important as the fighter. He maintained that the air war should be fought in the skies over the enemy's territory, and he therefore advocated a bomber force powerful enough to take the offensive, and attack an enemy's vital centres from the outset. He argued that this would rob an enemy of the initiative and throw his air force on to the defensive.

Eventually Trenchard's views were accepted by the British government, and in the air defence of Great Britain two-thirds of the squadrons were to be bombers and one-third fighters. But because it was thought that the bombers were offensive while the fighters were defensive in character, it was judged that the building up of fighter strength would not be liable to trigger off an arms race. The seventeen authorized fighter squadrons were in existence by 1930, but at that date no more than twelve of the thirty-five authorized bomber squadrons had been formed, most of them equipped with small short-range day bombers. In 1935 the alarm caused by German rearmament in the air occasioned a further shift of emphasis in favour of the fighters. A system of radio-location, later called radar, which would provide invaluable early warning and make it possible to track incoming raids, was pioneered by Robert Watson-Watt, and given all possible encouragement.

At the outbreak of war in September 1939 the odds against the RAF, in terms of modern aircraft, were about four to one. Although money had been poured out like water during the years since the Munich crisis, it had been too late to redress the balance. Only time—as much time as possible— could do that.

La Panne beach: destroyed AA guns abandoned at Dunkirk by the British Expeditionary Force

IN FRANCE DEFEAT
IN BRITAIN PREPARATION

Evacuees leave London (above) and they still carried their gas masks as they paddled

For the children, filling sand bags was all good fun

CHURCHMAN'S CIGARETTES

REMOVAL OF INCENDIARY BOMB WITH SCOOP AND HOE

CHURCHMAN'S CIGARETTES

THE CIVILIAN RESPIRATOR—HOW TO ADJUST IT

CHURCHMAN'S CIGARETTES

EQUIPPING YOUR REFUGE ROOM—8

CHURCHMAN'S CIGARETTES

TYPES OF SPLINTER-PROOF WALL

A woman warden on duty. (Left) Cigarette cards from a series on air raid precautions

LUFTWAFFE: THE FLAWED WEAPON

Heinkel He 111 B2

Gross weight: 22,046 lb. *Span:* 74 ft 2 in.
Length: 57 ft 5 in. *Engine:* 2 x 950 hp DB 600.
Armament: 3 x 7·9-mm machine-guns. *Crew:* 4.
Speed: 186 mph at ground level. *Ceiling:* 22,966 ft.
Range: 1,030 miles. *Bomb load:* 3,307 lb.
The B2 version of the He 111 served with the
Condor Legion in the Spanish Civil War,
outpacing all opposing fighters and carrying out
unescorted raids at will. But the resulting
over-confidence was shattered by opposition
from Spitfires and Hurricanes in 1940 and the
He 111 was soon relegated to night duties

**German Fighter Pilot,
2nd Lieutenant**

A German 2nd Lieutenant fighter pilot began
training at an elementary flying training school
which entailed gliding on Course 1, elementary
flying on Course 2, and single-engine fighter
training on Course 3. He then went on to
advanced training and lastly to his operational
training unit : altogether it took seven to eight
months and 107 to 112 hours at the controls.
He wore the national eagle emblem on his right
and pilot's insigne on his lower left breast. On his
visored cap, more rakish than others in the army,
was the national rosette flanked by oak leaves
and spreading wings surmounted by a

flying eagle. Yellow piping and a large 'W'
decorated his epaulettes ; his collar patch was an
eagle and oak leaves on a yellow background.
He wore jackboots, grey-blue wool-rayon
breeches, jacket with patch pockets, grey shirt,
black tie and a Sam Browne belt with
eagle-emblem buckle. His flying suit had
zippered slash pockets and his flying boots were
lined. He had passed a rigid physical
examination and was eligible for pilot training
after the age of 18. Under normal conditions,
Luftwaffe pilots enjoyed better food than the rest
of the army and the pay was higher

1	Visual dive indicator
2	Gun sight
3	Artificial horizon
4	Compass repeater
5	Speedometer
6	Boost pressure
7	Altimeter
8	Rev counter
9	Flap indicator
10	Intercom connection
11	Crash pad
12	Manual engine pump
13	Engine priming pump
14	Electrics panel (radio)
15	Oil cooler flap control
16	Rudder bar pedal
17	Target view window
18	Control column
19	Target view window flap control
20	Fuel metering hand priming pump
21	Throttle
22	Starter switch
23	Main electrics switch
24	Coolant temperature
25	Fuel contents
26	Oil temperature
27	Oil contents
28	Compass
29	Oil pressure gauge
30	Clock
31	Dive pre-set indicator
32	Fuel pressure gauge
33	Radio altimeter
34	Rate of climb indicator
35	Water cooler flap indicator

Junkers Ju 87 B2 'Stuka' Cockpit

Junkers Ju 87 B2 'Stuka'
Gross weight: 9,370 lb. *Span:* 45 ft 3½ in.
Length: 36 ft 1 in. *Engine:* 1,400 hp Junkers
Jumo 211 D. *Armament:* 3 x 7·9-mm
machine-guns. *Crew:* 2. *Speed:* 232 mph at
13,500 ft. *Ceiling:* 26,248 ft. *Range:* 370 miles.
Bomb load: 1,540 lb.   The famous Stuka
enjoyed tremendous success during the early
stages of Hitler's blitzkriegs in Poland, France and
Scandinavia. But during the Battle of Britain
Stukas suffered severe losses against the
superior Spitfires and Hurricanes, and were
withdrawn from the spearhead of the attack

Messerschmitt Bf 109 E-4

Gross Weight: 5,530 lb. *Span:* 32 ft 4½ in.
Length: 28 ft. 8 in. *Engine:* 1,150 hp DB 601A.
Armament: 2 x 7·92-mm machine-guns;
2 x 20-mm cannon. *Speed:* 357 mph at 12,300 ft.
Ceiling: 36,000 ft. *Range:* 412 miles.   This was
the aircraft of Adjutant of J.G.3 'Udet' Franz von
Werra, which crashed in Kent on 5 September
1940. Von Werra was the only German officer to
escape his captors and return to Germany during
the Second World War

MESSERSCHMITT Bf 109

Bf 109 V-1 (top)
Prototype of the Bf 109 which first flew in
September 1935, powered by a 695 hp Rolls-
Royce Kestrel V engine because of the shortage of
Jumo 210 units

Bf 109 B-1 (second)
Span: 32 ft 4½ in. *Length:* 28 ft 6½ in. *Engine:*
635 hp Jumo 210D. *Armament:* 1 x 20·mm
cannon ; 2 x 7·9-mm machine-guns. *Speed:*
292 mph at 13,100 ft. *Ceiling:* 26,575 ft.   One
of the fighter types which equipped the Condor
Legion during the Spanish Civil War

Bf 109 D-1 (third)
Powered by the 960 hp DB 600 engine which
gave an increased speed of 323 mph

Bf 109 E-3 (bottom)
Span: 32 ft 4¼ in. *Length:* 28 ft 3¾ in. *Engine:*
1,100 hp DB 601A. *Armament:* 3 x 20-mm
cannon ; 2 x 7·92-mm machine-guns. *Speed:*
354 mph at 12,300 ft. *Ceiling:* 36,000 ft.
Known throughout the Luftwaffe as 'Emil', this
was the principal fighter type used during the
Battle of Britain

Boulton Paul Defiant Mk I
Span: 39 ft 4 in. *Length:* 35 ft 4 in. *Engine:*
1,030 hp Rolls-Royce Merlin III. *Armament:*
4 x ·303 in. machine-guns in power-operated
turret. *Speed:* 303 mph at 16,500 ft. *Ceiling:*
30,350 ft.   A modernised version of the
two-seat patrol fighter concept of 1918, the
Defiant was an easy target for German
single-seaters

RAF Fighter Pilot, Pilot Officer
A Pilot Officer, lowest commissioned rank in the
RAF, began training as an Aircraftsman II at an
initial training school and first flew on his
two-month elementary course, soloing after about
seven hours' instruction on a Tiger Moth. After
another four months, on Proctors, he qualified for
his wings and commission, then went to an
operational training unit to fly fighters with
experienced instructors. Altogether he would
have spent over a year in training and up to
200 hours in the air as well as 'blind flying' time in
a Link trainer. His minimum age was 18,
maximum 35 ; average height was 5 ft $8\frac{1}{2}$ in. He
had passed a written entrance examination, a
physical examination, and a colour blindness
test. He wore either a serge woollen blue-grey
uniform or a four patch-pocket barathea with
blue shirt, black tie and black shoes. His rank
insigne was a 'half-narrow' blue and grey ring
around both sleeves ; his wings were white-drab
silk with a crown over the RAF monogram and
brown silk laurel wreath. He was paid 11
shillings a day, plus £25 a year flying pay and
dependents' allowance

ROYAL AIR FORCE: BATTLE AGAINST TIME

Cockpit of a Spitfire Mk II
Pilot's eye-view of the Spitfire's business end.
With an eight-gun armament, constant speed
propeller, retracting undercarriage, and 1,175
horsepower engine, a complex array of controls
had to be shoehorned into a small space. The
bucket seat took the pilot's parachute

THE SPITFIRE

Supermarine Spitfire II
Weight: 6,317 lb. *Length:* 29 ft 11 in. *Span:*
36 ft 10 in. *Engine:* 1 x 1,150 hp Rolls-Royce
Merlin. *Speed:* 357 mph at 1,700 ft. *Range:* 500
miles. *Crew:* 1. *Armament:* 8 x ·303 machine-guns.
The Supermarine Spitfire remains the symbol
of the Battle of Britain. Although outnumbered by
the Hurricane, its graceful lines, near perfect
handling, and eight-gun punch made it a legend
in the hands of the pilots of Fighter Command.
Although the Spitfire underwent development
throughout the war, the whine of a well-tuned
Merlin engine and the flash of an elliptical wing,
for an Englishman at least, will always evoke the
summer of 1940

Spitfire Mk Ia

Spitfire Mk II

Spitfire Mk IIa

DL◉M 8194

1

1. Messerschmitt 109E

Known to Luftwaffe pilots
as the 'Emil', the 109E was at
least as fast as the Spitfire
but was found to be less
manœuvrable, though more
so than the Hurricane.
Always handicapped by its
short range, its
performance as a fighter
was further restricted by a
bomb load later in the
battle, when pressed into
service in a fighter/bomber
role.
Armament: Two 7·9-mm
machine-guns and two
20-mm cannons.
Max speed: 357 mph

2

2. Messerschmitt 110

Göring's folly: the cream of
the Luftwaffe fighter
strength was deployed in
'destroyer' units, intended
to smash through the
fighter defences and
provide long-range escort
for the bombers. Against
the Spitfire and Hurricane,
however, the Me-110s had
finally to be provided with
escorts themselves, for their
lack of manœuvrability
meant that their powerful
armament was all too often
useless.
Armament: Two 20-mm
cannons, four 7·9-mm
machine-guns, one free-
mounted 7·9-mm gun.
Max speed: 349 mph

3

4

5

8

9

8. Supermarine Spitfire

The Spitfire fighter was the most agile machine in the battle—it could out-manoeuvre even the Me-109E. Another vital superiority was its fire-power: eight wing-mounted Brownings which, though out-ranged by the German cannon, held a decisive concentration of rounds per second. In the Battle of Britain the Spitfire also held the advantage of fighting on home ground, unfettered by the range handicap of the 109E.
Armament: Eight ·303-inch machine-guns.
Max speed: 361 mph

9. Hawker Hurricane

Britain's first monoplane fighter was the numerical mainstay of RAF Fighter Command in the Battle of Britain. The Hurricane's ideal role was that of bomber-interceptor; as a rule, only the Spitfire could tackle the Me-109 on level terms, though the Hurricane scored notable successes against the Me-110. During the battle the Hurricane was already being replaced by the Spitfire as the standard RAF fighter.
Armament: Eight ·303-inch machine-guns.
Max speed: 328 mph

3. Junkers 87

The famous gull-winged Stuka was the main weapon which Göring turned against the RAF fighter bases. But the easy victories of past campaigns had been won in the absence of adequate fighter opposition, and RAF pilots found the Stuka an easy prey. Severe losses in operations throughout August destroyed its reputation as the all-conquering weapon of the Luftwaffe, and the Ju-87 was withdrawn from the spearhead of the attack.
Bomb load: One 1,102-lb, four 110-lb bombs.
Max speed: 217 mph

4. Junkers 88

The Ju-88 was the most versatile aircraft in the Luftwaffe's armoury for the entire war, serving as level bomber, dive-bomber, and night-fighter, as well as carrying out valuable reconnaissance duties. It was used by the Luftwaffe as a medium bomber in the Battle of Britain; but neither speed nor its comparatively high number of defending machine-guns was adequate protection from the fire-power of Spitfires and Hurricanes.
Bomb load: 5,510 lb
Max speed: 292 mph

5. Heinkel 111

The standard level bomber of the Luftwaffe at the time of the Battle of Britain, the He-111 suffered from its design as a medium bomber ideal for Continental operations but handicapped — as were all German twin-engined bombers — by the distances to targets in the north of England. Göring was convinced that its use in mass would prove decisive; but the He-111, it was found, was unable to beat off determined RAF fighter attacks.
Bomb load: 5,510 lb
Max speed: 258 mph

6. Dornier 17

The Do-17 was the Luftwaffe's veteran bomber: the type first saw service in the Spanish Civil War. Despite subsequent modifications, it was very weak in defensive fire, especially to attacks from below and to the rear. Known as the 'Flying Pencil' from its slim fuselage, the Do-17 was often confused with the British Hampden bomber, many of which were fired at by their own anti-aircraft guns. Its slender lines dictated a light bomb load.
Bomb load: 2,210 lb
Max speed: 270 mph

7. Dornier 215

This variant was a development of the basic design of the Do-17 with the installation of more powerful Daimler-Benz engines. The Do-215 was faster than the Do-17—fast enough to tax the lower-rated British engines of the early Spitfires and Hurricanes in a chase. In its light bomb-load and weak defence armament, however, the Do-215 was as handicapped as the Do-17.
Bomb load: 2,215 lb
Max speed: 311 mph

6

7

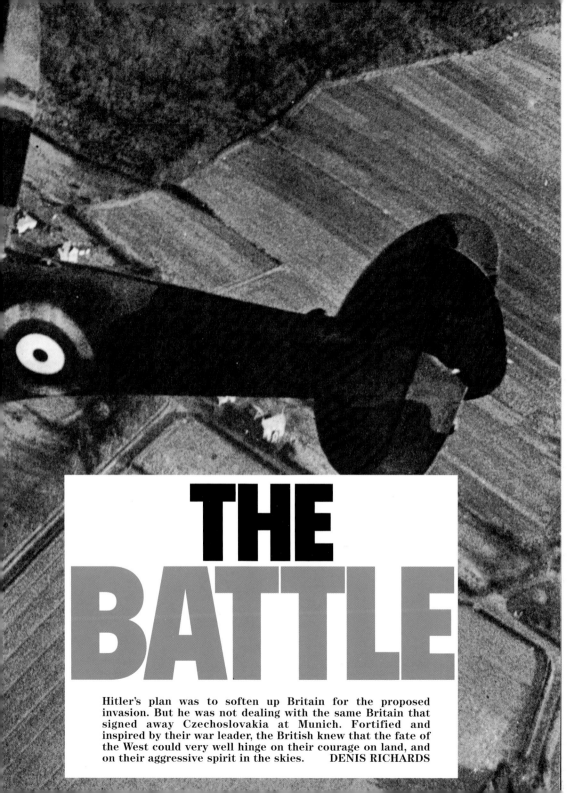

THE
BATTLE

Hitler's plan was to soften up Britain for the proposed invasion. But he was not dealing with the same Britain that signed away Czechoslovakia at Munich. Fortified and inspired by their war leader, the British knew that the fate of the West could very well hinge on their courage on land, and on their aggressive spirit in the skies. DENIS RICHARDS

R.A.F. Fighter Command
- ⊙ Command Headquarters
- ⊕ Group Headquarters
- ● Sector station
- ○ Fighter base
- + Low-level radar station
- ◆ High-level radar station
- 🔥 Towns bombed

German bases
- ○ Fighter
- ● Twin-engined Me 110
- + Bomber
- St (Stuka) Dive-bomber

0   50   100
Miles

LUFTFLOTTE 5 from Norway and Denmark

NORTH SEA

Glasgow

NORTHUMBERLAND

Belfast

Newcastle   Sunderland
FIGHTER COMMAND GROUP 13
Middlesbrough

YORKSHIRE
Driffield
Hull

Range of High-level Radar

Liverpool   Manchester
Merseyside   Sheffield

FIGHTER COMMAND GROUP 12

Nottingham

Birmingham   Coventry

Norwich

Range of Low-level Radar

Amsterdam
NETHERLANDS
Rotterdam

Debden
Ipswich   Martlesham

Stanmore
London
North Weald
Hornchurch
Rochford

FIGHTER COMMAND GROUP 11
Northolt
Uxbridge
Croydon   Biggin Hill
Kenley

Swansea
Cardiff
Bristol

Rochester
Eastchurch
Detling
Manston
Canterbury

Antwerp

Ghent

FIGHTER COMMAND GROUP 10

Andover
Middle Wallop   West Malling
Worthy Down
Southampton
Exeter
Portsmouth
Tangmere
Ventnor
Portland

Hawkinge
Lympne
Calais   +St

Lille
BELGIUM
LUFTFLOTTE 2

Plymouth

ENGLISH CHANNEL

+St
Amiens

Cherbourg   Le Havre

Paris

LUFTFLOTTE 3

FRANCE

+St

Rennes

A W Gatrell & Co Ltd

30

The moment drew near for the Luftwaffe's great assault

From the very outset of the war a great German air assault had been expected in Britain. It was for fear of this that mothers and children had been evacuated from the big cities, the blackout enforced, gas masks and Anderson shelters distributed, thousands of beds held vacant in the hospitals. But no 'knock-out blow' from the air, or indeed any kind of blow at all—other than minelaying and raids on Scottish naval bases and east coast convoys—had disturbed the uncanny peace of the British Isles during the autumn and winter of 1939-40.

This quiet remained unbroken even when, in the spring of 1940, the war in the west came abruptly to the boil. Strange as it seemed at the time, there were in fact good reasons for Britain's unexpected immunity. Britain herself had not launched a strategic bombing offensive against Germany during the 'Phoney War' for fear of retaliation while the Allies were still the weaker side in the air. Germany had not launched any such offensive against Britain because she did not think she could achieve decisive results from German bases and because the Luftwaffe was largely cast for the role of military support. This support the Luftwaffe had given, with exemplary effectiveness, during the campaign in Poland; and now, as the Germans struck in the west, it operated in similar fashion in Norway, the Low Countries, and France. Meanwhile, it did not waste its strength in irrelevant activity against England.

This self-imposed restriction lasted until the German army entered the smoking ruins of Dunkirk. Within less than 48 hours, on the night of June 5/6, the Luftwaffe began to show a more lively interest in the British homeland. Some 30 German bombers—far more than on any previous occasion—crossed the east coast to attack airfields and other objectives; and the following night similar forces repeated the experiment. Then came a lull while the German armies in France truck southwards, again supported by the Luftwaffe. It lasted until the French sought an armistice, whereupon within a few hours German aircraft resumed night operations over Britain. From then on until the opening of their full daylight air offensive in August, the Germans repeatedly dispatched bombers—70 of them on the busiest night—against widely separated targets in England. Their intention was to give their crews experience in night operations and the use of radio navigational aids, to reconnoitre, and to maintain pressure inexpensively (their usual losses were one or two aircraft each night) until captured airfields in France and the Low Countries could be made ready for operations of a more intensive kind.

Meanwhile there was always the chance—or so it seemed to Hitler—that such operations might not be necessary. The Führer accordingly put out 'peace-feelers', at the

The Luftwaffe was able to use the entire coastline of occupied Europe: the British resources were to be strained to their furthest limits ◁

same time encouraging preparations for the next stage of hostilities. This next stage, the invasion or occupation of Britain, was not one to which the Germans had already devoted long thought. The speed and completeness of the German victory in France had taken even the optimistic Hitler by surprise; and though his armed forces had given some casual attention in the autumn of 1939 to the general problems of invading Britain, it was not until German troops actually reached the Channel coast on May 20, 1940, that the project really came to life. From then on the German navy, anxious not to be caught out by Hitler, began serious planning; but the German army showed comparable interest only after the total defeat of France. On July 2 Hitler formally directed his services to proceed with this invasion planning, though on a purely provisional basis. On July 19 came his public peace offer; on the 22nd, its rejection.

If the Germans were to take advantage of the 'invasion season' in the Channel that year, their three services would now have to formulate and agree plans with extraordinary speed. This difficulty struck the German naval and military chiefs more forcibly than it did Hitler, who declared to his paladins that only the rapid elimination of Britain would enable him to complete his life's work by turning against Russia. On July 31 he accordingly disregarded the fast-waning enthusiasm of the German navy and army and ordered that an attempt must be made to prepare the invasion operation, to which the code-name 'Seelöwe' ('Sea Lion') was given, for September 15. The following day, August 1, he issued a directive concerning the only part of the venture on which all three German services were thus far agreed. It was for the preliminary battle, which must consist of the subjugation of the RAF. 'The German air force is to overcome the British air force with all means at its disposal, and as soon as possible.' With these words, Hitler finally decreed the Battle of Britain.

600 RAF sorties a day

While the plans for Sea Lion and the preliminary air battle were taking shape, the Luftwaffe was not of course idle. From its captured airfields it continued to harass Britain by night, and from July 10 onwards it waged increasing war by day against British shipping in the Channel. The German bombers were usually detected by the British radar stations, but since the attacks were delivered at the periphery of the British defensive system they set the Fighter Command a difficult problem. In such circumstances it was highly creditable to the command that the British fighters inflicted more casualties than they themselves suffered: between July 10 and August 10, as we now know, the Germans lost 217 aircraft, Fighter Command 96. On the other hand the German attacks, though sinking only a modest tonnage of British shipping, imposed a severe strain on Fighter Command, which was compelled to fly some 600 sorties a day at extended range at a time when it was trying to build up resources for the greater trials clearly soon to come. As Air Chief Marshal Sir Hugh Dowding, Air Officer C-in-C of the Fighter Command, pointed out to the Air Ministry and the Admiralty, if constant air protection was to be given to all British shipping in home waters, the entire British fighter force could be kept fully employed on that task alone.

These German attacks on shipping, how-

ever, were only a prelude to the air battle which the Luftwaffe had now to induce. The prerequisite of Sea Lion was that the Germans should gain air supremacy over the Channel and southern Britain. Only if the RAF were put out of business could the Germans hope to cross, land, and maintain communications without an unacceptable rate of casualties; for the destruction of the RAF would not only obviate British bombing attacks, but would also enable the Luftwaffe to deal, uninterrupted from the air, with the Royal Navy. And beyond this there was always the hope, ever present in the minds of Hitler and his service chiefs alike, that the Luftwaffe's success alone might be so great as to bring Britain to submission, or very near it. In that case, an invasion about which neither the German navy nor army was really happy could become something much more to their liking—a virtually unresisted occupation.

As the moment drew near for the Luftwaffe's great assault, the forces arrayed stood as follows. On the German side there were three *Luftflotten*, or air fleets. The main ones were Luftflotte II, under Field-Marshal Kesselring, in northern Germany, Holland, Belgium, and in north-eastern France; and Luftflotte III, under Field-Marshal Sperrle, in northern and western France. By day, these two air fleets threatened the entire southern half of England, up to and including the Midlands; and by night they could range still farther afield. In addition, to disperse the British defences and to threaten Scotland and north-eastern England there was also a smaller force, Luftflotte V, under General Stumpff, based in Denmark and Norway. Between them, the three air fleets on August 10 comprised over 3,000 aircraft, of which about three-quarters were normally serviceable at any one time. Roughly 1,100 of the 3,000 were fighters—for the most part Messerschmitt 109E's, virtually the equal of the opposing Spitfires of that date, but handicapped in a protective role by their limited range.

To escort bombers to the more distant targets, including those to be reached across the North Sea from Norway, there were some 300 Messerschmitt 110s; but these twin-engined fighters, though sturdy, could not compare in manoeuvrability with the single-engined Spitfire or Hurricane. The remaining 1,900 German aircraft were almost entirely bombers, mainly the well-tried if slow Heinkel 111, the slim, pencil-like Dornier 17, and the fast and more recent Junkers 88, but including also about 400 Junkers 87s—the Stukas, or dive-bombers. These had established a legendary reputation on the battlefields of Poland and France, but their range was very short and they had yet to face powerful opposition.

On the British side, the situation was a great deal better than it had been a few weeks earlier. On June 4, following the heavy losses of Hurricanes in France, Fighter Command had been able to muster only 446 modern single-engined fighters—Spitfires and Hurricanes—with another 36 ready in the Aircraft Storage Units (ASUs) as replacements. But on August 11, on the eve of the main air battle, Fighter Command had 704 of these aircraft in the squadrons and 289 in the ASUs. Its fighting strength had been virtually doubled during those ten critical weeks since Dunkirk, thanks to the fruition of earlier Air Ministry plans and the tremendous efforts of the air-

craft industry under the stimulus of the newly appointed Minister of Aircraft Production, Lord Beaverbrook.

Strengthening the shield

During those same ten weeks the British air defence system, built up against an enemy operating from Germany and possibly the Low Countries, had also been extended, thanks to schemes already worked out and in progress, to deal with forces operating from France and Norway. To the existing groups within Fighter Command – No. 11 Group, guarding the south-east, No. 12 Group, guarding the east and Midlands, and No. 13 Group, guarding the north-east up to the Forth – had been added another: No. 10 Group, guarding the south-west. The intermittent defences of the north-west, including Northern Ireland, had been thickened, as had those of Scotland.

This was not only a matter of providing more fighter aircraft and the pilots to fly them. It was also a matter of extending the main coastal radar chain, adding special radar stations to detect low-flying aircraft, extending Observer Corps posts for inland tracking over the south-western counties and western Wales, adapting more airfields for fighter operations, installing guns, searchlights, balloon barrages. All this was the concomitant, on the air defence side, of the gun-posts and the pill-boxes, the barbed wire and the dragon's teeth, that the inhabitant of southern England, enrolled perhaps in the newly formed Local Defence Volunteers and on watch at dawn and dusk for the arrival of German paratroops, saw springing up before his eyes along his familiar coasts and downlands.

The island's air defences had grown stronger and more extensive, but many grave deficiencies remained. Of the 120 fighter squadrons which the Director of Home Operations at the Air Ministry considered desirable in the new situation created by the German conquests, Dowding had less than 60 – and eight of these flew Blenheims or Defiants, no match for the Me-109s. Of the 4,000 anti-aircraft guns deemed necessary even before the German conquests, Anti-Aircraft Command still had less than 2,000. The early warning and inland tracking systems were still incomplete in the west and over parts of Scotland. There was a shortage of fighter pilots: new planes could be produced quicker than new skilled men to fly them. But whatever the deficiencies of the air defence system by day, they were as nothing compared with its alarming weaknesses by night, when ordinary fighters were useful only in the brightest moonlight, and when the men of the Observer Corps had to rely on ineffective acoustical detectors instead of their clear eyesight and a pair of binoculars.

Britain, however, had assets not yet mentioned. Among others, there was RAF Coastal Command, prepared both to carry out reconnaissance and to help in offensive operations; and there was RAF Bomber Command. Most of the latter's aircraft could operate safely only by night, and by night it was by no means certain that they could find and hit the more distant targets. The daylight bombers – about 100 Blenheims – were capable of much greater accuracy; but they needed fighter support, which could be supplied only at short range (assuming the Hurricanes or Spitfires could be spared). Against targets near at hand – airfields, ports, and shipping just across the Channel

– the British bombing force was capable of playing a vital part. Against distant objectives, its effectiveness at that date was more problematical.

In sum, the opposing forces, disregarding reconnaissance aircraft and units still stationed in Germany, consisted of about 1,900 bombers assisted by 1,100 fighters on the German side, and of about 700 fighters assisted to a limited extent by 350 bombers on the British side. The Germans had the advantage not only of numbers but of the tactical initiative – of the fact that they could strike anywhere within their range – while the British defences could react only to the German moves.

The British air defence system, however, though incomplete, was the most technically advanced in the world. The early warning supplied by the radar stations (which in the south-east could pick up enemy formations before they crossed the French coast), the inland tracking by the Observer Corps, the control of the British fighters from the ground in the light of this information and the continuous reporting of the fighters' own position – all this, designed to obviate the need for wasteful standing patrols, meant that the British fighters could be used with economy and could take off with a good chance of making interception.

One other factor, too, helped the British: the Luftwaffe's offensive against Britain was largely an improvised one; and Luftwaffe C-in-C Göring, though an able man, was also a vainglorious boaster who in technical proficiency was not in the same class as the opposing commander. The single-minded Dowding, in charge of Fighter Command since its formation in 1936 – the man whose obduracy had preserved Britain's fighter resources against the clamour to squander them in France – knew his job. Göring, as much politician as airman, scarcely knew his; while theoretically controlling and co-ordinating the entire offensive, in practice he was incapable of more than occasional acts of intervention. On the next level of command, Kesselring, in charge of the main attacking force – Luftflotte II – was for all his successes in Poland and France a novice in the forthcoming type of operation; while Air Vice-Marshal Keith Park, commanding the main defending force – Group 11 – had earlier been Dowding's right-hand man at Headquarters, Fighter Command. Unlike their opposite numbers, the two principal British commanders had lived with their problem for years. Their skill, experience, and devotion, like those of their pilots, offset some of the British inferiority in numbers.

Operation Eagle

By August 10 the three Luftflotten stood ready to launch the major assault – Operation Eagle ('Adler') – which would drive the RAF from the skies of southern Britain. Four days, in the opinion of the German Air Staff, would see the shattering of the fighter defences south of the line London-Gloucester, four weeks the elimination of the entire RAF. Allowing for the ten days' notice required by the German navy for minelaying and other final preparations before the actual D-Day, the date of the invasion could thus be set for mid-September.

August 11 was a very cloudy day, and the Germans confined their activity to bombing Portland and some east coast shipping. On the following day came what seemed to the British to be the beginning of the main attack: five or six major raids and many

minor ones, involving several hundred aircraft, including escorted Ju-87s, struck at airfields and radar stations along the south coast and at shipping in the Thames Estuary. Of the six radar stations they attacked, the raiders damaged five but knocked out only one – that at Ventnor on the Isle of Wight. It could not be replaced until August 23 – a sharp blow. Among the airfields, they hit Lympne, a forward landing ground, and Manston and Hawkinge, two important fighter stations in Kent, but all were back in action within 24 hours. Fighters from No. 11 Group challenged all the major raids and frustrated completely one aimed at Manston. In the course of the fighting the Germans lost 31 aircraft, the British 22.

According to the German records, the next day, August 13, was Eagle Day itself – the opening of the Eagle offensive proper. The attack went off at half-cock in the morning when a message postponing operations till later in the day failed to get through to some of the German squadrons. In the afternoon the main assault developed with a two-pronged thrust, Luftflotte II attacking over Kent and the Thames Estuary, while Luftflotte III, challenged by No. 10 Group, ranged over Hampshire, Dorset, and Wiltshire. The raiders hit three airfields severely – Eastchurch, Detling, and Andover – but none of these belonged to Fighter Command; their attacks on fighter stations such as Rochford were beaten off.

In the whole day's operations – which witnessed 1,485 German sorties and ended with a successful night attack on a Spitfire factory at Castle Bromwich, near Birmingham – the Germans lost 45 aircraft, Fighter Command only 13 (with six of the British pilots saved). This was a poor sort of Eagle Day for the Germans, but they were nevertheless well satisfied with their progress. They calculated that between August 8 and 14, in addition to successful attacks on some 30 airfields and aircraft factories, they had destroyed more than 300 British fighters in combat. In fact, they had destroyed less than 100.

After lesser activity on August 14 – a matter of some 500 German sorties, directed mainly against railways near the coast and against RAF stations – the Luftwaffe on August 15 attempted the great blow with which it had hoped to open the battle some days earlier. In clear skies the Germans sent over during the day no less than seven major raids, using all three Luftflotten in a series of co-ordinated attacks on widely separated areas. The first clash came at about 1130 hours, when some 40 escorted Ju-87s of Luftflotte II struck at Lympne and Hawkinge airfields in Kent. Then, about 1230 hours, some 65 He-111s escorted by 35 Me-110s of Luftflotte V, operating from Stavanger in Norway, headed in to the Northumberland coast in an attempt to bomb airfields in the north-east. These formations were barely retiring when at 1315 hours another force of Luftflotte V, consisting of about 50 unescorted Ju-88s operating from Aalborg in Denmark, approached the Yorkshire coast on a similar mission. Little more than an hour later at 1430 hours, and once more at 1500, Luftflotte II struck again, on the first occasion north of the Thames Estuary against Martlesham airfield and on the second against Hawkinge and Eastchurch.

▷ **Seen through German eyes: a British fighter pilot bales out of his stricken Hurricane; his parachute canopy is about to open (top)** seat in the sun—but both sides are at instant readiness for take-off. On RAF and Luftwaffe bases, the youth, the pipes, and the flying-kit were much the same. There is little to distinguish these pilots except the national markings on their aircraft

irfields and aircraft factories at Rochester. Next it was the turn of Luftflotte III: at 720 hours some 80 bombers, heavily escorted, came in to the south coast at Portland, bombed the harbour, and then attacked airfields at Middle Wallop and Worthy Down. Finally, at 1830 hours, 60 or 70 aircraft of Luftflotte II again penetrated over Kent, hitting West Malling airfields and the airfield and aircraft factories at Croydon. To round off the day's work, another 60 or 70 bombers made sporadic attacks during the hours of darkness.

All this German effort was fiercely challenged. Though the bombing had its successes, notably at Middle Wallop, Martlesham, and Driffield (Yorkshire) airfields and at Croydon, in no case did the British fighters allow the raiders to operate unmolested, and in many cases the primary objectives escaped unscathed. Especially significant was the fighting in the north-east, where No. 13 Group, involved for the first time in the battle, intercepted the formations from Norway well out to sea, and with the help of the anti-aircraft guns on Tyne and Tees destroyed eight He-111s and seven Me-110s, with no British losses. A little farther south, too, No. 12 Group and the local guns, tackling the formations from Denmark, brought down eight of the enemy with no loss on the British side. The Germans thus failed in their main hope – that Dowding, in his anxiety to protect the vital and heavily threatened south-east, would have left the north almost undefended. Instead, they discovered, to their cost, that their attacks across the North Sea were met before they reached the British coast, and that the Me-110s in a long-range escorting role were useless against Spitfires and Hurricanes. The lesson was sufficiently expensive to convince the Germans not to launch any further daylight attacks from this area.

The fighting on August 15 was the most extensive in the whole Battle of Britain. With 520 bomber and 1,270 fighter sorties, and attacks stretching from Northumberland to Dorset, the German effort was at its maximum. But so too was the German loss – 75 aircraft as against 34 British fighters. This did not prevent an effort of almost equal magnitude on the following day, when the Germans sent across some 1,700 sorties, attacked a number of airfields (with particular success at Tangmere), and lost 45 aircraft in the process. With Fighter Command losing 21, the balance remained in the British favour.

The Luftwaffe switches strategy

The four days of intensive attack calculated to clear the skies of southern England were now over, and the Germans took stock. In the opinion of their Intelligence, Fighter Command, if not exhausted, was down to its last 300 aircraft. This appreciation was very wide of the mark, for Dowding still had nearly twice that number of Hurricanes and Spitfires in the front line, in addition to another 120 or so Blenheims, Defiants, and Gladiators. However, it encouraged the Germans to believe that another day or two of major effort might see the end of British opposition. On August 18 the Luftwaffe accordingly struck again in full force, chiefly against airfields in Kent, Surrey, and

A Ju-87: the legendary Stuka, the terror of Europe – now, matched at last by comparable fighter opposition, now the hunted and not the hunter ◁

Sussex; but in doing so they lost 71 aircraft while the British lost no more than 27. Clearly Fighter Command was still unsubdued. After a few days of minor activity owing to bad weather, the Germans therefore made their first great change of plan.

Up till then, the main German objectives had been airfields fairly near to the coast; after August 12 they had given up intensive attacks on radar stations – fortunately for Fighter Command – because they found them difficult to destroy. The airfields and other coastal targets they had continued to attack, partly to deny the airfields to the British during the proposed invasion period, but still more to force Fighter Command to join battle in their defence. The German theory was that by such attacks they might, without severe losses to themselves, inflict heavy losses on the RAF – for raids on coastal targets or those not far inland did not involve prolonged exposure to the British defences – while at the same time the Me-109s would be free from worries on the score of endurance and accordingly able to give maximum protection to the German bombers. Such was the German strategy when the battle began. It had not disposed of Fighter Command, so it was now changed in favour of attacks farther inland.

The first phase of the battle was thus over. So far, Fighter Command had more than held its own: 363 German aircraft had been destroyed between August 8 and 18, as against 181 British fighters lost in the air and another 30 on the ground. The period had also seen what proved to be the last daylight attack by Luftflotte V, and the last attempt by Luftflotte II to make regular use of its Ju-87s – both notable successes for the British defences.

At the same time, however, there was one aspect of the struggle which gave Dowding and the Air Ministry acute anxiety. During the same ten days, when Fighter Command had lost 211 Spitfires and Hurricanes, the number of replacements forthcoming from the aircraft industry had fallen short of this total by at least 40. In the same period, Fighter Command had lost 154 experienced fighter pilots: but the output of the training schools had been only 63 – and those less skilled than the men they replaced. Fighter Command, while inflicting nearly twice as many casualties as it was suffering, was thus in fact being weakened – though not, as yet, at anything like the speed desired by the enemy.

It was to increase the rate of destruction of the British fighter force – which unchanged would have left Fighter Command still in existence in mid-September – that the Germans now switched to targets farther inland. They reckoned that by making their prime objective the fighter airfields, and in particular the sector airfields of No. 11 Group from which the British fighters in the south-east were controlled, they would not only strike at the heart of the British defences, but would also compel Fighter Command to meet their challenge with all its remaining forces. In the resulting air battles, they hoped to achieve a rate of attrition that would knock out Fighter Command within their scheduled time: though they also knew that in penetrating farther inland they were likely to suffer greater losses themselves. To guard against this, and to destroy as many Hurricanes and Spitfires as possible, they decided to send over a still higher proportion of fighters with their bombers.

The sector stations of No. 11 Group stood

in a ring guarding London. To the south-west, in a forward position near Chichester, lay Tangmere. Nearer the capital and south of it there were Kenley in Surrey and Biggin Hill in Kent, both on the North Downs. Close to London in the east lay Hornchurch, near the factories of Dagenham; and round to the north-east was North Weald, in metropolitan Essex. Farther out there was Debden, near Saffron Walden. The ring was completed to the west by Northolt, on the road to Uxbridge, where No. 11 Group itself had its headquarters – which in turn was only a few minutes' drive from that of Fighter Command at Stanmore. All the sector stations normally controlled three fighter squadrons, based either on the sector station itself or on satellite airfields.

Strikes at the source

The Germans had already severely damaged two of the sector stations – Kenley and Biggin Hill – on August 18. Now, on August 24, they struck hard at North Weald and Hornchurch. On August 26 they attempted to bomb Biggin Hill, Kenley, North Weald, and Hornchurch, were beaten off, but got through to Debden. On August 30 they hit Biggin Hill twice, doing great damage and killing 39 persons. The following day – the most expensive of the whole battle for Fighter Command, with 39 aircraft lost – they wrought great damage at Debden, Biggin Hill, and Hornchurch.

On September 1 Biggin Hill suffered its sixth raid in three days, only to be bombed again less than 24 hours later; and on September 3 the attack once more fell on North Weald. On the 5th the main raids again headed towards Biggin Hill and North Weald, only to be repelled, while on the 4th and 6th the attacks extended also to the Vickers and Hawker factories near Weybridge. The Hawker factory, which produced more than half the total output of Hurricanes, was a particularly vital target. Its selection showed that the Germans, perplexed by the continued resilience of Fighter Command, were also trying to cut off the British fighter supply at its source.

Between August 24 and September 6 the Germans made no less than 33 major raids, of which more than two-thirds were mainly against the sector and other stations of Fighter Command. This assault imposed on the command a still greater strain than the preceding one, against targets in the coastal belt. The fighting was more difficult for the British pilots, in that the proportion of German fighters to bombers became so high, and sections of the fighter escort so close; and over the whole fortnight a daily average of something like 1,000 German aircraft, of which 250 to 400 were bombers, operated over England. Twice, on August 30 and 31, the number of intruders was nearer 1,500.

In the course of the combats and the ensuing night operations the British defences destroyed 380 German aircraft, as against a Fighter Command loss of 286: but many other British fighters were seriously damaged, and no less than 103 fighter pilots were killed and 128 wounded out of a fighting strength of not much more than 1,000. In addition six of the seven sector stations of No. 11 Group sustained heavy damage: and though none was yet out of action, Biggin Hill could control only one squadron instead of its normal three.

So Fighter Command was being steadily worn down. The wastage, both of fighters

◁ A Dornier in action: a stick of bombs streams from its bomb-bay

▷ Target and tracer-fire: camera-gun film from a British fighter records the end of a Me-110 fighter. The 110, at full throttle, streams smoke trails from its twin engines (top); tracer fire misses the starboard wing, then the first hit glows on the port engine which explodes (bottom)

◁ Two Dorniers fly over fires started by the first wave

▽ The Luftwaffe strikes at Fighter Command: on an RAF fighter base, a Spitfire in its bomb pen survives a low-level strafing run

The nose-gunner of an He 111 engages a Spitfire at close range

and of pilots, was far exceeding the output. In one sense the command was winning the battle; in another – if the Germans could maintain the pressure long enough – it was losing it.

The Germans, however, were not intending to fight a prolonged battle. They, too, could not afford heavy losses indefinitely – as may be seen from their decision after August 18 to hold back most of the vulnerable Ju-87s for the actual invasion, from their caution in employing Me-110s, and from their increasingly closer and more numerous fighter escort. Their attack, as we have seen, was meant to be a brief one, geared to Operation Sea Lion; and for Sea Lion they were now running short of time. This Hitler recognised at the end of August when he agreed that D-Day, provisionally set for September 15, should be postponed to September 21. For this date to be kept the German navy had to receive the executive order by September 11: and Göring's Luftwaffe had thus to administer the *coup de grâce* to the British fighter forces within the next few days. The attack on sector stations and other inland targets might be doing well, but in itself it was not proving decisive. On September 7 the Germans accordingly switched to another target, farther inland than most of the sector stations and, as they believed, still more vital – London.

Target London

The German decision to attack London was inspired by three beliefs. In the first place, operations against London could be expected to bring about still greater air battles and so – the Germans hoped – still higher wastage in Fighter Command. It was for this reason that Kesselring, though not Sperrle, strongly supported the change of plan. Second, an assault on the capital, if reinforced by attacks during the night against other main cities as well, might paralyse the British machinery of government in the final period before the invasion, or even terrorise the British people into submission. Third, an attack on the British capital would be, as the Germans saw it, an act of retribution. On the night of August 24/25, during the course of the Luftwaffe's usual scattered night operations, some badly aimed or jettisoned bombs had fallen on central London – the first of the war. Churchill and the War Cabinet had immediately ordered retaliation against Berlin; and during the following nights RAF bombers had found and hit the German capital – an occurrence which Göring had assured Hitler could never happen. The enraged Führer promptly vowed revenge and with Göring's eager concurrence unleashed the Luftwaffe against its supreme target.

On the night of September 4 German bombers laid flares over London; on the following two nights small numbers of aircraft dropped bombs on Rotherhithe and other places near the docks. These were the warming-up operations.

In the late afternoon of September 7 some 300 German bombers escorted by 600 fighters crossed the Kent and Sussex coasts or penetrated the Thames Estuary in a series of huge waves. A few bombed the oil installations at Thameshaven, still burning from earlier attacks; the rest, instead of bombing the sector stations, which the British fighters were alert to guard, held on until they reached the outskirts of the capital itself. Though nearly all the British squadrons ordered up eventually made contact, most of the raiders were able to put down their high explosive and incendiaries before they were molested. The attacks fell in full force on London's dockland east of the City. Huge fires sprang up among the dockside warehouses, especially at Silvertown, and these the Germans used as beacons to light their way to further attacks during the ensuing hours of darkness. That night, when 250 German bombers ranged over the capital in a prolonged assault from dusk to dawn, millions of Londoners had their first experience of what they imagined was Blitzkrieg, and what they were soon to call 'The Blitz'.

The climax of the battle was now approaching. Göring took personal charge of operations, and the bombers from Norway and Denmark joined Kesselring's forces for what were meant to be the final and deciding blows. Meanwhile, however, the German invasion preparations had not gone unobserved: since August 31 Spitfires and Hudsons of RAF Coastal Command had been returning with an impressive photographic record of the growing number of barges and other invasion craft in the ports and estuaries across the Channel. On August 31 at Ostend, for instance, there were 18 barges; by September 6 there were 205.

As the concentrations increased, Bomber Command began to attack them, using at first its daylight Blenheims. By September 6 the enemy preparations were sufficiently obvious for the British authorities to order Invasion Alert 2: 'Attack probable within three days.' The following day, when the German bombers turned against London, it seemed that the hour of supreme trial might be at hand. Alert 2 then gave place

Hawker Hurricane Mk I
Span: 40 ft. *Length:* 31 ft 5 in. *Gross weight:* 6,447 lb. *Engine:* 1,030 hp Rolls Royce Merlin II. *Armament:* 8 x ·303 machine-guns. *Speed:* 324 mph at 17,500 ft. *Ceiling:* 34,200 ft. The Hurricane was developed in 1934 from the Hawker Fury and is best known for its part in the Battle of Britain when it shot down more enemy aircraft than all other air and ground defences combined. The aircraft illustrated was flown by the British ace Squadron Leader Stanford Tuck, whose machine bore 25 victory swastikas beneath the cockpit

to Alert 1: 'Invasion imminent, and probable within twelve hours.'

That night, as the German bombs began to crash down on London, the code-word 'Cromwell' went out to the Southern and Eastern Commands of Britain's Home Forces, bringing them to immediate readiness. In the prevailing excitement a few commanders of Home Guard units rang church bells to call out their men, so spreading the impression that German paratroops had actually landed. Meanwhile, forces of the Royal Navy waited at immediate notice, and the Hampdens of Bomber Command – 'heavy' bombers of the time – joined Blenheims, Hudsons, and Battles in intensified attacks on French and Belgian ports.

It was with the British fully alert to what the next few hours or days might bring that the Luftwaffe now strove to repeat the hammer blows of September 7. On September 8 bad weather limited their daylight activity; but at night Luftflotte III was able to send 200 bombers against London in a lengthy procession lasting more than nine hours. The zone of attack now extended from dockland to the capital as a whole, with special attention to railways and power stations, and by the morning every railway line running south of London was for a brief time unserviceable.

On the next day, September 9, clouds again restricted activity in the morning, only for a further assault to develop in the late afternoon. More than 200 bombers with full escort headed for London; but such was the promptness and vigour of the interception that less than half reached even the outskirts of the capital, and the bombs fell widely over the south-eastern counties. No. 12 Group's Duxford wing of four squadrons, led by the legless pilot Squadron Leader Douglas Bader, enjoyed a notable success. All told, the British pilots shot down 28 German aircraft for the loss of 19 of their own.

Very different once more was the story at night. Again nearly 200 aircraft bombed the capital in attacks lasting over eight hours; this time some 400 Londoners were killed and 1,400 injured – all with negligible loss to the Luftwaffe.

Hitler again shifts D-Day

September 10 was a day of cloud, rain, and light German activity – though at night there was the usual raid on London, while other German bombers attacked South Wales and Merseyside. The next afternoon, while the Germans tried to jam some of the British radar stations, Luftflotte III attacked Southampton, and Luftflotte II sent three big raids against London. Many of the bombers got through to the City and the docks; and the balance of losses – 25 German ones, against 29 by Fighter Command – for once tilted against the British. On their return, some German pilots reported that British fighter opposition was diminishing. But though the Luftwaffe still hoped to complete its task, the date was now September 11, and Fighter Command was still in existence. With the German navy requiring ten days' notice before D-Day, an invasion on September 21 thus became impossible. Accordingly Hitler now gave the Luftwaffe three more days' grace, till September 14, in the hope that a decision could then be taken to invade on September 24.

As it happened, September 12 and 13 were days of poor visibility, unsuitable for major attacks. Even the nightly efforts against London – which was now enjoying the heartening noise of greatly reinforced gun defences – were on a reduced scale. When September 14 came, Hitler could only postpone the decision for a further three days, till September 17. This set the provisional D-Day for September 27 – about the last date on which the tides would be favourable until October 8. The Führer's order was contrary to the advice of his naval chiefs, who urged indefinite postponement – a tactful term for abandonment. Their worries had been sharply increased by the mounting intensity of the RAF's attacks on the invasion barges, large numbers of which had been destroyed the previous evening.

The Luftwaffe now strove to clinch the issue in the short time still at its disposal. Despite unfavourable weather, on the afternoon of September 14 several raids struck at London. Some of the German pilots reported ineffective opposition, and Fighter Command lost as many aircraft as the enemy. The night proved fine, but on this occasion no more than 50 German bombers droned their way towards London. The Luftwaffe was husbanding its efforts for the morrow.

Sunday September 15 was a day of mingled cloud and sunshine. By 11 am the British radar detected mass formations building up over the Pas-de-Calais region. Half an hour later the raiders, stepped up from 15,000 to 26,000 feet, were crossing the coast in waves bent for London. Park's fighters met them before Canterbury, and in successive groups – two, three, then four squadrons – challenged them all the way to the capital, over which No. 12 Group's Duxford wing, now five squadrons strong, joined the conflict. In the face of such opposition, the raiders dropped their bombs

Fiat C.R. 42 Falco (Falcon)
Span: 31 ft 10 in. *Length:* 27 ft 1 in. *Engine:* 840 hp Fiat A.74 air-cooled radial. *Armament:* 1 x 12·7-mm. 1 x 7·7-mm machine-guns later increased to 4 x 12·7-mm. *Speed:* 267 mph at 17,450 ft. *Ceiling:* 34,500 ft.   C.R.42s formed the fighter component of Mussolini's token Corpo Aereo Italiano based in Belgium for raids on eastern England

LAND AND SEA SUPPORT

September 1940 : Ack-ack girls practise air raid drill. Women from the Auxiliary Territorial Service worked in anti-aircraft units and performed non-combatant duties, like plotting and ranging enemy aircraft, releasing men for active service

RAF Air-Sea Rescue Launch
The intensity of air operations over the Channel during the early stages of the Battle of Britain focused attention on the need for fast rescue launches co-operating with sea-planes to bring airmen bailing out over the sea back into the battle. The Germans used similar techniques from their side of the Channel

Heinkel He 59
Span: 77 ft 9 in. *Length:* 57 ft 1 in. *Engine:* 2 x 660 hp BMW VI 6·0 ZU. *Armament:* 3 x 7·9-mm machine-guns. *Speed:* 137 mph at sea level. *Range:* 1,087 miles. *Bomb load:* 2,200 lb or one torpedo. Designed as a torpedo bomber, the so-called 'Red Cross' aircraft of the German air-sea rescue service were attacked on sight by the RAF whilst shadowing British convoys

3·7-inch Anti-Aircraft Gun
Crew: 9/11. Max. effective altitude: 32,000 ·

Associated Press

43

Fiat BR 20
Gross weight: 22,266 lb. *Span:* 70 ft 9 in.
Length: 52 ft 9 in. *Engine:* 2 x 1,000 hp Fiat
A80 RC41. *Armament:* 2 x 7·7-mm ; 1 x 12·7-mm
machine-guns. *Speed:* 267 mph at 13,120 ft.
Ceiling: 24,935 ft. *Range:* 1,700 miles.
Bomb load: 3,500 lb.　　　　Based at Melsbroek
airfield in Belgium in the autumn of 1940, these
Italian bombers were badly mauled in their only
daylight raid on eastern England

Focke-Wulf Fw 200 'Condor'
Gross weight: 50,045 lb. *Span:* 107 ft. 9½ in.
Length: 76 ft 1⅓ in. *Engine:* 4 x 1,200 hp BMW
Bramo 323 R-2. *Armament:* 2 x 7·9-mm ;
3 x 13-mm ; 1 x 20-mm machine-guns. *Crew:* 7.
Speed: 224 mph at 15,750 ft. *Ceiling:* 19,000 ft.
Range: 2,210 miles. *Bomb load:* 4,620 lb.　　　The
Fw 200 'Condor' was designed as a trans-Atlantic
airliner for Lufthansa, but during the Battle of
Britain, numbers of militarised Condors were
encountered in the reconnaissance and
anti-shipping role in the Western Approaches and
around the British coast

Dornier Do 215 B-1
Gross weight: 19,600 lb. *Span:* 59 ft ⅔ in.
Length: 51 ft 10 in. *Engine:* 2 x 1,100 hp
DB 601A. *Armament:* 6 x 7·92-mm
machine-guns. *Crew:* 4. *Speed:* 292 mph at
16,400 ft. *Ceiling:* 31,170 ft. *Range:* 965 miles.
Bomb load: 2,200 lb.   A reconnaissance
bomber which carried three cameras as well as
twenty 110-lb. bombs

Heinkel He 115K
Gross weight: 20,020 lb. *Span:* 75 ft 10 in.
Length: 57 ft. *Engine:* 2 x 850 hp BMW.
Armament: 4 x 7·92-mm machine-guns.
Crew: 3/4. *Speed:* 217 mph. *Ceiling:* 21,500 ft.
Range: 1,300 miles. *Bomb load:* 1,760 lb
bombs or torpedo.   Piloted by mixed Navy
and Luftwaffe crews, this adaptable float plane
was used for a wide variety of roles

inaccurately or jettisoned them, mainly over south London.

Two hours later a further mass attack developed. Again British radar picked it up well in advance: and again – since they had had time to refuel and rearm – Park's fighters challenged the intruders all the way to, and over, the capital. Once more the Germans jettisoned their bombs or aimed them badly, this time mainly over east London, and, as before, further British formations harassed the raiders on their way back. Meanwhile a smaller German force attacked Portland. Later in the day other raiders – some 20 Me-110s carrying bombs – tried to bomb the Supermarine aircraft works near Southampton, only to meet spirited and effective opposition from local guns. When darkness fell, 180 German bombers continued the damaging but basically ineffectual night assault on London, while others attacked Bristol, Cardiff, Liverpool, and Manchester.

So closed a day on which Göring had hoped to give the death-blow to Fighter Command. In all, the Germans had sent over about 230 bombers and 700 fighters in the daylight raids. Their bombing had been scattered and ineffective, and they had lost the greatest number of aircraft in a single day since August 15 – no less than 60. Fighter Command had lost 26, from which the pilots of 13 had been saved.

This further German defeat on September 15 – combined with the attacks of British bombers against barge concentrations – settled the issue. When September 17 came, Hitler had no alternative but to postpone Sea Lion indefinitely. A few days later, he agreed to the dispersal of the invasion craft in order to avoid attack from the air. The invasion threat was over.

Göring orders more raids

Göring, however, was not yet prepared to admit failure: he still clung to the belief that given a short spell of good weather the Luftwaffe could crush Fighter Command and thereafter compel Britain to submit, even without invasion. Between September 17 and the end of the month his forces strove to attack London by day, whenever weather permitted, in addition to aircraft factories elsewhere. On only three days – September 18, 27, and 30 – was he able to mount a major assault on the capital, and on each occasion British fighters prevented intensive bombing and took a heavy toll of the raiders. The loss of 120 German aircraft during these three days (as against 60 by Fighter Command) was not one which afforded Göring much encouragement to continue.

Had the Luftwaffe's corpulent chief known them, he would not have derived any greater encouragement from the casualty figures during the whole three weeks his air force had been attacking London. Between September 7 and 30 Fighter Command had lost 242 aircraft, the Luftwaffe 433. Equally important, though Dowding was still gravely worried by the continuing loss of pilots (on September 7 his squadrons had only 16 each instead of their proper 26), his anxieties about aircraft were diminishing. From the time the Germans abandoned their attack on sector airfields in favour of an assault on London, the wastage of Hurricanes and Spitfires had been more than counterbalanced by the output of the factories.

The prize of victory had thus eluded Göring's grasp. On October 12 Hitler recognised this by formally postponing Sea Lion

until the spring of 1941. In fact, this meant abandonment: Hitler's mind was now fixed on Russia. Until the German war machine could roll east, however, there was everything to be said, from the German point of view, for maintaining pressure on Britain, so long as it could be done inexpensively. During October the Luftwaffe, assisted by a few Italian aircraft, kept Fighter Command at stretch in daylight by sending over fighter and fighter-bombers, which did little damage but were difficult to intercept. At night the German bombers, operating with virtual impunity, continued to drop their loads on London.

The story of the 'Night Blitz' is one of civilian suffering and heroism, of widespread yet indecisive damage – and of slowly increasing success by the British defences. In the battle of wits against the intruders, perhaps the most vital developments were the discovery (and distortion) of the German navigational beams, the provision of dummy airfields and decoy fires, and the advances in radar which made possible accurate tracking overland.

Radar advances resulted in gun-laying radar that gave accurate readings of heights, and so permitted the engagement of the target 'unseen', and in ground-controlled interception (GCI) radar stations which brought night fighters close enough to the enemy for the fighters to use their own airborne radar (AI) for the final location and pursuit. It was only towards the end of the Blitz, however, that the GCI/AI combination emerged as a real threat to the attackers, who began to lose three or four aircraft in every 100 sorties, instead of merely one.

Meanwhile, the Luftwaffe was able to lay waste the centres of a score or more of British cities. After the early raids in August, the weight of attack by night fell for a time almost entirely on London. Between September 7 and November 13 there was only one night on which London escaped bombing, and the number of German aircraft over the capital each night averaged 163. With the final postponement of Sea Lion, the attack then extended also to longer-term, strategic objectives – the industrial towns, and later mainly the ports, so linking up with the blockading actions of the German submarines.

On November 14 the devastation of Coventry marked the change of policy; thereafter Southampton, Birmingham, Liverpool, Bristol, Plymouth, Portsmouth, Cardiff, Swansea, Belfast, Glasgow, and many other towns felt the full fury of the Blitz. In the course of it all, until Luftflotte II moved east in May 1941 and the attacks died away, the Germans killed about 40,000 British civilians and injured another 46,000, and damaged more than 1,000,000 British homes, at a cost to themselves of some 600 aircraft. On the economic side, they seriously impeded British aircraft production for some months, but in other directions the damage they did was too diffuse to be significant.

Hitler's first setback

The 'Blitz' ceased not because of the increased success of the British defences, but because most of the German aircraft were needed elsewhere. Had Russia collapsed within the eight weeks of the German – and the British – estimate, they would doubtless have returned quickly enough, to clear the way for invasion or to attempt to pulverise Britain into submission. As it was, Russia held, and though the British people were

subjected to further bombardments, they were not again called upon to face a serious threat of invasion.

Though the Night Blitz was inconclusive, the daylight Battle of Britain was thus one of the turning points of the war: it was the air fighting of August and September 1940, together with the existence of the Royal Navy and the English Channel, which first halted Hitler's career of conquest. The 1,000 or so pilots of Fighter Command who bore the brunt of that fighting – including the 400 or more who lost their lives – saved more than Britain by their exertions. By earning Britain a great breathing space in which the further progress of events was to bring her the mighty alliance of Russia and the United States, they made possible the final victory, and the liberation of Europe from the Nazi terror.

1940

August 1: Hitler decrees the Battle of Britain with the command: 'The German air force is to overcome the British air force with all means at its disposal, and as soon as possible.'
August 13: 'Eagle Day': the Luftwaffe launches its air offensive against Britain, with 1,485 sorties. The Germans lose 45 aircraft, the RAF 13.
August 15: In the most intense attack of the Battle of Britain, the Luftwaffe sends a total of 1,790 sorties over England. They lose 75 aircraft, while Britain loses 34.
August 17: The Germans establish an 'operational area' around Britain; in it, all ships are to be sunk without warning.
August 25: The RAF conducts its first raid on Berlin.
September 3: Britain cedes to the USA bases in the West Indies and elsewhere in exchange for 50 destroyers.
September 7: Some 300 German bombers, escorted by 600 fighters, penetrate the Thames Estuary and bomb London's dockland.
September 13: *Italy invades Egypt.*
September 15: The RAF claims to have shot down 183 German aircraft during daylight Luftwaffe raids on Britain – a figure subsequently found to have been greatly exaggerated.
September 17: Hitler postpones Operation Sea Lion 'until further notice'.
September 23/25: *British and Free French forces attempt to take Dakar.*
October 12: Operation Sea Lion is postponed until 1941.

A formation of the much-vaunted Me-110s; they had long range but rather poor manoeuvrability, and thus they suffered heavy losses in the battle ▷

Cockpit Armament Bf 110
1 Rheinmetall MG 15 machine-gun with
750 rounds. Rate of Fire: 1,100 rpm.

Nose Armament Bf 110
4 x 7·92 MG 17 machine-guns with 1,000
rounds per gun

MESSERSCHMITT Bf 110

Span: 53 ft 4¾ in. *Length:* 39 ft 8½ in.
Armament: 4 x 7·9-mm machine-guns; 2 x 20-mm
MG FF cannon. *Engine:* 2 x 1,150 hp
Daimler-Benz DB 601A. *Crew:* 2. *Speed:* 349
mph. *Range:* 530 miles.   The concept of the
long-range super-fighter, heavily armed and able
to smash through enemy fighter defence, was a
major part of Göring's plan of attack.
Unfortunately for the Luftwaffe the chosen
instrument proved a complete failure. The big
Messerschmitt packed a fearsome punch in its
nose batteries of cannon and machine-guns but
was too sluggish and unwieldly to take on RAF
opposition. Indeed their very presence became a
major defensive liability for the hard-pressed
Bf 109E pilots

Squadron Leader 'Sailor' Malan, the ex-merchant seaman who became the third highest scoring RAF ace with thirty-five enemy aircraft shot down. The RAF's top scorers were M T St John Pattle with forty-one kills, and Johnny Johnson with thirty eight.

Squadron Leader Stanford Tuck. Between May 1940 and January 1942, he shot down twenty-nine German aircraft making him the eighth highest RAF scorer for the war. In 1942 he was shot down over France and captured.

Left: A German Heinkel being shot down. *Main picture:* A formation of Spitfires in flight

THE ACES

Major Adolf Galland, top German scorer in the Battle of Britain. A captain in the Condor Legion fighting for Franco, Galland rose to be chief of the Luftwaffe fighter arm, but ended the war flying combat missions with the Me 262 jet-fighter. Although behind a desk for three years, he shot down 103 aircraft on the Western Front and was the Luftwaffe's fourth highest scorer in that theatre.

Lieutenant Colonel Werner Mölders. Like Galland, Mölders started his combat career in Spain where fourteen victories made him the top-scoring German Ace. In the Battle of Britain he scored fifty-five kills. Flying from the Eastern Front to the funeral of Ernst Udet, the fighter ace of the First World War, Mölders died when his Heinkel transport crashed.

Imperial War Museum

Keystone Press

A formation of Bristol Blenheims, the RAF's maids-of-all-work

RADAR: THE SECRET WAR

Scientists had been aware of the principle of radar many years before they realized that a practical application was possible. Before 1920 it was known that radio waves produced echoes and in 1924 E.V. (later Sir Edward) Appleton used this phenomenon to prove the existence of the ionosphere and to discover the height of its various layers by measuring the time required for a radio echo to return to the ground.

Ten years elapsed before a system for the detection of aircraft in a radio beam was devised.

In June 1934 A.P. Rowe, an Air Ministry scientist uneasy about the way the situation in Germany was developing, on his own initiative leafed through the fifty-three available files on air defence. He found that hardly any effort had been made to tackle the whole problem scientifically. Rowe reported his findings to Wimperis, director of scientific research at the Air Ministry, who then proposed to the secretary of state for air, Lord Londonderry, that a Committee for the Scientific Survey of Air Defence should be set up. This became the celebrated committee under Henry (later Sir Henry) Tizard.

For many years inventors had submitted propositions for a death ray which would immobilize an aircraft or incapacitate the crew. Before the first meeting of the Tizard Committee Wimperis informally asked R.A. (later Sir Robert) Watson-Watt of the Radio Research Station, Slough, whether in fact enough radio energy could conceivably be transmitted to damage an aircraft sufficiently. Watson-Watt passed the problem to one of his staff, A.F. Wilkins, who in half an hour's work showed that, although damage to an aircraft could be dismissed, the detection of radio energy reflected from an aircraft and, therefore, the determination of its distance could be found.

This information was digested by the Tizard Committee when it first met at the end of January 1935. On 26th February the first test of radio detection was held. A van containing suitable radio receivers halted in a field about ten miles from the short-wave transmitters of the Daventry broadcasting station. A pilot was instructed to fly over a course near the radio station. The van's instruments detected the aircraft as it flew through the radio transmissions at a distance of eight miles. It has been written, not without cause, that this simple experiment determined in large measure the fate of Great Britain and even of the world.

The authorities speedily grasped the importance of the experiment and gave permission and funds for research to begin. A small team of scientists under Watson-Watt secretly developed the first practical radar equipment at Orfordness on the Suffolk coast. Rowe had given the cover name PDF to the experiments—R standing for radio (because the tall aerial masts could not be disguised) and DF because direction finding was external to the original proposal. RDF became 'radar' (RAdio Detection And Ranging) later in the war and by then included a number of devices not all of which made use of radio echoes. The radar researchers soon moved to Bawdsey Manor, south of Orfordness and Bawdsey became the

prototype of a chain of coastal radar stations.

By the late 'thirties radar had reached a similar state of development in Germany, France, Holland, and the United States. In Germany, although the equipment was technically in advance of the British, the Services, anticipating a short war, made no plans for long term research. They failed, moreover, to discover the purpose of the British radar chain and, when war came, failed to destroy the vital radar stations. In the United States there appeared to be no pressing need for radar. So the US Navy was caught napping at Pearl Harbour. France was the first country to devise a radio navigational system—for the liner *Normandie*—but little attention was paid to military uses.

Two factors were essential to the success of the warning system; one was the speed with which the radar information was despatched to the appropriate quarter by landline or radio; the other was the need to maintain the continuity of a hostile aircraft's track under a permanent reference designation from Command Headquarters downwards to fighter groups and sectors.

The heart of the system was at Headquarters, Fighter Command, at Stanmore, Middlesex, where, in an underground filter room, the radar plots of the position, strength, height, and direction of the raiders were received, sifted, and reported when a track became discernible by specially selected and

Below left: Robert Watson-Watt who led the team of scientists which developed the first practical radar equipment, with his wife. *Below right:* The original magnetron invented by Randall in 1940 and the copper anode which forms the heart of this device. *Bottom:* WAAFs plot raids in operations room, Fighter Command HQ

Keystone Press

Science Museum

Camera Press

trained filter officers. In the early stages of the war the height-finding technique was liable to some degree of error and the filter officers had occasionally to resort to simple probability exercises. The tracks provided by the filter officers went to the adjoining operations room where the controller and his assistants sat on a raised dais and watched the airmen and WAAF plotters as they moved the counters on the glass-topped table, representing hostile and friendly aircraft, with their long croupier-like rakes according to the information received through their headphones. From here the air raid warning system was set in motion. The fighter groups and sectors, each equipped with identical operations and filter rooms, also received the raiders' tracks. In the early days of the war all the filtering was done at Stanmore, but after the deployment of German formations along the French coast information went directly to the appropriate groups.

As the coastal radar sets could not 'look' backwards, it was the responsibility of the Observer Corps to provide warning inland, and information on the approach of hostile aircraft was sent to the Observer Corps control rooms.

In the fighter sector operations rooms the controllers directed their squadrons to attack at the right place and time and afterwards brought them safely back to base. The medium of communication was the high frequency radio telephone. High frequency direction finders situ-

ated in each sector provided the position of every aircraft and, in addition, every fighter aircraft was provided with an automatic device known as 'Pipsqueak' which switched on the pilot's high frequency transmitter for fourteen seconds in every minute. Each aircraft had IFF (Identification, Friend or Foe) which characterized its radar 'blip'.

At night, the fighter pilot and his observer had enough to contend with in the business of taking off and landing and of navigating in total darkness and trying to locate an enemy bomber without control from the ground was like looking for a needle in a haystack. It was necessary for the controller to know at one and the same time the position, track, speed, and height of both the night fighter and the bomber. Provided with this information the controller could radio to the pilot the direction and height at which the latter should fly and, if necessary, to reduce speed in order not to overshoot his target. Control by night was made practicable by the Plan Position Indicator (PPI). This device was used in conjunction with a rotating radar beam with which it was possible to estimate an aircraft's range (up to about ninety miles) and direction.

The PPI which next to shortwave radar was the most important radar development during the war, was incorporated in the Ground Controlled Interception equipment. This resembled a domestic TV set with a map of the area imposed on the screen. The controller was able to plot the position of the enemy bomber and the pursuing fighter from the bright spots on the tube face, and by calculating the speed and direction of flight of the enemy was able to direct the night fighter towards it by the shortest route. In the final stages of the pursuit the fighter homed onto its quarry using its own Aircraft Interception set (AI).

But the early AI sets had severe limitations as did the sets for detecting surface vessels, and particularly surfaced submarines. Very narrow radio beams were required which could detect small objects, like a surfaced submarine, from the air, and without interference from ground echoes or from enemy jamming. The Bawdsey scientists had long foreseen the need for microwaves, but at that time there was no valve adequate to generate the high power required. Again, Great Britain made a revolutionary step forward in radar history. Early in 1940, at the instigation of the Admiralty, J.T. (later Sir John) Randall, and his colleagues at Birmingham University, devised the magnetron—a valve no bigger than a child's fist, which eventually provided a reliable output of hundreds of kilowatts in short pulses.

When, in August 1940, it was decided to divulge to the Americans, sixteen months before they entered the war, the latest British scientific achievements, the magnetron was the most important item taken to the USA by the Tizard Mission. The Americans, who had not yet solved the problem of generating microwaves, were now able to produce short wave sets for the detection of night bombers and surface vessels from the air, and for the control of anti-aircraft fire. **Guy Hartcup**

53

▽ Radar plotted the incoming bomber formations, alerting the AA defences and RAF Headquarters. Fighter Command had to anticipate feints by the incoming bombers in addition to the weight of the German attack itself

Fighter reports   Auto radio plots   Radar reports   AA land line   Observer reports   Combat orders

B

C

ighters take off to intercept attack, but land to refuel when it
s for 3. Attack swings away from fighters at 3, returning to 1
2, where the fighters are still grounded

B: Parade-ground 'Vic' was
rigid and inadequate for the
needs of modern air fighting

C: RAF pilots adopted the
German 'Schwarm': better
known as the 'Finger-four'

RAF Commander (X THEATRE OF WAR)	Luftflotte (EQUIVALENT OF ARMY GROUP)
Group	**Fliegerkorps**
Wing Fighter Command Bomber Command Coastal Command	**Geschwader** Kampfgeschwader – Bomber Jagdgeschwader – Fighter Stukageschwader – Dive-bomber
(No Direct Equivalent)	**Gruppe**
Squadron	**Staffel**

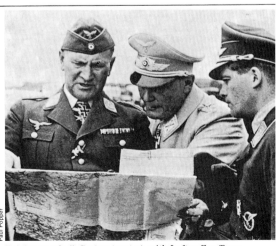

Marshal Sir Hugh Dowding   WAAFs plot the battle

Reichsmarschall Göring (centre), with Luftwaffe officers

Junkers Ju 88A-1
Gross weight: 27,500 lb. *Span:* 59 ft 11 in.
Length: 47 ft 1⅜ in. *Engine:* 2 x 1,200 hp
Junkers Jumo 211. *Armament:* 3 x 7·92-mm
machine-guns. *Crew:* 4. *Speed:* 286 mph at
18,000 ft. *Ceiling:* 30,150 ft. *Range:* 1,550 miles.
Bomb load: 5,510 lb.　　The Ju 88, designed in
1936 as a fast bomber, became famous in the
Second World War as an aircraft capable of
taking on any role, serving as everything from
dive-bomber to night fighter. During the Battle it
showed its paces as bomber, reconnaissance and
anti-shipping aircraft

Searchlights over London: 'the initiative in the air offensive now lay with the Germans'

Peter Elstob

ONE MAN'S BLITZ

Londoners got their first taste of the Blitz on the night of September 7, 1940, when 250 German bombers struck hard at the capital. For the rest of that year, and into the next, they were subjected to relentless pounding from the air

In September 1940 I took a week's holiday owing to me and so missed the first serious night raids. When I got back to London I tried to find out what it had been like, but the young couple I was living with seemed unable to describe it. I was, however, made to feel that I had missed great goings-on, that not having shared the experience I didn't belong to the exclusive club. I almost wished for an air raid —a little one, not too near.

About a week later I got my air raid. The warning went just after dinner but, apart from checking the blackout curtains, no notice was taken and we sat down to our weekly bridge game. At first there was quiet outside but slowly the noises which were to become so familiar built up. I wasn't playing very well because I was listening to the noise and trying to sort out what was going on outside. The others didn't seem to notice anything, rubbing their small experience into the new boy.

Edith dealt and, as an explosion shook the house gently, reminded me that we were vulnerable. I didn't make the obvious joke because I didn't feel at all funny.

'One heart,' she bid briskly. Somewhere high above us anti-aircraft shells exploded.

'Pass,' said Roland, her husband. A louder noise as a nearer battery had a go. Surely that was the throb-throb of a bomber's engine I could hear?

'Your bid,' Edith said impatiently.

'Two diamonds.' My words were drowned out by a terrific explosion. I checked an impulse to dive under the table because no one else seemed to have noticed it.

'Two diamonds.' I tried again but again there was an enormous explosion. This time I couldn't help ducking.

'You really *must* try and raise your voice above the bombs,' Roland said quite seriously.

And, within a fortnight or so, I, like most other Londoners, had also achieved a certain amount of sang-froid. My initiation came a few nights after the bridge game.

This time the raid started about one in the morning and I was awakened by it. I hadn't remembered to pull aside the blackout after putting out the light so the room was pitch black. I had awoken with a start and there was a taste of dust in my mouth, so I realised that one must have fallen close enough to shake my room. There was a series of explosions, as a stick of bombs straddled our neighbourhood. The third one seemed to be under my bed for I was lifted straight up and dumped on the floor and sprinkled with dust and plaster. The explosion was quite the loudest bang I had ever heard.

Reasoning that it was now too late to go down into the shelter I crept back under the blankets and, strangely, fell asleep at once.

In the morning I went to the window but, before pulling aside the blackout, braced myself for the dreadful destruction I was sure to see. To my amazement nothing had changed: the back gardens with their little sheds and clothes lines were exactly as always and not even a window was cracked. We found out, of course, where the particular bomb had fallen, but there wasn't a great deal to see, for it had gone through the roof of the house nearly opposite ours and had burst deep in the cellar. The casualties had been taken away, the small fire put out, and the road cleared of rubble.

One evening after the sirens had sounded their usual warning and nothing had happened, there was a sound like stones being thrown against the house or a number of slates falling off the roof. We ran to the front door and found an incendiary bomb burning brightly on the mat. Roland dashed upstairs for the bucket of sand he kept for just such an emergency; I ran into the kitchen and snatched up a bowl of washing-up water. The suds doused the bomb, snuffing it like a candle.

From the doorway we could see that there were many other incendiaries, some burning out harmlessly in the road or basement areas, some on houses, and one on the back seat of a car, having burned through the roof. Roland dumped his bucket of sand on that one and was pleased that it obediently went out. The bombs were about 9 inches long and burned with a white light for three or four minutes, leaving only the tail fins.

There were many people in the street shouting instructions to each other. Roland, Edith, and I were busy with bucket and stirrup pump when someone ran up shouting that the stables were on fire. These were at the end of a cul-de-sac behind our house and in them were kept a number of milkcart horses. We ran round to find thick smoke rolling out of the large open doors and were told that the terrified animals wouldn't come out.

There didn't seem to be any flames so I thought that probably some wet straw was smouldering. I bent low and felt my way along the wall towards the stalls. The lights were still on and I unlatched a stable door and found myself face to face with a large, very frightened horse. I shouted and clapped my hands but he took no notice of me, standing rooted to the spot. I got hold of his mane and tried to pull him out but he tossed his head and showed his yellow teeth. Fortunately someone had had the wit to go for two of the milkmen who lived near by. They quickly got bridles on the animals and were able to lead them out.

The daughter of a trapped woman was standing on her doorstep crying hysterically. Roland asked her which room her mother was in.

'Second floor back, but she's dead. Oh, poor mum, she's dead, I know she's dead.'

Roland gave me a full bucket of water and kept the stirrup pump himself. We soaked handkerchiefs, tied them over our nose and mouth and went up the smoke-filled stairs on our hands and knees. He kicked open the bedroom door. The room was full of smoke but there was a red glow in one corner and he crawled towards this. I pumped and he directed the spray.

The incendiary had crashed through the roof and the bedroom ceiling, landing on the bed. All the smoke in the house was coming from the burning mattress and bedding. The bomb had long since burned itself out and the spray soon had the fire out. As the smoke cleared we could see an old lady in the bed. She was quite dead.

Once outside again we were grabbed by a little old man in a white muffler who begged us to put out some incendiaries lodged in his attic. We got these out fairly quickly but he then pointed to a ladder and an open skylight, saying there were more on the roof. Somehow I found myself edging along the peak of the roof clutching a stirrup pump while Roland came behind with the bucket.

From up there we could see down into the street and away over the rooftops. It was an extraordinary sight: all around the horizon fires glowed, searchlights slowly raked the dark sky, anti-aircraft guns flashed silently, there being no apparent connection between them and the almost continuous noise of the guns. High above us shells burst like fireworks. But the most insistent noise came from the street immediately beneath us. It was the excited sound of many people shouting as they scurried in and out of their houses.

I started to spray the incendiary lodged by the chimney when I heard the sound of more bombs coming down and hugged the peak of the roof. Moments later a stick of small, 50-pound high-explosive bombs fell in a line across houses and street.

The bombers, earlier in the evening, had dropped nothing but hundreds of incendiaries. But this wave, a couple of hours later, came back with instantaneous high-explosive bombs where the fires were brightest and most people were in the streets.

The explosions caused panic; people ran back into burning houses or threw themselves into basement areas. I heard screams above the explosions as I tried to dig myself into the slates of the roof.

The rain of bombs lasted only a few minutes but it was dawn before the fires were all out and the injured had been taken away. We sat in the kitchen of our house drinking cocoa with neighbours who had lived near each other for years but had never spoken. Now they were talking and gesticulating in a most un-English manner as they described the narrow escapes of the night.

From the street shelters came the ones who had been down there during all the excitement. The rest of us looked at them sorrowfully, knit together by the experience we had shared.

△ Old Bailey in ruins: many landmarks were hit by the Blitz

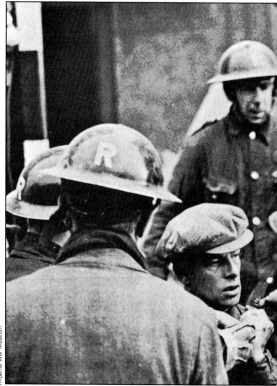

△ Rescue workers bring out a man buried by rubble for 14 hour

△ Adding to the havoc of the bombing were the fires that raged in the Blitz's wake: firemen work while others hunt for survivor

By May 1941 bombs had killed some 40,000 British civilians

△ Street damage like this often cut power and water lines

△ The bombing of Coventry marked a shift to strategic targets

Heinkel He III H3
Weight: 19,130 lb. *Span:* 74 ft 1¾ in. *Length:*
53 ft 9½ in. *Armament:* 5 x 7·92-mm machine-
guns ; 1 x 20-mm cannon. *Engine:* 2 x 1,200 hp
Jumo D-1. *Crew:* 5/6. *Speed:* 258 mph.
Range: 760 miles.   The twin-engined
Heinkels were the principal weapon in the
German heavy bomber squadrons and had
proved their tactical value in campaigns from
Spain to the fall of France. As a strategic bomber
however, attacking the industries and defences
of Britain, the type proved lacking in offensive
power and defensive armament

"The defence of Southern England will last four days and the Royal Air Force four weeks. We can guarantee invasion for the Führer within a month."

Reichsmarschall
Göring, 11 July 1940

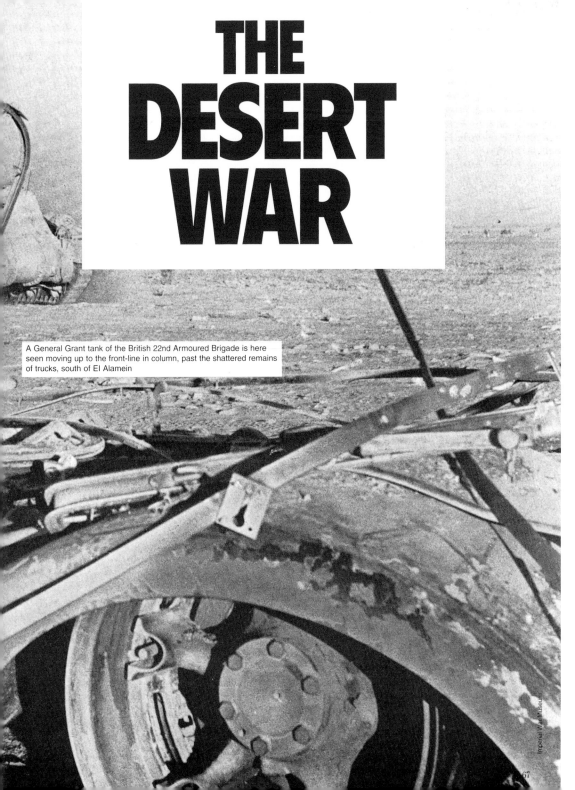

THE DESERT WAR

A General Grant tank of the British 22nd Armoured Brigade is here seen moving up to the front-line in column, past the shattered remains of trucks, south of El Alamein

Imperial War Museum

THE FIRST SWING OF TH

Sandwiched between French Algeria and British Egypt, Mussolini's North African colony of Libya represented, at the outset of war, a vulnerable outpost of the Axis Empire. Until the Fall of France in June 1940, that is. Immediately the situation was reversed. Now there was only the British presence in Egypt barring the road to the Nile and the oil-rich states of the Persian Gulf. And against General Wavell's 30,000-strong Western Desert Force, the Italians — under General Graziani — could muster no less than 250,000 men.

From the moment Italy joined the Second World War, on June 10, 1940, Mussolini's ambitions in North Africa were clear. Graziani was to sweep through Egypt, cross the Nile, and raise the Italian flag over the oilfields of the Middle East. Graziani however, could only make a hesitant advance of 65 miles into Egypt. There, at Sidi Barrani, he dug in and refused to go any further, saying his lack of armour, guns and equipment was such that any further offensive was impossible.

Over the top. Pith-helmeted infantrymen of Graziani's Italian desert army attack during their initial, hesitant thrust of 65 miles to Sidi Barrani in Egypt

Light field-gun support for the advancing Italian troops

PENDULUM

om Rome nonetheless there came a
muniqué announcing Graziani's
ance and making naïve claims that 'all
uiet and the trams are again running in
town of 'Sidi Barrani'. But the grossly
numbered British Western Desert
ce in Egypt harboured no such delusions.
Italian army, static and dug in at
Barrani, presented a target that Gen.
vell was not slow to appreciate.

t: **Autoblinda 40:** medium armoured car of the Italian
ert army. Turret gun: 20-mm Machine-gun: 8-mm.

Below and left: **Italian M15/42 medium
tanks moving across ideal terrain into
Egypt. Badly designed and poorly
armed, they proved no match for the
British Matildas of the day**

Paul Popper

The Italian C-in-C: Marshal Graziani

WAVELL'S 30,000

In a short and memorable campaign during the last weeks of 1940 and the beginning of 1941, the British managed to drive the Italians out of Egypt, Libya and Cyrenaica. It was the first British offensive of the Second World War and the first victory on land. Even as it happened it was transformed into a legend – a legend, that is, until other events – victories and defeats – pushed it into the background of men's minds.

On any numerical calculation, the success of Graziani's invasion of Egypt was a certainty, so large was the size of the invading army compared with the British force available to defend Egypt. But its mobility was low, and the handicap that limited mechanisation imposed on manoeuvre – for surprise – was increased by administrative inefficiency. After a 70-mile advance through the Western Desert, the Italians halted at Sidi Barrani, and there stuck for a couple of months.

The British Commander-in-Chief in the Middle East, General Wavell, decided to try the effect of an upsetting stroke by the Western Desert Force – the embryo of the 8th Army – under General

An Italian heavy machine-gun fitted with anti-aircraft sights dug in on the desert front

Fort Capuzzo, captured on December 14, 1940

O'Connor. It was visualised in the nature of a powerful raid rather than an offensive. There were only two divisions available, the 7th Armoured and the 4th Indian; after this stroke the latter was to be brought back to the Nile and sent down to the Sudan, to help in dealing with the threat of the Italian army in Eritrea and Ethiopia.

The 'raid', however, turned into a decisive victory, thanks to the paralysis and dislocation produced by General O'Connor's surprise move through the desert on to the enemy's rear. This sudden blow was delivered on December 9, 1940. A large part of Graziani's army was cut off and 35,000 captured, while the remainder only regained the shelter of their own frontier after a panic retreat that reduced them to a disorderly rabble.

The whole campaign might have ended at this point if Wavell had not insisted on the 4th Indian Division being withdrawn in accordance with the original plan. Deprived of its backing, the 7th Armoured Division was naturally unable to penetrate the Bardia defences, and several weeks elapsed before a fresh infantry division, the 6th Australian, could be brought from Palestine to act as a 'tin-opener'. Then Bardia was captured, on January 3, with 40,000

Wavell (on right) with O'Connor, his architect of victory

British barrage hammers   **Italian desert fort to the south of Sidi Barrani**

British howitzer bombards besieged Bardia

British light tank at speed

Right: The **Gloster Gladiator.**
Highly manoeuvrable but outclassed in both speed and fire-
power by the newer monoplane
fighters, this plane last saw active
squadron service with the RAF in
North Africa, a backwater in the
air war for both Axis and Allies
alike. **Max speed:** 246 mph
Armament: four Browning .303
machine-guns

Above: **Fiat CR-42.** This was the last single-
seater biplane to be used by any combatant
in the Second World War. **Armament:** two
12.7-mm machine-guns **Max speed:** 261
mph

Below: **Breda Ba-65.** This saw service in
Ethiopia in 1935 and was basically a
ground-attack plane. An observer could be
carried for scouting. **Armament:** four 12-mm
machine-guns **Max speed:** 267 mph

prisoners. Tobruk fell on the 22nd, with a further 25,000. In both cases the infantry/tank battalion, the 7th Royal Tanks, with its thickly armoured Matildas, proved decisive – as it had at Sidi Barrani.

The surviving part of Graziani's army retreated past Benghazi towards Tripoli, but was intercepted by an indirect pursuit that proved one of the most brilliant and daring strokes of the war. The 7th Armoured Division made a dash through the desert interior to reach the sea south of Benghazi on February 5, 1941. Its leading elements covered 170 miles in 36 hours over difficult and unknown country. While one group under Colonel Combe established a block across the enemy's line of retreat at Beda Fomm, another group – the 4th Armoured Brigade under Brigadier Caunter – pummelled his forces until they surrendered. The two groups combined amounted to only 3,000 men, yet by their audacity in thrusting across the path of a vastly superior enemy they secured a 'bag' of 21,000 prisoners.

Such Italian troops as remained, besides being ill-equipped to meet a tank thrust, were badly shaken by the fate of their main army. O'Connor was eager to exploit his victory at Beda Fomm, and was convinced that he could carry out the fresh bound with little delay for the replenishment of supplies. But a halt was called by the British government in order to provide the means of dispatching the ill-starred expedition to Greece. Wavell was instructed to leave only a minimum to hold Cyrenaica. O'Connor also went back to Egypt, and the control was left in less capable hands.

Italians under RAF attack during their retreat in the desert

Left: **Fiat BR-20 Cicogna.** One of Italy's heaviest bombers, this plane served everywhere in Mussolini's empire except East Africa. **Bomb load:** 3,300 lb **Max speed:** 267 mph

Below: **Savoia SM-79.** Like the Luftwaffe's Do-17, this had been blooded in the Spanish Civil War and was the standard long-range bomber of the Regia Aeronautica. **Bomb load:** 2,205 lb **Max speed:** 260 mph

ENTER THE AFRIKA KORPS: ROMMEL'S FIRST ATTACK

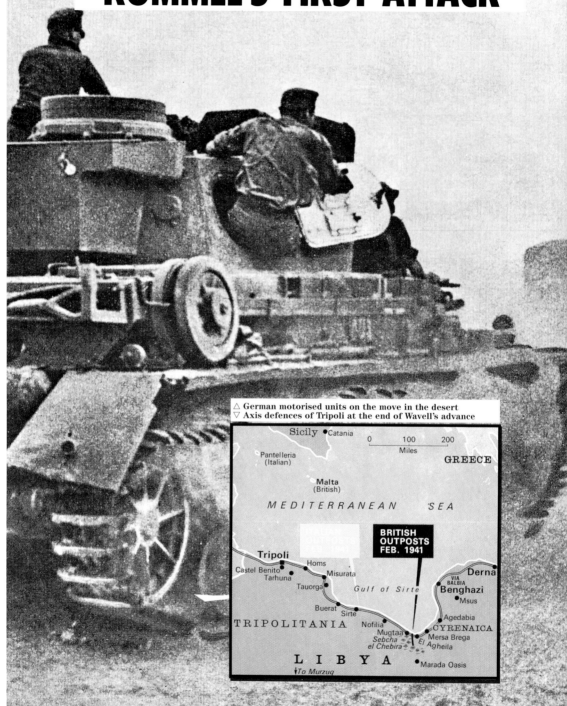

△ German motorised units on the move in the desert
▽ Axis defences of Tripoli at the end of Wavell's advance

Sicily •Catania

Pantelleria
(Italian)

GREECE

Malta
(British)

M E D I T E R R A N E A N   S E A

0   100   200
Miles

ITALIAN
OUTPOSTS

**BRITISH
OUTPOSTS
FEB. 1941**

Tripoli   Homs
Castel Benito   •Misurata   **Derna**
Tarhuna   VIA
BALBIA
Tauorga   *Gulf of Sirte*   **Benghazi**
•Msus

Buerat   Sirte
•Agedabia
TRIPOLITANIA   Nofilia   CYRENAICA
Mugtaa   •Mersa Brega
Sebcha   El
el Chebira   Agheila

L I B Y A   •Marada Oasis
↓To Murzuq

Struggle with the desert: in heavy going, a German heavy tank is given marshalling directions

The scorching pace of the conquest of Cyrenaica had exhausted the men and machines of Wavell's 'Thirty Thousand', some of which were withdrawn for service on other fronts. They were replaced by untried commanders and troops, with nondescript armoured vehicles – and were to receive damaging treatment from Rommel and the Afrika Korps, who used superior tactics and had better fighting vehicles.

Rommel arrived in Africa on February 12, 1941, followed by the Afrika Korps, which at that time was limited in numbers and supported by a relatively small airforce. The XV Panzer Division did not arrive until the end of May and the leading formation, V Light Division, was not complete until mid-April, although 105 medium and 51 light tanks had landed by March 11. The Italian army had five divisions and 60 light tanks of doubtful value.

Convinced that the British lacked a plan of aggression, Rommel easily captured El Agheila on March 24, and then attacked the British 2nd Armoured Division's positions at Mersa Brega on March 31. When Mersa Brega fell after a day's fierce fighting, Rommel launched a full-scale offensive to recover Cyrenaica. By swift moves round his opponents' flank and into their rear, he disrupted their advanced dispositions, and then by an encircling bluff produced the surrender of their main force at Mechili. The only in-

Rommel (right) plans his first attack

tact body to survive the net were -the two brigades of the Australian 7th Division, which withdrew under fire to join the Australian garrison at Tobruk. Within two weeks Rommel reached the Egyptian frontier, but he had overstretched his supply lines and was compelled to halt.

The only thorn in his side was Tobruk, where the improvised defences held out against the first attacks of his leading units.

Supply and defence for the Germans: Junkers 52 transports and Me 110 fighters

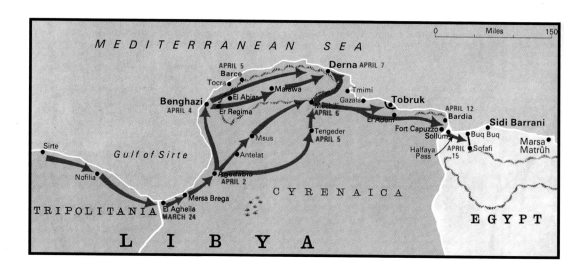

Below: **Panzer III.** This tank was the mainstay of the early German war offensives. In use with the Afrika Korps it was superior to any Allied armour before 1942.
Crew: 5 **Weight:** 19.5 metric tons **Armament:** MG34 machine-guns, front and co-axial 37-mm or 50-mm main armour-piercing gun **Armour:** 20-57 mm
Range: 165 km road; 95 km x-country

Rommel's next assault was well planned and executed, but although the perimeter was penetrated the attack failed. The Australians at Tobruk were not easily intimidated and calmly allowed the German tanks to over-run their lines so they could tackle the supporting infantry. It was the first time that the Germans had driven their tanks through infantry that did not automatically surrender. It was also the first time in the war that the Germans were defeated: they could not take Tobruk from the Australians.

Setting aside Tobruk, which was to remain in a state of siege for eight months, all that had been achieved by Wavell and O'Connor in four months had been swept away in one month by Rommel. No longer was the war to be one-sided: after this, the battle was to be one of constant movement between forces of roughly equal strength whose success or failure depended on the superior skill or luck one commander might have over the other. For the next two years it was to be the virtuosity of Rommel versus a succession of unhappy contenders.

Above: German **Sd.Kfz-251/7.** In common with the other vehicles illustrated below, this half-track personnel carrier was one of the mainstays of the Afrika Korps' light-armoured force. **Speed:** 31 mph **Range:** 185 miles **Crew:** 2 plus 9 troops

Right: German **Sd.Kfz-222** light armoured car. **Speed:** 50 mph **Range:** 180 miles **Crew:** 3 **Armament:** one 20-mm cannon, one 7.92-mm machine-gun

Right: German **Sd.Kfz-251** half-track reconnaissance vehicle. **Speed:** 31 mph **Range:** 185 miles **Crew:** 2 **Armament:** 7.92-mm machine-guns

Below: German **Sd.Kfz-231** heavy armoured car with drive and steering to all wheels. **Speed:** 53 mph **Range:** 187 miles **Crew:** 4 **Armament:** one 20-mm cannon, one 7.92-mm machine-gun

THE SIEGE OF TOBRUK

Tobruk was threatened by the German salient at Ras el Madauar, but Rommel had underestimated the strength of the western defences. The perimeter was in fact more vulnerable from the south-east corner, where O'Connor broke through the defence in 1941

Tobruk is a small but important port on the coast of Cyrenaica. Its pre-war population numbered about 4,000 people, living in a few hundred white buildings standing out starkly against the sun-baked, rocky ground sloping down to a tiny quay. The square in the centre of the town boasted a few dusty palm trees; and in times of peace the busiest installation in Tobruk was probably the water distillation plant which, with one or two wells, produced 40,000 gallons a day.

The importance of Tobruk lay in the fact that its harbour was the only safe and accessible port for over 1,000 miles, between Sfax in Tunisia and Alexandria in Egypt, apart from the even tinier harbour at Benghazi. Like Benghazi, Tobruk had been built by the Italians as one of the principal defences of Libya from the east and as a naval base.

In peace, it was important as the main outlet for the products of a vast area of hinterland. But in war, during the struggle for North Africa, its importance was greatly increased because any advance beyond it, either to the east or west, was doubly imperilled. First, the possession of Tobruk was essential as an unloading point for supplies and reinforcements, which otherwise had to be brought along difficult and lengthy lines of communication, either from Alexandria in one direction or Benghazi in the other. Secondly, in the hands of a determined and aggressive garrison, it could represent a serious offensive threat to the flank of any advance which by-passed it.

Winston Churchill himself described it as a 'sally port' and declared: 'Nothing but a raid dare go past Tobruk.'

The original Italian maps of the Tobruk defences show two lines of strong-points, completely sunk into the ground. These covered a perimeter of some 35-40 miles with a radius of about 20 miles (see map). The outer defences consisted of a series of heavily concreted dugouts — many cleverly improvised from natural caves — each holding 30 to 40 men. These dugouts were interconnected by trenches with locations every few hundred yards for machine-guns, mortars, or anti-tank guns. The trenches were roofed in with thin boarding and covered lightly with sand so that they were invisible from even a few yards away. In front of the outer defences barbed wire was laid, varying in some places from a single coil in width to a belt 30 yards wide elsewhere.

In front of the barbed wire the Italians had built an anti-tank ditch, often cleverly adapting an existing natural ravine. Straight-sided, and averaging 7 feet deep and 10 feet wide, the ditch was designed to thwart any attempted crossing by a tracked vehicle. The inner defence line was some 2,000 to 3,000 yards behind the outer line and constructed to the same pattern, but without the anti-tank ditch.

When Rommel launched his forces against the Western Desert Force in April 1941, and the opposition crumbled before him, one of his first thoughts was to capture Tobruk so as to eliminate it as a hazard, and to shorten his lines of communication for his drive into and beyond Egypt.

He did not anticipate any great difficulty. Wavell's forces had captured it from the Italians in two days, and the confident Rommel thought that it would not take much longer — if as long — to wrest it back.

However, the hastily improvised defence by the 9th Australian Division — augmented by 18th Brigade from 7th Australian Divi-

German armoured cars in a night battle for Tobruk: Rommel was becoming impatient, and threw his force into a full assault

sion and the remnants of 3rd Armoured Brigade, with field and anti-aircraft regiments, all under Major-General Leslie Morshead – was more than a match for the dying momentum of Rommel's push.

Siege warfare – modern style

From then on, Tobruk was in a constant state of siege. But it was not a siege in the same sense as those of Ladysmith and Mafeking in the Boer War, or of Lucknow in the Indian Mutiny, where isolated garrisons were surrounded by a numerically superior enemy and completely cut off from friendly forces. Constant contact was maintained between Tobruk and the main Allied forces by the Royal Navy – although it should not be imagined that this was in any way a 'milk run'.

Yet it was certainly a siege in the sense that Tobruk was a fortified position under continuous attack by the enemy. Every inch of the defended area was within range of the German and Italian artillery, and the harbour working-parties came under fire almost as much as the troops in the outer perimeter.

Beyond dispute the survival of Tobruk depended upon the harbour being kept in working order and the continuance of supplies along the tenuous sea-lane leading to it from Egypt. Nothing of use to the survival of an army was indigenous to Tobruk except for the shelter given by the natural caves. Everything had to be brought in from Egypt; and Rommel, realising this, concentrated almost as much on neutralising the harbour and interrupting the sea life-line as he did on planning a landward assault.

Since the days of Wavell's offensive the British army in Cyrenaica had been supported and supplied from the sea by ships of the Inshore Squadron, a heterogeneous armada comprising anything from a destroyer to a monitor, sloop, gunboat, trawler, sponge-fisher, or lighter. In Tobruk's most heated hour, these ships, supported sometimes by the Mediterranean Fleet, as often as possible covered by fighter aircraft, regularly braved the perils of mines, shells, bombs, and torpedoes to run men, machines, and supplies (including water), along the enemy-held coast to the besieged fortress.

Losses among the Inshore Squadron were heavy, particularly by day, and at times it became permissible to voyage only on the moonless nights. Daylight attacks such as those aimed at the anti-aircraft sloops *Auckland* and *Paramatta* on June 24, when they were escorting the valuable petrol-carrier *Pass of Balmaha*, give an indication of the scale of Axis efforts. On this occasion, combined raids by torpedo-bombers and 96 dive-bombers accounted for *Auckland* and stopped *Pass of Balmaha*. At the other end of the scale, a captured Italian fishing schooner *Maria Giovanni*, skippered by an Australian, Lieutenant Alfred Palmer, ran the gauntlet night after night until tricked into disaster by the Germans. In common with others, Palmer guided himself into Tobruk harbour by a shaded green light at the entrance, but he was not to know that one night the Germans had lit a decoy to the east. To his surprise Palmer ran himself hard ashore and was taken prisoner by the Germans as he and his crew were industriously digging a channel through which to refloat the ship.

Against the backcloth of coastal sea and air battle, the fight on land muttered and grumbled amid bombardments and patrol-scuffles while Rommel, chastened by his first rebuffs, raised his strength for a full assault. He was becoming impatient. Any other advance beyond the frontier was out of the question until Tobruk had been taken, but he was not ready until April 30.

The attack on that day began with a continuous pounding from Stuka dive-bombers and artillery, against which the defenders' powers of retaliation were limited. They engaged the dive-bombers with anti-aircraft and small-arms fire, and the British artillery put down counter-fire on the enemy gun-positions. But because the garrison could not expect fresh supplies of ammunition until the next moonless night – a week away – ammunition had to be husbanded and every shot made to count.

The German dive-bombers were unchallenged in the air, for the RAF Hurricane squadron, unable to operate from airstrips under continuous fire – with their runways frequently cratered and with workshops and petrol-dumps shelled every day – had been withdrawn on April 25.

As the dive-bombers drew off from their targets, the attacking infantry and tanks moved in against the western sector of the defences. But the defenders were far from subdued, and the Germans and Italians were met by ferocious fire from the British artillery and tanks and the Australian infantry.

It was a grim and bitter battle. Writing of it later Rommel said: 'The Australians fought with remarkable tenacity. Even their wounded went on defending themselves with small-arms fire, and stayed in the fight to their last breath. They were immensely big and powerful men, who without question represented an élite formation of the British Empire, a fact that was also evident in battle.'

By the end of the day the Germans and Italians had succeeded in penetrating the defences of Tobruk and had established a 2-mile salient into the Australian positions on the western sector of the perimeter. The salient included the important hill of Ras el Madauar, which dominated a large part of the defended area.

Still determined to subdue Tobruk, Rommel next day put in fresh troops, to exploit the Ras el Madauar salient, but although the fighting raged unabated until May 4, the attackers were unable to advance farther.

The salient of Ras el Madauar, however, remained a constant threat to the besieged garrison and – although there was sporadic activity on the other sectors of the defended perimeter – from May 4 onwards the defence of Tobruk was, in essence, the defence of its western sector. Here the hard outer shell of permanent defence works had been breached, and the opposing forces faced one another from hastily improvised foxholes. It was, in a way, the soft under-belly of Tobruk: the Germans and Italians expected that if the breakthrough came anywhere it would come in the western sector, and this was the area to which they devoted most of their attention.

By the time Tobruk had been under siege

The 'Rats of Tobruk' spent much of their time underground in shelters – the ventilators for this one came from the clutter of wrecked ships in Tobruk harbour

for a month the area around the town was littered with burned-out tanks, vehicles, and all the debris of war. The town itself was reduced to a heap of rubble in which only one house remained standing, and in this—despite the fact that it stood out among the flattened buildings like a sore thumb—General Morshead maintained his operational headquarters.

For the defenders of Tobruk each day brought a fresh crop of problems. Problems, that is, in addition to those normally associated with desert fighting—the strange disorientation brought on by a featureless landscape which induced a tendency to walk in circles; and daily temperatures in the hundreds, so that to touch a tank left standing in the sun meant a burned hand. There were problems of food; not a shortage, perhaps, but a monotonous sameness with everything coming out of cans. There was, like elsewhere in the desert, a shortage of water, and what little there was was salty. There was an almost total absence of bread, and a superabundance of fleas, flies, and rats.

Added to these discomforts was a problem rare in the annals of defended strongholds. The Axis airfields from which sorties were made against Tobruk were sufficiently close for the defenders to hear the aircraft starting up prior to take-off. Two of the airfields, El Adem and Acroma, were only about 10 miles away, and some of the defenders swore that in the still, desert night air they could hear the ground crews singing as they worked on the aircraft.

There was only one permanent line of defence against the bombers once the RAF fighters had been withdrawn on April 25, and that was the anti-aircraft guns of the Royal Artillery, supplemented by the guns of ships in harbour. Two regiments of 3·7-inch and captured Italian 102-mm guns, plus three regiments with 40-mm Bofors stayed for the whole siege, pitting their wits against each new variation and combination of attack by high-level and dive-bombers. Throughout countless raids the gunners emulated their colleagues at Malta by maintaining a miniature 'Grand Barrage' in the face of the fierce bravery of German pilots who sometimes swept at less than 500 feet over the gun pits. By July the dive-bombers actually began to let up, and it became possible even to unload ships in daylight. Alone, the anti-aircraft gunners prevented bombing with impunity and so they, above all, enabled the supply vessels to unload and maintain the garrison.

The western sector, around the Ras el Madauar salient, had its own fixed problems. The rocky nature of the ground made deep digging almost impossible and, on those days when fighting was not actually taking place, both sides lay in their shallow trenches unable to move. A German account of conditions in the salient at the time says: 'The Australians were crack shots. Their sniping was superb. Even the most trivial movement from the foxhole—rump too high—and ping! You'd had it.'

For night patrolling, the Australians wore crêpe-soled shoes, long trousers, pullovers, and berets. They were armed with submachine guns and grenades, and their objective in most cases was a single enemy stronghold. They would descend on it silently on a moonless night, throw their grenades and empty the magazines of the sub-machine guns into the enemy emplacement, then disappear back into their own positions as swiftly and silently as they had arrived.

The Germans used much the same technique against the Australians and British, and on occasions a patrol from either side would encounter one another in No-Man's-Land, and a short sharp action would develop, often involving fierce, hand-to-hand fighting.

Conditions worsen

As time went on, conditions in the besieged area became steadily worse, a fact of which Rommel himself was very much aware. Writing home to his wife in June he said: 'Water is very short in Tobruk, the British troops are getting only half-a-litre a day. With our dive-bombers I'm hoping to cut their rations still further. The heat is getting worse every day and . . . one's thirst becomes almost unquenchable.'

Churchill, too, was highly sensitive to the importance of Tobruk, and the role it should and could play in the Middle East campaign. After Tobruk had successfully beaten off one of the many attacks by the Axis forces, he cabled: 'Bravo, Tobruk! We feel it vital that Tobruk should be regarded as a sally port.'

This the Australians and British did, although often their efforts were overshadowed by events elsewhere. The eyes of the world were on the airborne invasion of Crete, the German assault on Russia, and—somewhat nearer to the beleaguered garrison—the abortive Operation 'Battleaxe'. Nevertheless, the Australian and British troops in Tobruk continued to play a decisive part in the tactical moves of both sides in the Western Desert.

Then, in August, Churchill began to receive demands from the Australian government for the withdrawal of their troops from Tobruk. Already, in response to this pressure, Auchinleck had relieved one Australian brigade by the Polish Carpathian Brigade (Lieutenant-General S. Kopanski), but this was not enough. By early September the Prime Minister of Australia (Mr Fadden) had become firmly determined that the Australian troops must be withdrawn from Tobruk. The reason he put forward at the time was: '. . . in order to give them an opportunity for refreshment, restoration of dis-

cipline and re-equipment, and to satisify public opinion in Australia.' The Australian government was also said to be 'anxious about the decline in health resistance of their troops in the fortress and the danger of catastrophe resulting from further decline and inability to withstand a determined attack'.

There seems to be no evidence that the Australian troops were themselves clamouring to be relieved. They had fought with vigour and determination under the most trying conditions for five months, but they would probably have borne the strain longer if called upon to do so. Nevertheless, during September the rest of the Australians were replaced by the 70th British Division (Major-General R. M. Scobie, who also assumed command of the garrison).

It was not an easy change-over. The ships which brought in the 70th Division and took out the Australians were subjected to severe air attack in the process, the minelayer *Latona* being sunk and the destroyer *Hero* damaged.

When the Polish Brigade arrived in mid-August, General Morshead allocated them at first to the comparatively quiet southern sector, but after a few weeks they took over, with the Durham Light Infantry and Black Watch, the western sector with the salient.

By then the sector was showing all the

The Australians at Tobruk showed that the Afrika Korps was not invincible

signs of the four months' siege. The 'No-Man's-Land' between the forward posts was thickly carpeted with mines and booby-traps, and strewn with the unburied bodies of soldiers of both sides. But the defences – if such they could be called – were still in the same primitive condition; narrow and shallow trenches in which there was no room for the occupants to sit or kneel. In some places there was nothing but small, improvised stone breastworks.

The exposed nature of the forward defences in the western sector made any daylight approach to them impossible. Once the sun had risen, the defenders could not move out, nor could their reserves or supplies get up to them. Life would have been impossible had it not been for the fact that, by one of those unspoken mutual arrangements which sometimes come about in war, both sides observed an unofficial two-hour armistice, beginning at dusk. During this period, neither side opened fire on the other and the troops on both sides could emerge safely from their cramped positions. Food, water, and ammunition could be brought up to forward defended positions and life could be made slightly more bearable on both sides.

Each night the Germans signalled the end of the two-hour armistice by a burst of tracer-bullets fired straight up into the air, and from then on it was 'business as usual'.

Another mutually accepted custom was the raising of a Red Cross flag when a man was wounded. Fire immediately switched from that point and stretcher-bearers could safely approach to remove the wounded man. Indeed, on one or two occasions when casualties were heavier than usual, ambulances were allowed to drive up unmolested to the Red Cross flag to remove the wounded.

When the Poles took over the western sector from the Australians, their first instinct was to reject these cease-fire arrangements. They were all men who had, at great risk to themselves, escaped from a Poland occupied by the Germans, who were applying barbarian methods of treatment. There was a powerful emotional barrier inhibiting the Poles' acceptance of anything in the nature of a pact with the Germans.

However, General Kopanski realised that any change in the established customs would alert the Germans to the fact that a change of units had taken place, and this, of course, the defenders wished to keep secret as long as possible. Accordingly he ordered his battalion commanders to continue to observe the armistice and cease-fire arrangements of the Australians and this they did, although with some reluctance. After a few days in the sector, however, they began to appreciate the practical value of the two-hour nightly armistice, realising that without it the forward companies would inevitably have died from thirst and starvation. But they discontinued the hoisting of the Red Cross flag as soon as possible. Each section was equipped with medical supplies and with the aid of these, plus some improvised surgery, it was possible in the majority of cases for the wounded to wait for evacuation until the two-hour armistice at dusk.

Nevertheless, on their side the Germans and Italians continued the custom of hoisting a Red Cross flag and evacuating wounded in daylight, and although the Poles did not fire on the casualty clearing party, the flag –

Tobruk harbour as another German raid explodes on the town and its defences

Imperial War Museum

as General Kopanski put it – 'greatly facilitated our pinpointing their strongholds, and destroying them very efficiently and inflicting new casualties later on'.

With the relief of the 9th Australian Division by the 70th British Division complete, there were now in Tobruk three infantry brigades (14th, 16th, and 23rd), a tank brigade (32nd, comprising 1st and 4th Royal Tank Regiments and a squadron each from 7th Royal Tank Regiment and the King's Dragoon Guards), seven artillery regiments, plus an anti-aircraft artillery brigade, a Czech battalion, a machine-gun battalion of the Royal Northumberland Fusiliers, an Australian battalion and – later on – two New Zealand battalions with supporting artillery.

This was the force with which General Scobie intended to break out from Tobruk and link up with a co-ordinated offensive by the 8th Army: Operation 'Crusader'.

Inside the besieged fortress General Scobie decided that the Tobruk garrison should break through the lines of the enemy on the eastern sector, in order to meet the approaching units of the 8th Army. This was to be the task of the 14th Infantry Brigade (Black Watch, Bedfordshire and Hertfordshire Regiment, York and Lancaster Regiment) under its commander Brigadier B. H. Chappel, with the support of the tanks of the 32nd Tank Brigade and the machine-gunners of the Royal Northumberland Fusiliers.

The break-out was planned for dawn on November 22. But three hours before the break-out, the Polish Brigade was to launch a feint break-out from the western sector, preceded by a heavy artillery barrage.

During the hours of darkness on the night November 21/22, the Tobruk troops moved to their arranged jumping-off points. In the distance they could hear the sounds of the fierce battle in the Sidi Rezegh area, where the 8th Army was fighting to reach them.

All those awaiting zero hour – British, Poles, Czechs, New Zealanders, and Australians – were hopeful that the siege was about to be ended. But much hard fighting lay ahead. Operation 'Crusader' was destined to continue for many weeks and the siege of Tobruk was not to end until December 10, when land communications between the garrison and the main body of the 8th Army were once again firmly established. Then the Royal Navy could relax from its task of being the only link between Tobruk and the rest of the Allies – a task which had included delivering to the garrison 34,000 men, 72 tanks, 92 guns, and 34,000 tons of stores over a period of 242 days.

40-mm Bofors Anti-Aircraft Gun. The Swedish-designed Bofors was one of the most widely used weapons of the war. Not only an AA gun, it was also used – as at Alamein – to fire tracer as a guide-line for infantry. **Weight:** 2.4 tons **Weight of shell:** 2 lb **Rate of fire:** 120 rpm **Ceiling:** 12,000 ft **Crew:** 6

In one month Rommel's first offensive had taken him all the way from Tripolitania to the border of Egypt; but the British could not allow him to consolidate his hold on the strategically important passes at Sollum and Halfaya. The Allies' high hopes, though, were soon dashed. Rommel proved himself as tenacious and resourceful in defence as he was daring and fluid in attack.

When Wavell received news that a convoy of tanks and aircraft was on its way (the Tiger Convoy) he planned a limited operation – Operation Brevity – to drive the Germans from the frontier. Brigadier Gott's force attacked on May 15 with all available tanks but they were unable to consolidate their gains and retreated when the Germans counterattacked. On May 27 the Germans reoccupied the Halfaya Pass.

The Tiger Convoy docked at Alexandria on May 12 and disgorged 238 tanks and 43 Hurricane fighters. Churchill insisted that his 'Tiger Cubs' be used in an immediate offensive, and although unhappy about the operational readiness of his newly-equipped forces, Wavell launched his last desert offensive – Operation Battleaxe – on June 14. The British attacked with tanks and infantry looking for a decisive battle – tank against tank – which they hoped to win with their superior numbers. But Rommel had other ideas. With calculated deliberation he held his hand, letting the defensive positions break the British tank attacks on their own. Although he had lost a fair proportion of his infantry and guns, his tank force was practically as fresh as it had been at the start of the battle and, as a result of attrition, actually superior in numbers to the British.

DUELS WITH THE AFRIKA KORPS

Operation Brevity

Operation Battleaxe

then launched a well-judged armoured counterstroke wide round enemy's desert flank, and sent the British scurrying back.

n November 1941 the British mounted a bigger offensive – eration Crusader. By this time Wavell had been replaced by neral Auchinleck as Commander-in-Chief, while the enlarged ces on the Libyan frontier had been constituted as the 8th Army, ter General Cunningham. The offensive opened on the 18th, with esert flank advance which placed the British close to Rommel's r. In meeting the superior numbers and mobility of the British chanised forces, the Germans skilfully applied tactics which ed the British tanks into traps that were lined with their own cealed tanks and deadly 88-mm guns. Rommel thus strikingly

e German '88' flak guns knocked out many British tanks.

demonstrated, as already in Operation Battleaxe, the defensive-offensive method and baited gambit in modern mechanised warfare – blunting the edge of his opponent's 'sword' on his own 'shield', preparatory to the delivery of his thrust.

Next day Rommel, judging the situation to be ripe for bolder action, launched the mobile part of his forces on a daring swoop round the 8th Army's desert flank and over the frontier on to its communications. As it burst through into the British rear areas it spread confusion and panic. The effect might have settled the issue of the battle if the decision to persist or retreat had remained with Cunningham. But Auchinleck, who flew up at this crucial moment, insisted on a continuance of the battle, and then, on returning to Cairo two days later, appointed Ritchie to command in place of Cunningham. Auchinleck's intervention brought victory out of defeat – yet it was basically more of a gamble than Rommel's strategic raid, because it staked the 8th Army's survival on the maintenance of its far advanced position.

While Rommel's deep thrust failed in its aim only by a narrow margin, the penalty of failure was large. For while he and his three armoured divisions (two German and one Italian) were operating over the frontier, far away from the remainder, the split-up British forces which he had left behind were able to recover their balance, resume their offensive pressure, and link up with the garrison of Tobruk, before he returned to the relief of his non-mobile formations. Although he succeeded in regaining the advantage temporarily after several days' hard fighting and close-quarter manoeuvring, it was a barren success. His losses were much heavier than in the opening phase, and a bigger subtraction from his limited tank strength than he could withstand, particularly in view of the larger reinforcements available to the British. On December 6, 1941, Rommel was forced to break off the battle around Tobruk and retreat, first to Gazala, and then back to the frontier of Tripolitania.

Operation Crusader

r left: Operation Brevity, which started on ay 15, 1941, was the British attempt to ow the Germans back from the frontier d pave the way for future operations in renaica. The British started well but had on to withdraw in the face of German unterattacks. Left: Operation Battleaxe as more ambitious, but failed because of mmel's excellent defensive tactics. ght: Operation Crusader. After losing the tial battle Rommel immediately fell back his defensive position at El Agheila.

atildas on the move: the battle for lfaya ended their reputation as the ulnerable queen of the battlefield, for 88s, used as anti-tank guns, pene-ted their thick armour with ease

ROMMEL STRIKES BACK

By mid-January 1942, Auchinleck's spearheads had reached the Gulf of Sirte, and Cyrenaica seemed lost for Rommel's exhausted Panzer army. But in fact the pattern of the desert was was repeating itself: as Rommel's forces fell back on their bases in Tripolitania, the 8th Army advanced farther and farther from its bases in Egypt. Both sides had suffered heavy losses in men and equipment and a race was on to bring the opposing armies up to strength. This time, however, the German and Italian armies had the advantage of a shorter supply route from Tripoli and better protection for their convoys – thanks to the attacks on Malta. The Afrika Korps was once again ready to attack.

Rommel's Panzers deploy for the attack on the British outposts at El Agheila

Rommel's second offensive in Cyrenaica followed the lines of his debut in March and April 1941. It began with a timely blow against the Allied outposts, at Mersa Brega and Agedabia, which disrupted all hopes of the 8th Army for an invasion of Tripolitania. Rommel had hoped merely to delay the British attack by striking while the 8th Army was off balance and spread over a large area; but when he saw the confusion he had caused, Rommel ignored the orders of Commando Supremo, the Italian High Command in Rome, and fed in his Panzer forces until the strike became a full-scale offensive which kept the 8th Army on the run. This time Rommel was not able to press on to Tobruk, but was halted west of Gazala. In three weeks, nonetheless, he had reconquered western Cyrenaica for the Axis – the 'Desert Fox' had done it again.

Far left: A mobile piece of German artillery in action during the advance to Mechili

Left: A Mark IV Panzer of the Afrika Korps. This was the best tank in the desert at the time

Right: Rommel and his staff. With renewed confidence Panzerarmee Afrika gathered momentum

THE FIGHT AT GAZALA

From February until mid-May 1942 there was a l[...] in the desert war as both sides renewed their force[...] But Rommel was anxious to continue his reconque[...] of Cyrenaica, and Churchill was continually urgi[...] his commanders to resume the offensive. Romm[...] attacked first, but it soon seemed that he had m[...] calculated—that lack of fuel and water wou[...] destroy the Afrika Korps. However, the 'Dese[...] Fox' was saved by his own willingness to improvi[...]

and by the slowness of the British commanders. The result, the fall of Tobruk, was not only a terrific blow to Allied morale but also meant that the road to Egypt and Suez now seemed open—and Rommel urged on his men and tanks towards a spot on the map called Alamein.

Of the opposing forces the British were in greater strength on the ground with 100,000 troops and 849 tanks, as opposed to Rommel's 90,000 troops and 560 tanks. But the Axis had an overwhelming superiority in the air while their tank formations contained a proportion of the best tanks in the desert. Furthermore Rommel possessed a more finely-tempered, though considerably smaller, army. The Italians were hardly outstanding soldiers, but the Afrika Korps embodied a rare degree of experience and skill. Nor can there be anything but admiration for the way in which the enemy commanders handled their armour. With rare exceptions, they kept their tanks concentrated, and wisely protected them behind an effective artillery screen until the moment for the *coup de grâce* had come.

The 8th Army, on the other hand, was at this time a mixture of tired veterans and brash newcomers, who were given scant time to settle in before the blow came. And the much-vaunted Gazala Line

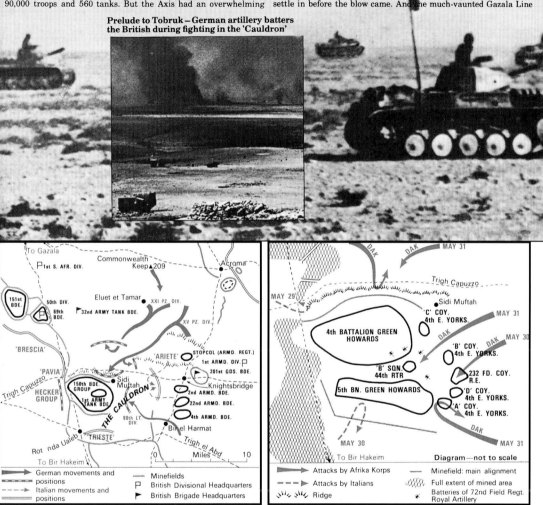

Prelude to Tobruk – German artillery batters the British during fighting in the 'Cauldron'

German movements and positions	Minefields
Italian movements and positions	⊓ British Divisional Headquarters
	► British Brigade Headquarters

Attacks by Afrika Korps	Minefield: main alignment
Attacks by Italians	Full extent of mined area
Ridge	Batteries of 72nd Field Regt. Royal Artillery

Diagram—not to scale

◁ **Phase 1: The Gazala Line is turned.** The front-line brigades of General Ritchie's 8th Army were deployed along the Gazala Line in an inter-connected system of 'brigade boxes' and Ritchie hoped to exhaust Rommel's attacks against these defences. But the Gazala Line had one great weakness: its southern flank at Bir Hakeim extended into empty desert—and Rommel opened the battle with a vast sweep around the Gazala Line with his Afrika Korps, while Cruewell and the Italians pinned down the rest of the line. Within 24 hours, German spearheads were astride the 8th Army's communications. But the Bir Hakeim garrison held out in the German rear.

△ **Phase 2: Rommel turns on 150th Brigade box.** This box nearly wrecked Rommel's attack: General Bayerlein later said: 'We never even knew that it was there; by the evening of the third day we were surrounded and almost out of petrol.' As Rommel's armour moved west into the 'Cauldron', it seemed to Ritchie that all was going well and that Rommel would be trapped against the Gazala minefields with no supplies. The battle now devolved on Rommel's attempt to crush the 150th Brigade box, while his sappers fought to keep open his supply-lines through the British minefields. This was the time for a counterattack by 8th Army—but Ritchie held back and missed his chance

△ **Phase 3: The fight for 150th Brigade box.** For almost 72 hours, Rommel's entire efforts were concentrated on this vital sector—but again the 8th Army missed its chance to throw in a heavy counterattack. This 'battle within a battle' was one of the unsung epics of the desert war, as the box garrison was forced steadily back by the German attacks. Since the battle had opened, the 150th Brigade box had exhausted the supplies calculated to last for 21 days—and the end finally came on June 1, heralded by a crushing Stuka bombardment. Rommel had secured his lifeline through the Gazala Line—but Bir Hakeim still held out at the southern flank of the battle-front was more suited to be the springboard of a fresh offensive than to provide a well-balanced line of in-depth defence fortifications.

In May 1942 Rommel attacked first with a diversion in the north by the Italian infantry, followed by a wide flanking manoeuvre with his armour which, in the night of the 26th, threw the 8th Army off its balance. He was checked, however, before he could reach the

▽ **Phase 4: Rommel's breakthrough.** Ritchie's counterattack came too late: his attempts to smash Rommel's hold on the 'Cauldron' were beaten off, and in a fierce attack Rommel shattered 30th Corps. This time he made no mistake about Tobruk, and broke through in the south-east corner

◄── 8th Army attacks   ━━► Rommel resumes attack toward Tobruk

Auchinleck meets Rommel

1942 June 23: The Middle East Defence Committee authorises the withdrawal of 8th Army from the Egyptian frontier to Marsa Matrûh.
June 25: General Auchinleck takes command of 8th Army; General Ritchie is sent on leave. Auchinleck appoints Major-General Dorman-Smith as his acting Chief of the General Staff.
June 26: Auchinleck cancels the order to stand on the Matrûh-Sidi Hamza line – 8th Army will withdraw eastwards as the enemy advances. Rommel begins to move his forces forward, with his armoured divisions astride the southern escarpment, and 90th Light Division to the north, aiming to cut the coast road east of Matrûh.
June 27: 1200 hours: The Germans have reached a position from which they threaten the withdrawal of 13th Corps; 10th Corps is ordered to attack to relieve this pressure.
1920 hours: 13th Corps issues the withdrawal codewords. 8th Army HQ orders 10th Corps to withdraw as well, but it does not receive the order until early the next morning.
June 28: 10th Corps is trapped with its back to the sea. At 1200 hours Auchinleck orders 10th Corps to break out that night, but 13th Corps, which is intended to launch a diversionary attack, is not informed of this plan until 2100 hours, by which time 10th Corps is moving out to the south – leaving over 7,000 prisoners.

Matrûh was Auchinleck's first battle after ▽ taking over command of 8th Army: his disorganised forces tried to hold the threadbare defences, but Rommel simply repeated his encircling tactics. The next stop was Alamein

Rommel leads the Axis Panzerarmee to the ▷ height of its success: the invasion of Egypt. His first attack in January had recovered western Cyrenaica for the Axis; the battles of May/June hurled 8th Army back into Egypt

coast and cut off the British forces holding the Gazala Line. Thereupon he took up a defensive position with his back against the British minefields – which led the British to feel that he was cornered, and bound to surrender. But their countermoves were too direct and they fell into the defensive traps which Rommel had quickly improvised when he was checked. With its reserves entangled and expended, the 8th Army was unable to meet Rommel's next flanking move, and was beaten piecemeal – once again the 'Desert Fox' had turned the tables of defence into offence.

While one portion was falling back to the frontier, another portion withdrew into Tobruk. Rommel's armoured forces swept past Tobruk, as if heading for the frontier, then suddenly switched round and struck at Tobruk in reverse, before the forces there had settled down. Penetrating the defences at a weak point, the Germans overran the garrison and captured almost the whole of it – together with such an abundance of supplies and transport as to provide the means for a prolonged advance on their own part – an advance that was not long in coming.

Not unnaturally, the news of Rommel's heavy defeat of 8th Army and his capture of Tobruk caused a wave of exhilaration to run through Germany and Italy. Overnight, Erwin Rommel's detractors in high places – and they were not lacking in either Rome or Berlin – became his staunchest champions, and there was widespread approval for the Führer's announcement that he was immediately conferring the rank of Field-Marshal on the brilliant desert commander. It seemed that the war in the Western Desert, already a little over two years old, was on the point of being resolved.

To the east of the Egyptian frontier, the brave but bewildered and exhausted formations of General Ritchie's defeated army began painfully to regroup themselves. In a desperate bid to stop the Axis onrush, General Auchinleck took command of the 8th Army, but the improvised defences at Marsa Matrûh were no match for Rommel's army and the British fell back to El Alamein. For the first time this desert bottleneck was about to become the hinge on which the outcome of the Desert War would swing.

"For you the war is finish!"

We learnt yesterday that we are now definitely cut off here in Tobruk. Jerry has driven along to the south through El Adem and Sidi Rezegh and cut the coast road, probably near Gambut.

We are in a big, wide, flat area which has been used as an aerodrome and lies between the road to Bardia and the sea, and is to the south-east of the town.

9 am – Eric and I are squatting in our new and still unfinished trench. There is a hell of an attack on and it's been going on for the last two hours. A colossal barrage of AA is going up, and dive-bombers, mainly Junkers 87s, are very numerous. We haven't seen one of our planes yet! No 'drome to work from, I suppose. I only hope my luck holds.

Mid-day – Have just snatched a little grub. Things are looking bloody black. Jerry is slowly pushing our tanks and guns back from the eastern edge of the perimeter defences and he is now up on the escarpment to the south-east of us. It has been one long roar of bombs, guns, and shells all morning.

After making the last entry we spent a terrifying afternoon in our dug-outs and trenches. Hour after hour we were cooped up while Jerry's creeping artillery barrage crept nearer and nearer, and beyond that a mass of tanks of all sizes spitting all they had got. Of what use are our puny .303 Lee Enfield rifles against that lot? This morning we could at least bang away at the Stukas and feel we might hit the bastards.

The last two hours were hell indeed. It seems fantastic now that so many of us got through unscathed. Shells were bursting all round, making the sides of the trench crumble in upon us. They were evidently aiming mainly to knock out the Coastal Defence and AA gun emplacements just behind us, and, being in between, the shells were roaring low over our heads, seeming only a foot or two above the ground. They made a whistle and roar like a train, and the shrapnel a horrible tearing sound. Many of them also fell short, exploding on con-tact with the rocky surface round about. But our big main danger and fear were the AP shells bursting in the air. How we wished our tin helmets were 12 ft in diameter instead of 12 inches!

At last, at about 5 o'clock, and after ten hours of practically continuous shelling, a mass of Jerry tanks and armoured vehicles rumbled into our location, nosing around trenches, dug-outs and wagons, lids down and guns slewing, ready to blast the slightest signs of opposition. So we were taken prisoners.

We scrambled out of our trenches and were soon marched off after being allowed to hurriedly collect a few things together. However, the Germans – Rommel's Afrika Korps – treated us with reasonable consideration and I saw several signs of compassion and nothing of the snarling Nazi we had been led to expect – let's hope it stays that way. As we marched by, a German officer, smiling triumphantly, leant down from the turret of his huge tank and said to me 'For you, the war is finish. Thank God you have got away alive!'

First we were marched here and then there. We must have covered several miles, our numbers constantly swelling as more prisoners were brought in. What a disaster this is for us out here in North Africa. Firing and fighting was still going on a short distance away and we passed very close to a heavy Jerry field gun in action.

The reason for the fall of Tobruk was plain to see, as Jerry had a colossal number of very heavy guns and the perimeter defences did not appear to have been prepared for a second siege at all.

At last they decided where to put us, and, after a short march up to and over the coast road we lay down and slept on the open desert surrounded, of course, by armed guards.

I shall never never forget the heat, thirst, and exhaustion of this day.

[*A first-hand account by M. W. Brown.*]

Associated Press

FIRST ALAMEIN:
8TH ARMY OUTWITS ROMMEL

A General Grant tank of the 8th Army moves up to the battle area at El Alamein

If Rommel was to be stopped El Alamein was the place to do it. Although the distance between the impassable Qattara Depression and the sea at El Alamein was only 30 miles, Auchinleck had neither the time nor the forces to construct a static defence line of linked fortified positions. Instead he took a leaf out of Rommel's book and relied on mobility, flexibility and tactical judgment.

Auchinleck reasoned that Rommel would try to by-pass the strong point of El Alamein on the coast and cut the coastal road to Alexandria behind it, so he organised his defences in depth south of the El Alamein perimeter. Rommel's forces were also depleted, although

morale was very high. He launched his attack early on July 1 south of the El Alamein perimeter as Auchinleck had expected, and much to his surprise his army was checked. As the battle wore on Rommel was severely hampered by the counterattacks launched on his Italian formations. On July 3 the New Zealand Division destroyed the Ariete Division with a bayonet attack; while on July 11 the Australian 9th Division knocked out the Sabratha and Trieste Divisions in the north. By July 18 Rommel was overextended and on the defensive — he could neither advance nor retreat.

Auchinleck's success at El Alamein had upset the Axis grand strategy for the Mediterranean. Operation Hercules, the proposed airborne assault on Malta, was cancelled and the troops sent to reinforce Rommel's battered army. Mussolini, who flew to North Africa for the victory celebrations, went back to Rome.

First Alamein: The Opening Moves

Few would have banked on 8th Army's power to halt Rommel at El Alamein, but Auchinleck intended to fight a decisive battle there. With only two operative infantry divisions and a still unorganised armoured division, Auchinleck prepared to 'occupy' what has become

inaccurately known in history as the 'El Alamein Line'. Indeed, the coming battle was to be one of the most fluid in the entire desert war, for Auchinleck knew that mobility would have to make up for his lack of troops. He was out to fight Rommel to a standstill, and this he did. Allowing Rommel to commit the weight

of his attack in the centre, Auchinleck then prepared to strike hard towards Tell el Eisa, thus forcing Rommel to extend the Panzerarmee's line to the sea and dig in. But the prelude was to be Rommel's series of attacks along the Ruweisat Ridge—and his first check since Gazala

- ▚ 8th Army Corps headquarters
- ▯ 8th Army Divisional headquarters

Miles: 0 — 10

JULY 7/8 AUCHINLECK PREPARES TO STRIKE TOWARDS TELL EL EISA

To Sidi Abd el Rahman 7 miles

Tell el Eisa · ITALIAN XXI CORPS

Tell el Makh Khad · 90th LT. DIV.

MEDITERRANEAN SEA

El Alamein

EL ALAMEIN PERIMETER

Tell el Aqqaqir · DAK

3rd S. AFR. BDE.

To Alexandria 55 miles

ITALIAN XX CORPS

ITALIAN X CORPS

XV PZ. DIV.   XXI PZ. DIV.

Miteiriya Ridge

JULY 1 4th ARMD. BDE. ARRIVES JUST AHEAD OF DAK'S 90th LT. DIV.

▯ 1st S. AFR. DIV.
• Alam el Onsol

30th CORPS

Deir el Abyad

1800 HRS. JULY 1

1st S. AFR. BDE. COL.   2nd S. AFR. BDE. COL.

Deir el Shein

18th IND. BDE.

R u w e i s a t   R i d g e

El Mreir   Pt. 63   ▲ Pt. 64   22nd ARMD. BDE.

▯ 1st ARMD. DIV.

Alam el Halfa Ridge

July 2/4 ROMMEL TWICE REPULSED

6th N.Z. BDE.

Bab el Qattara   Alam Nayil

▚ 13th CORPS

Deir el Munassib   N.Z. DIV.

7th MOTORISED BDE.

Naqb Abu Dweis   5th IND. BDE.

▯ 7th ARMD. DIV.
Barrel Track

Qaret el Himeimat

To Cairo 130 miles

Qattara Depression

◁ July 3: Defeat for the DAK and Ariete. Rommel was then forced to abandon his hopes of by-passing Alamein as he had Matrûh

▷ July 10/11: Auchinleck crushes the Sabratha Division. By July 9, Rommel was extended from the Depression to the sea. The Australian attacks on Tell el Eisa in the next two days destroyed 'Sabratha' and mauled 'Trieste'; when Rommel counterattacked with the DAK on July 13/14, he suffered heavy German losses as well. Auchinleck's defence plans were working well — and were inflicting damaging losses on Rommel's Panzerarmee

▽ **Left: July 14/15.** Auchinleck strikes at the western Ruweisat Ridge. Although the New Zealanders on the left flank gained their ridge objectives, these could not be consolidated. Rommel's counterattacks on the 15th recaptured Point 63 — but the rest of 13th and 30th Corps consolidated on their ordered objective. This was another devastating blow to Rommel's hopes, for the Italian X Corps suffered damaging losses.
▽ **Right: July 21/22.** The second attack on western Ruweisat kept up the pressure on Rommel, but it gained no ground. Now the battle was crystallising: minefields defined the front. ◁ A German sapper lifting British mines — the perilous task which was to be the essential preliminary to all future attacks by both sides on the Alamein front

Ullstein

ALAM HALFA

△ 'The strength of the defence came as a complete surprise to me' – *Gen. Bayerlein*

△ Vehicles of the Afrika Korps assemble before their vain attempts to break through

▽ British minefields held up the Axis advance so that their infantry made few attacks. Again, it was up to the armour

The Battle of Alam Halfa was Rommel's last attempt to break through to the Nile Valley. It was also Lieutenant-General Bernard Montgomery's first battle in the Western Desert after taking command of the 8th Army. Thus both commanders came to grips under conditions of unusual tension, each aware that his personal reputation depended on the outcome—the German feverishly anxious to gain another quick success with dwindling resources

if he were not to fail forever; the Briton careful to consolidate his hold upon the hearts and minds of a convalescent army, as a prerequisite to the battle of annihilation he planned to fight at a later date.

Rommel launched his attack on August 31 with a strong armoured thrust along the Qattara Depression, intending to turn north behind Alam Halfa Ridge. However, he was delayed getting through the British minefields, giving Montgomery time to take the necessary counter-measures. With a threat to his flanks developing from 7th Armoured Division in the south and 10th Armoured Division in the north, Rommel turned in early against Alam Halfa Ridge which was heavily defended by the British. There the battle raged until September 2, when the shortage of fuel and supplies, the stubborn Allied resistance, and the incessant air attacks forced the Germans to break off the attack and retreat to their own lines.

Rommel repeated the tactics which had served so well at Gazala—diversionary attacks while the main strength of Panzerarmee swung round to the south to outflank the British and cut their supply lines. But the threat of attack by 7th Armoured Division forced him to shorten the attack, and lack of fuel and stubborn Allied resistance destroyed it

ALAMEIN: THE

Western Desert, October/November 1942

Major-General Sir Francis de Guingand

Now began what in British eyes has long seemed the most important battle of the war – popularly known as the Battle of Alamein. This title ignores the First Battle of Alamein, fought over virtually the same ground 16 weeks before, at which Rommel's advance was halted and the Afrika Korps given the first inkling of its fate. For now the supply situation favoured the British. Between July and October many changes had been wrought in the 8th Army: the men were rested, conscious of their hard training, aware that for the first time their weapons and equipment were superior in both quality and quantity to the enemy's. And most important of all, they had seen the enemy beaten back at Alam Halfa and knew that he was no Superman. Now it would be demonstrated to the world

When the Axis armies in Africa rose to meet the onslaught of the 8th Army on October 23 they were at a disadvantage in almost every department. Not least of their deficiencies was the absence of their great leader, for Rommel was a sick man and had returned to Germany for rest and treatment on September 23. In his place General Stumme held command – disgruntled in the knowledge that, if an attack came, Rommel would return at once, convinced that he alone was capable of taking the right decisions in an emergency on the Alamein front against the British.

Yet even Rommel regarded a defence against an enemy as strong in material as the British as a 'Battle Without Hope' while, from his masters in Rome and Berlin, he had obtained many promises but little practical help. So, daily, his reserves of men, tanks, guns, ammunition, fuel, and supplies fell lower, making comparison with the British an even gloomier exercise. For instance, Rommel was aware of a British superiority of 2 to 1 in tanks when, in fact, it was nearer 2½ to 1 overall (including 300 Italian tanks) and 5½ to 1 counting Germans alone. And the Royal Air Force now dominated the air, making the Luftwaffe's despairing efforts appear puny by comparison. While in Rome, Rommel told Mussolini that unless the supply position was improved the Axis would have to get out of North Africa, but he sensed his failure to transmit the gravity of the situation and in Berlin he recoiled before a wall of blind optimism and false promises.

At the front, meanwhile, all Panzerarmee could do was prepare an even denser fortified area in the neck between the sea and the Qattara Depression, based on the prime con-

sideration that, if they were driven out into the open, they would be overwhelmed for lack of sufficient vehicles or fuel to withdraw or fight a mobile rearguard action. Thus they planned to hold each piece of ground at all costs, cleaning up each enemy penetration with an immediate counterattack.

The German system of defence which evolved was not unlike that to be found on the Western Front at the end of the First World War – a battle zone spread out in depth behind a screen of outposts, in an effort to acquire time for mobile reserves to assemble and counterattack. One technical feature, in particular, amplified the 1918 concept – anti-tank and anti-personnel mines. Some 500,000 of them, supplemented by buried British bombs and shells, were sown thickly around each defended locality, creating a deep belt along the length of the front.

In each sector Italian troops, well laced with Germans to give stability, waited for impact with mounting anxiety. The pattern they formed contained an invitation to a Battle of Attrition – it only needed the British commander to accept that invitation and a drawn-out battle would be in prospect.

Before the Battle of Alam Halfa was fought Winston Churchill paid us a visit on his way back from Moscow (August 19) and stayed at our headquarters at Burgh-el Arab.

General Montgomery took special care to see that the Prime Minister and his party would be comfortable. He gave up his own caravan and sited it within a few yards of the sea, so that our distinguished guest could bathe when he felt so inclined.

TIDE TURNS

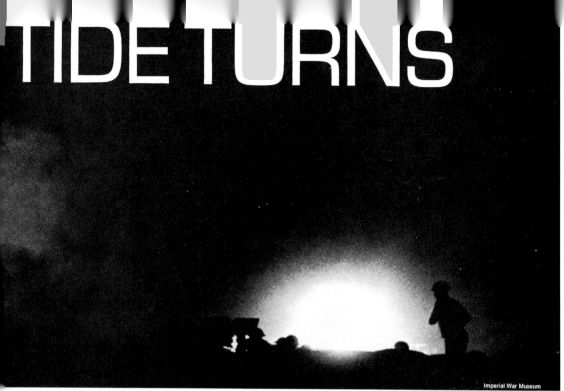

Imperial War Museum

Churchill gave us the most vivid description of his visit to Moscow and how he had talk 'cold turkey' before it was accepted at Great Britain was doing something to in the war, but he had come away with a ery deep impression of Stalin's leadership; nd enthralled us with details of our gathering war effort, and what we were preparing or the enemy. I well remember him saying: 'Germany has asked for this bombing warre, and she will rue the day she started, for her country will be laid in ruins.'

Once Rommel had failed in his last desperate offensive, he was faced with two alrnatives. Either to stay and await the ttack which he knew would most surely be unched against him, increasing in the eantime the strength of his defences; or withdraw to some favourable position efore we were ready to follow him up in fficient strength, thereby shortening his nes of communication and so rendering his upply position less precarious.

He chose the first of these courses, no oubt largely because he lacked the necesary transport and petrol for a withdrawal; ut in any case a retreat would have been gainst his character and would certainly ave proved very unpopular with the Axis igh Command. His decision meant therere that the longer we waited before unching our offensive, the more formidable is defences would become – particularly ith regard to minefields, wire, and the onstruction of prepared positions.

It was therefore obvious that it was to our dvantage to attack as soon as possible and his view was strongly held by Churchill, ho started to press General Alexander – ommander-in-Chief Middle East – for an

early offensive. He wanted this to take place in September. He had an additional important reason and that was the fact that Operation 'Torch', the Anglo/US landings in North Africa, was due to take place early in November, and therefore hard and prolonged fighting on our front would be of great benefit.

One day Alexander arrived at our headquarters, bringing with him a signal from Churchill saying that he more or less demanded that we should attack in September. After reading the document Montgomery said 'Hand me a pad, Freddie', and seizing it he wrote down these points:

● Rommel's attack had caused some delay in our preparations.

● Moon conditions restricted 'D' day to certain periods in September and October.

● If the September date was insisted upon the troops would be insufficiently equipped and trained, and failure would probably result. But if the attack took place in October then complete victory was assured.

Turning to Alexander, he handed over the pad and said: 'I should make these points in your reply; that should fix it.' A signal was subsequently dispatched on these lines and produced the required result; for what could any Prime Minister do with this clearcut military opinion before him! Montgomery in his memoirs recalls that he told Alexander 'privately' that if the attack was ordered for September they would have to find someone else to do the job.

Taking all considerations into account, Montgomery decided that we should attack during the October full moon and the exact date fixed was the 23rd. It was essential that we should attack at night owing to the

formidable minefield problem.

I now come to the plan itself. There was no way round the enemy positions; the sea and the Qattara Depression saw to that, so a hole had to be punched through their defences. Montgomery had decided to launch the main attack on the right flank with General Leese's 30th Corps, together with a secondary attack on the southern flank by General Horrocks' 13th Corps. The plan was to pass 10th Corps (General Lumsden) through the gap made by 30th Corps to sit astride the enemy's supply line, and so force him to deploy his armour against us, when it would be destroyed. This was in accordance with normal teaching. Having destroyed the enemy's armour, his troops could be dealt with more or less at leisure.

The Army Commander had laid down three basic fundamentals which would govern the preparatory period. These were: leadership – equipment – training. He soon put the first matter in order, and the re-equipment of the army was going well. But early in October he realised that the training of the army was still below what was required, and in view of this weakness made one of his rapid decisions. He would alter the conception of the plan so that instead of first going all out to destroy the enemy's armour, he would eat away the enemy's holding troops – who were for the most part unarmoured – and use our armour to stop the enemy from interfering. Without their infantry divisions to hold the line, providing firm bases for their mobile forces, the enemy's armour would be at a grave disadvantage and their supply routes would be constantly threatened. It was unlikely that they would stand idly by while this 'crumbling' process was going on, and so it was probable that we would force his armour to attack *us*, which, once we were in a position to receive it, would be to our advantage.

The final plan in outline as given out by the Army Commander on October 6 was as follows:

● Main attack by 30th Corps in the north on a front of four divisions [to secure a bridgehead – objective 'Oxalic' – beyond the enemy's main defended zone]. Two corridors were to be cleared through the minefields, and through these lanes 10th Corps was to pass.

● 13th Corps in the south was to stage two attacks. One directed on Himeimat and the Taqa feature. The other into the area of Gebel Kalakh and Qaret el Khadim. These attacks were to be made with the primary object of misleading the enemy and thereby containing forces that might otherwise be used against 30th Corps.

● Both the above corps were to destroy the enemy holding the forward positions.

● 10th Corps was to deploy itself [to a line 'Pierson', just west of 'Oxalic'] so as to prevent 30th Corps' operations from being interfered with. And its final object [by an advance to area 'Skinflint'] was the destruction of the enemy's armour.

● The attack was to start at night during the full moon.

The artillery plan was very carefully prepared. We would go into battle with great gun power and considerable supplies of ammunition. The battle was to open with a very heavy counter-battery bombardment, and then most of our artillery would concentrate on the enemy defences by barrage and concentrations.

The air plan was a good one. Before the battle Air Vice-Marshal Coningham's Desert Air Force had been wearing down the enemy's air effort. On one or two occasions he had shown brilliant leadership by taking advantage of fleeting opportunities when isolated rain storms had grounded portions of the enemy's air force. Low-flying attacks laid on with great rapidity had taken a very heavy toll of the enemy's aircraft and petrol.

During the first night our air forces were to undertake attacks against enemy gun positions, and so help our counter-battery plan. Later they were to switch to the areas where the enemy armoured divisions were located. Our available air strength on 'D' day was 500 fighters and 200 bombers – at that time a considerable force.

The 'going' was one of the matters which gave us a lot of anxiety, and we went to endless trouble to obtain information as to what the ground was like in the area over which we were making our thrusts. Air photos, interrogation of prisoners, questioning of our own troops who had at one time or another traversed the area – these were some of the means employed. We built six tracks leading up to 30th Corps' starting line, and this in itself was a tremendous task, constructed as they were through very soft sand.

Montgomery's dummy army

The deception arrangements were particularly interesting. We had decided quite rightly that strategic surprise was out of the question, for the enemy knew we were going to attack. On the other hand tactical surprise was quite possible. We considered we could delude the enemy as to the weight,

the date, the time, and the direction of our attack. Our plans were all made with this in view, and they proved most successful.

The first problem was to try to conceal our concentration as much as possible from the enemy. The staff worked out the complete layout on the day of the attack – the number of guns, tanks, vehicles, and troops. A very large 'operations' map was kept which showed this layout in various denominations. We then arranged to reach the eventual density as early as possible, and to maintain it up to the last moment, so that the enemy's air photography would show no particular change during the last two or three weeks. To achieve this we used spare transport and dummy transport. These were gradually replaced by those belonging to the assault units and formations as they came up to take over their allotted sectors. These changeovers took place at night, and we had special dummy vehicles made under which guns could be concealed. All moves forward were of course rigidly controlled, and slit trenches were dug and camouflaged at night in which the assault infantry could be concealed.

The next task was to make the enemy think that the main attack would be launched in the southern sector. This, I might add, was not very popular with 13th Corps, but they nobly accepted the plan for the common good. Besides various other methods adopted, we built large dummy dumps away to the south, and also a dummy pipe line and water installations. It was so arranged that the work would appear to the enemy to be aimed at completion a week or two *after* the actual date of our attack. Finally on the night of the attack itself the wireless traffic of the headquarters of an armoured division was so employed as to indicate that a large move of armoured forces was taking place in the southern sector.

On the night of the 23rd we arranged for a feint landing to take place behind the enemy's lines. About 4 pm a convoy sailed westwards out of Alexandria. After dark all but a few fast craft put back, but those remaining staged a dummy landing. Shelling of the coast, mortar and machine-gun fire, and light signals were used. It was timed to take place about three hours after our attack had started, and it was hoped that this would tie down enemy reserves. The loading of the ships was no doubt witnessed by enemy agents, who could see tanks being shipped and troops marching aboard. There is no doubt that all these measures helped materially to confuse the enemy and gained us tactical surprise.

On the administrative side there was a great deal to be done. The whole basis of administration had to be altered. Befor⟨e⟩ when we were on the defensive, the weig⟨ht⟩ of resources was held back; now that w⟨e⟩ intended to attack they had to be placed ⟨as⟩ far forward as possible. The conseque⟨nt⟩ carrying forward of supplies and the camo⟨u⟩flaging of the dumps was no small task, a⟨nd⟩ preparations were made to construct th⟨e⟩ railway forward as rapidly as possible. W⟨e⟩ also made preparations to open ports whe⟨n⟩ they were captured and perfected o⟨ur⟩ organisation for the recovery and repa⟨ir⟩ of tanks and vehicles.

Montgomery's change in plan as regard⟨s⟩ the use of our armour nearly caused a cris⟨is⟩ between himself and General Herbe⟨rt⟩ Lumsden, who had been selected to co⟨m⟩mand the 'Corps d'Elite' – the 10th Arm⟨oured⟩ Corps. Lumsden had fought with co⟨n⟩spicuous gallantry when commanding ⟨an⟩ armoured division in the 'bad old days'. H⟨e⟩ was a cavalryman through and through a⟨nd⟩ not unnaturally thought in terms of th⟨e⟩ mobile battle and yearned for the day whe⟨n⟩ his armoured formations, equipped wi⟨th⟩ modern tanks, would be launched throug⟨h⟩ a gap made by the infantry, to roam far an⟨d⟩ wide. The Army Commander's new instruc⟨⟩tions were therefore not to his liking.

Shortly after this Lumsden held a cor⟨ps⟩ conference at which he explained his pla⟨ns⟩ and views to all the commanders in h⟨is⟩ corps. Montgomery was temporarily abse⟨nt⟩ from the army on this occasion and I there⟨⟩fore decided to attend this conference myse⟨lf.⟩

It soon became clear to me that this ne⟨w⟩ conception of the use of armour had no⟨t⟩ been fully accepted by the corps command⟨er⟩ and at the end of the meeting I had a tal⟨k⟩ with Lumsden pointing out the Army Co⟨m⟩mander's determination to fight the comin⟨g⟩ battle this way. But I could see that he wa⟨s⟩ anything but happy and there appeared t⟨o⟩ be a recrudescence of the bad old habit⟨ of⟩ questioning orders.

On the Army Commander's return, I r⟨e⟩ported fully on what had taken place an⟨d⟩ he lost little time in making his view⟨s⟩ crystal clear to the commander of 10⟨th⟩ Corps; and Lumsden, being a good soldie⟨r,⟩ accepted the position and made the nece⟨s⟩sary changes in his plans.

Large-scale rehearsals for the comin⟨g⟩ battle were carried out, and the lesso⟨ns⟩ learned gone into very carefully by th⟨e⟩ various commanders. And by the end of th⟨e⟩ third week in October we realised that a⟨ll⟩ these vast preparations were successfull⟨y⟩ reaching their conclusion. From the sta⟨rt⟩

**Left map legend:**

⬭ German & Italian armour

⬭ German & Italian infantry

▧ Axis minefields

➡ 8th Army intended thrusts as planned on Oct. 6

〰 Western edge of 8th Army minefields

0 — Miles — 10

**Right map legend:**

0 — Miles — 4

⬭ German & Italian infantry units

At Alamein in October the 8th Army was faced by an enemy position which could not be turned, but must be breached by direct attack. Montgomery at first intended to use 30th Corps to push two corridors into the enemy lines through which the tanks of 10th Corps would flood to force an armoured battle and cut the Axis supply lines. But weaknesses in his forces' training made him decide to alter this plan: 30th Corps was still to open two corridors through to 'Oxalic', but it was then to concentrate upon 'crumbling' the enemy's holding troops. The tanks were to go no further than 'Pierson', where they would cover the infantry and await the German armoured counterattacks on ground of their own choosing. Further south, diversionary attacks by 4th Indian Division and 13th Corps would hold a large proportion of the Axis armour during the vital opening phase of the battle. On the Axis side, Stumme had split his armour (XV Panzer in the north, XXI Panzer in the south) to cover both possible lines of attack. This unprecedented step weakened his ability to mount a concentrated counterattack, but General Bayerlein believed that it had been approved by Rommel before he left Africa

After an extremely heavy artillery barrage, troops of 30th Corps, on a four-division front, advanced into the enemy minefields. By dawn on October 24 the infantry had reached most of the objectives of 'Oxalic', but stubborn enemy resistance and congestion in the corridors prevented the tanks from clearing the minefields. At first German reactions seemed hesitant and unsure – not only were Panzerarmee's commanders still uncertain as to where the real attack would come, but Stumme had died of heart failure on the first day, and for vital hours the Axis forces had no leader until General von Thoma was able to take over. It was not until the third day of the attack that a new Axis certainty about counterattacks showed that Rommel had returned. Throughout the 24th and 25th, 30th Corps inched forward, while 13th Corps successfully held XXI Panzer in the south. But Montgomery had realised that the impetus had gone out of the initial attacks, and, using attacks by 9th Australian Division in the north to cut off enemy forces in the salient and force Rommel to concentrate on their relief, he halted and began to redeploy 8th Army for a new breakout attempt

---

point of view there was a healthy slackening in the tempo of work, denoting that the stage was now set.

Montgomery had been indefatigable, and had satisfied himself that all was in readiness. He very rightly had decided that in order to get the best out of his troops it was necessary for them to know the whole plan so that they would realise how their particular contribution fitted in with the general scheme of things.

On October 19 and 20 he addressed all officers down to lieutenant-colonel level in 30th, 13th, and 10th Corps. These talks were some of the best he had ever given, clear and full of confidence. He touched on the enemy situation, stressing their weaknesses, and

said he was certain a long 'dog-fight' or 'killing match' would take place for several days – 'it might be ten'. He then gave details of our great strength, our tanks, our guns, and the enormous supplies of ammunition available. He drummed in the need never to lose the initiative, and how everyone – *everyone* – must be imbued with the burning desire to 'kill Germans'. 'Even the padres – one per weekday and two on Sundays!' This produced a roar. After explaining how the battle was to be fought, he said that he was entirely confident of the result.

The men were let into the secret on October 21 and 22, from which date no leave was granted, and by the 23rd a tremendous state of enthusiasm had been produced. Those soldiers just knew they would succeed.

On the morning of October 22, Montgomery held a press conference. He explained the plan, his intentions, and his firm conviction of success. Many of the war correspondents were rather shaken by the confidence – this bombastic confidence – which he displayed. They felt there must be a catch in it – how could he be so sure? Some, I think, thought the maze of minefields and deep defences that the enemy had constructed were too difficult a problem to justify such a sanguine attitude.

In the afternoon of the 23rd we drove up to our battle headquarters, tucked away on the coast within a few minutes of 30th and 10th Corps Headquarters. We had well protected buried cables running back to our main headquarters and to the various corps; vehicles

Panzerarmee Afrika

Gen Stumme (until Oct 26) and Fld Mshl Rommel

Reserve
German 90th Light Division
Italian **Trieste** Motorised Division
Luftwaffe XIX Flak Division

North
German XV Panzer Division
German 164th Motorised Division
Italian **Littorio** Armoured Division
Italian XXI Infantry Corps – **Trento** Division

Centre
German XXI Panzer Division
Ramcke Parachute Brigade
Italian XX Infantry Corps – **Brescia**
and **Bologna** Divisions

South
Italian **Ariete** Armoured Division
Italian X Infantry Corps – **Pavia**
and **Folgore** Divisions

8th Army

Lieut-Gen Montgomery

30th Corps – Lieut-Gen Leese
51st (Highland) Division – Maj-Gen Wimberley
4th Indian Division – Maj-Gen Tuker
9th Australian Division
New Zealand Division – Lieut-Gen Freyberg
1st South African Division – Maj-Gen Pienaar
23rd Armoured Brigade Group
9th (UK) Armoured Brigade

13th Corps – Lieut-Gen Horrocks
7th Armoured Division – Maj-Gen Harding
50th Division – Maj-Gen Nichols
44th Division – Maj-Gen Hughes
1st Free French Brigade Group
2nd Free French Brigade Group
1st Greek Infantry Brigade Group

10th Corps – Lieut-Gen Lumsden
1st Armoured Division – Maj-Gen Briggs
10th Armoured Division – Maj-Gen Gatehouse
8th Armoured Division – Maj-Gen Gairdner

Rommel
Nehring
Thoma
Bayerlein

Allied leadership was new and backed by great material resources, but Axis command suffered from changes and resultant indecisiveness. When the offensive began, Panzerarmee was led by General Stumme, but after his death on the first day of the attack it was commanded by General von Thoma until Rommel, who had been ill, returned on October 26

Montgomery
Leese
Horrocks
Lumsden

50,000 German, 54,000 Italian **104,000**

195,000

211 German – 85 Mark IIIs, 88 Mark III Specials. **489**
8 Mark IVs, 30 Mark IV Specials
278 Italian, mainly M13/40s

1,029

170 Grants, 252 Shermans, 216 Crusader 2-pdrs
78 Crusader 6-pdrs, 119 Stuarts, 194 Valentines

475 Field and Medium – 200 German, 275 Italian
744 Anti-tank – 444 German (86 – 8·8 cm, 68 – 7·62 cm) **1,219**
290 – 5·0 cm) 300 Italian

2,311

908 Field and Medium
1,403 Anti-tank – 554 2-pdrs, 849 6-pdrs

275 German (150 serviceable) **675**
400 Italian (200 serviceable)

750 (530 serviceable)

were dug in as we were rather far forward and near the desert road, which would undoubtedly become – as it did – a target for enemy air attack. I decided to make this tactical headquarters my base, and it worked very well. My people could talk to me on direct lines and come up for conferences within the hour.

It was a lovely evening, and I drove out after dark to see by the light of the moon the move forward of some of the troops. All was going well, and everyone looked cheerful. This was the day for which so many of us had been preparing and waiting.

As the time drew near we got into our cars and drove to a good view-point to see the opening of the battle. We passed the never-ending stream of tanks and transport – all moving with clockwork precision. This was 10th Corps moving up to its starting line, with the moon providing sufficient light to drive by, but the night protecting them from

the prying eyes of enemy aircraft. We had some of our own machines flying over the enemy's forward positions making distracting noises; otherwise all seemed fairly quiet and normal. An occasional Very light and burst of machine-gun fire, a gun firing here and there, as would happen any night. We looked at our watches, 2130 hours – ten minutes to go. I could hardly wait.

A 1,000-gun barrage begins
The minutes ticked by, and then the whole sky was lit up, and a roar rent the air. Over 1,000 of our guns had opened up. It was a great and heartening sight. I tried to picture what the enemy must be thinking, did he know what was coming? He must do now. How ready was he? Up and down the desert, from north to south, the twinkling of the guns could be seen in an unceasing sequence. Within the enemy's lines we could see an occasional deep red glow

light up the western sky. Each time this happened Brigadier Dennis, the commander of 30th Corps artillery, let out a grunt of satisfaction. Another Axis gun position had been blown up. We checked each change in the artillery plan; the pause while the guns switched to new targets. It was gun drill at its best. Now the infantry started forward. We could see the periodic bursts of Bofors guns which, with their tracer shell, demarcated the direction of advance. Behind us great searchlight beams were directed towards the sky, to help the forward troops plot their positions, and so find out where they had reached their objectives, for few landmarks existed in this part of the desert.

About 2300 hours I crept away and drove back to our headquarters. I knew we could expect to hear little of interest for some time yet, and so I snatched an hour or two's rest before being wakened up to hear the first reports come in.

As I closed my eyes I felt full of confidence and hope, but never did I think that this was the opening of a campaign that would bring us to the very gates of Carthage.

Although the Battle of El Alamein was a comparatively small affair in relation to later battles fought during the war, for a number of reasons it must rank high in importance. To start with it meant the turn of the tide in Britain's fortunes. In fact the victory stood out as a priceless jewel after a series of depressing defeats. Then it provided a much-wanted stimulus to British morale, for it convinced our armed forces that, given the right leadership and weapons, they could beat the Germans, and it also inspired confidence among the British people in ultimate victory.

By previous standards in the Middle East, however, it was a great offensive and probably some of the bitterest fighting in the whole war took place over those sandy wastes. Our new commander never once lost his confidence or the initiative, while his troops were always convinced that they would win through in the end. I do not propose to give a very detailed description of the operations, but will confine myself to the broad framework of the battle and concentrate upon the highlights.

On that night of October 23/24, 30th Corps attacked with four divisions down two corridors cleared through the minefields. This attack was made on a fairly narrow front of 6 to 7 miles, with the northern flank tied to the Tell el Eisa feature, and the Miteiriya Ridge forming the southern limit.

The enemy's and our own dispositions at the outset of the battle are interesting for three reasons:

● The greater part of the enemy static defences was manned by Italians.
● The German infantry divisions, 164th Division and 90th Light Division, were protecting the vital coastal road sector.
● The German armour (Afrika Korps) was held in reserve and distributed equally between the northern and southern sectors.

Besides 30th Corps' main attack, a brigade of the 9th Australian Division carried out a feint between Tell el Eisa and the sea. This, together with the phoney seaborne operation, had a worrying effect on the enemy, while farther south the 4th Indian Division launched a strong raid from the area of the Ruweisat Ridge.

Then, at 0200 hours on October 24, the leading elements of the 1st and 10th Armoured Divisions crossed their start lines.

The Germans reel . . . and recover

Progress was good, and the task of clearing the lanes through the minefields went on well, but by the morning the armour had not managed to troop out beyond them. Throughout the night, the Miteiriya Ridge was a very unpleasant place to be, and fierce fighting took place there, for once the enemy had recovered from the initial shock, he concentrated his artillery and mortar fire on the corridors, and XV Panzer Division carried out a counterattack. The Army Commander examined the situation on the morning of the 24th, and decided that although a very good start had been made, it was important that there must be no slackening in the efforts to get the armour through, and that the 'crumbling' operations by the New Zealand Division must start at once.

In the south, 13th Corps had started on schedule. The French had successfully assaulted the high ground about Himeimat, but the soft sand had prevented their supporting weapons reaching them in time, and they were driven off again by a German counterattack. The other 13th Corps' attack, after making initial gains, was held up between the belts of minefields. The 24th was, therefore, spent in 'crumbling' operations in this area. These were, however, secondary to the main attack by 30th Corps, and in spite of these small set-backs their main object was achieved, for the XXI Panzer Division was held in the southern sector.

Now started a week of terrific fighting. By the evening of the 24th, the 1st Armoured Division had managed to get some elements out of the minefields in positions beyond, but 10th Armoured Division was not so fortunate, and was having a very difficult time. An attack they made at 2200 hours that night, supported by the corps artillery, made little progress.

Altogether I gained the impression that a feeling was developing in some quarters which favoured suspending the forward move, and pulling back under cover of the ridge. I decided, therefore, that this was an occasion when the Army Commander must intervene, and so I called a conference for 0330 hours at our Tactical Headquarters, asking Leese (30th Corps) and Lumsden (10th Corps) to attend. Then I went along to his caravan and woke him up. He appeared to be sleeping peacefully—in spite of a lot of attention from the enemy air force. He agreed with the action I had taken, and told me to bring the two corps commanders along to his map lorry when they arrived.

In due course I led the generals along the little path to the lorry. Montgomery was seated on a stool carefully examining a map fixed to the wall. He greeted us all most cheerfully, motioned us to sit down, and then asked each corps commander to tell his story. He listened very quietly, only occasionally interrupting with a question. There was a certain 'atmosphere' noticeable, careful handling was required, and Lumsden was obviously still not very happy about the role his armour had been given. After a while Montgomery spoke to the commander of the 10th Armoured Division on the telephone, and heard his version of the situation. He then made it quite clear that there would be no alteration to his orders. He also ordered the headquarters of this division to be moved farther forward.

The decision to make no change in the plan at that moment was a brave one, for it meant accepting considerable risks and casualties. But if it had not been made, I am firmly convinced that the attack might

361st PZ. GREN. REGT.

26th AUST INF. BDE.

20th AUST INF. BDE.

125th PZ. GREN. REGT.

200th PZ. GREN. REGT.

24th AUST INF. BDE.

Tell el Eisa

⌒ 9th Australian Division's front on Oct. 28
--- German and Italian forces

Sidi Abd el Rahman

90th LT. DIV.

Rahman Track

XXI PZ. DIV.

NOV. 4 1st ARMD. DIV.

151st INFANTRY BRIGADE

9th ARMD.

0100 HRS. NOV. 2 ATTACK BEGINS

BRIGADE

AXIS MINEFIELDS

Tell el Aqqaqir

XV PZ. DIV.

152nd INFANTRY BRIGADE

NOV. 2 9th ARMD. BDE. SUFFERS HEAVY CASUALTIES

Kidney Hill

NOV. 4 10th ARMD. DIV.

ITALIAN XX CORPS

8th ARMY LINE NOV. 1

164th DIV.

Miteiriya Ridge

⟋ German and Italian armour
--- German and Italian infantry
◢ Rommel's counterattacks
⟸ Rommel begins withdrawal night of Nov. 3/4

well have fizzled out, and the full measure of success we achieved might never have been possible.

By 0800 hours on October 25 the leading armoured brigade of the 10th Armoured Division was reported to be 2,000 yards west of the minefield area, and in touch with the 1st Armoured Division to the north. In addition, we heard that the New Zealand Division and the 8th Armoured Brigade were clear of the main minefields, and were advancing south-westwards in accordance with the plan, drawing the XV Panzer Division into several counterattacks against us, which were all repulsed with heavy losses.

The attack switches to the north

By about mid-day Montgomery realised that the 'crumbling' operations by the New Zealand Division would prove very expensive and decided to switch the axis northwards, telling the 9th Australian Division to destroy the Germans in the salient. The 1st Armoured Division was ordered to fight its way westwards with the object of threatening the enemy's supply routes in the Rahman track area, where it would also threaten the rear of the enemy holding the coastal salient, but this attack made no appreciable progress until the night of October 26/27.

The Australian attack under General Morshead went well–ground was gained and heavy casualties inflicted on the enemy. Here the enemy's defences were very strong (the garrison was mainly German) and I believe this area saw the most determined and savage fighting during the whole battle and made a major contribution to ultimate victory.

On the 26th the New Zealand and South African Divisions made slow progress, and the Army Commander decided to regroup. The 30th Corps required a pause to reorganise and, although we had forced our way through the main minefields, the enemy still had well organised anti-tank defences opposing us.

This regrouping produced the reserves required for the decisive phase of the battle. The New Zealand Division was pulled out of the line, their place being taken by moving the 1st South African and 4th Indian Divisions northward. The New Zealanders were given first priority for all tank replacements, and spent a day or so resting and bathing. We could see this cheerful body of men spread out along the beach from our headquarters, the horrors of the Miteiriya Ridge behind them, preparing themselves for the ordeal ahead.

During October 27 news came in that two enemy tankers and a merchantman had been sunk near the entrance to Tobruk harbour, and their loss may have had a considerable influence on the battle. At 1400 hours the Army Commander held a conference at which the regrouping plan was explained, and also plans for the continuance of the Australian attack. The 13th Corps was ordered to make final arrangements for moving the 7th Armoured Division and other troops to the northern sector, for during the night of October 26/27 the XXI Panzer Division had moved northwards, and so these forces could be spared. In the morning we had located, by wireless direction-finding, the headquarters of this German armoured division.

For most of the day, the two German Panzer divisions launched attacks against our positions. This suited us well, and the 1st Armoured Division excelled themselves, claiming 50 enemy tanks knocked out, as well as others damaged. In addition, the RAF was doing good work bombing the enemy as they formed up, so altogether it was an exciting and successful day–from our headquarters we could see the tell-tale pillars of black smoke towering up into the sky when tanks and vehicles were destroyed.

Now Montgomery decided that the 1st Armoured Division needed a rest, and withdrew it into reserve, turning their sector to defence, with infantry brigades, moved up from 13th Corps, and available for subsequent operations.

On the night of the 28/29 the Australian Division attacked again, and drove a wedge into the enemy positions which almost

reached the road between Sidi Abd el Ra man and Tell el Eisa, and although on th 29th the enemy did all in their power t destroy this wedge, these attacks made wit both tanks and infantry completely faile

October 29 was a very interesting day a plans and preparations went ahead for th launching of the break-out attack – given th code name of 'Supercharge'.

The Army Commander's intention was t launch this attack as far north as possibl but some of us felt that better results wou be gained by adopting a more souther axis; the farther north we went, the mo Germans, mines, and prepared defence would be met.

During the morning we were paid a vis by Commander-in-Chief General Alexande Minister of State Casey, and Alexander' Chief-of-Staff, Lieutenant-General M Creery. The Army Commander describe the situation and his plans, and radiate confidence. He stressed that he had alway predicted a ten-day 'dog-fight', and he wa quite certain that he would win the battl However, I soon realised that the Cabine in London, if not some people in Cair were beginning to wonder whether Mon gomery would after all fulfil his promise o 'Complete Victory'. It was inevitable there fore that interest was focused upon Super charge and in discussions with McCreer I found that he also felt that it should b launched farther south.

After Alexander, Casey, and McCreery ha departed, I felt more than ever worried abou the sector chosen for Supercharge. appeared to me that Rommel would do a

German
tanks

 British
tanks

 Burned-out
British tanks

British
mine-clearers

British infantry
and 6-pounder
anti-tank guns

 British tanks
attacking

 German
50-mm gun

 German
88-mm gun

 Minefield

 British 25-pounder
shell-bursts on
German positions

A Set-Piece Desert Battle

Alamein was the first set-piece battle the 8th Army had to fight against an enemy firmly entrenched behind minefields which could not easily be turned. Although on a far larger scale than most subsequent engagements, it set a pattern for a series of later actions in which the 8th Army had to breach the defence lines set up by the retreating Panzerarmee. This diagram shows a typical desert engagement. In the foreground a corridor has been cleared through the Axis minefield, the armour (Crusaders, Grants, and Sherman tanks) has passed through; and one formation is waiting to go in on the near side of a ridge. Meanwhile, infantry are coming up in trucks with their 6-pounder anti-tank guns and the engineers are clearing a second lane. In the centre another tank unit is launching an attack; well spaced out—at least 100 yards between vehicles—they move against the Axis troops who have their 50-mm PAK anti-tank guns in front, and their 88-mm guns lying back. Axis armour waits on the flanks of the position which is being shelled by British 25-pounders

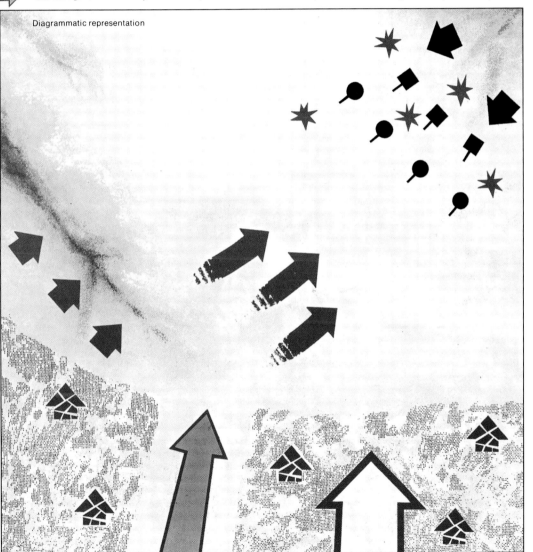

Diagrammatic representation

Rulers of the Desert Battlefield

To achieve a decisive breakthrough, 8th Army had to breach and clear strong Axis defence lines and minefields. Thus in the early stages new mineclearing vehicles—like the Baron—played an important part. although clearing by hand was still the most reliable and common method. But when the tank-to-tank battles began, in spite of Allied re-equipment and material strength, the Germans still had the outstanding mobile weapon—their Mk IV tank with the devastating long-barrelled 75-mm gun

BARON. A mine-sweeping tank built on the hull of a Matilda, with two additional engines to drive the revolving drum which carried the chains. The tank would be driven at 2 mph with the drum revolving at 72/80 revolutions per minute

5-cm Pak Gun (above) was the mainstay of the Wehrmacht's *Panzerjäger* (anti-tank) units, and during 1941 it had been steadily augmenting the artillery in Rommel's Panzer army. This process paralleled the British build-up for 'Crusader'. After the frontier tussles of 'Brevity' and 'Battleaxe', the number of 5-cm German Pak guns rose until out of 158 Pak guns, only 62 were the older 37-mm Pak. **Maximum range:** 1,000 yards **Gun crew:** 4

Pzkw MK IVG: *Weight:* 24 tons. *Crew:* 5. *Speed:* 25 mph. *Range:* 130 miles. *Armament:* One long-barrelled 75-mm Kwk 40 (L-43) gun, and two 7.92-mm Type 34 machine-guns n his power to protect his main supply dumps and his lines of communication which used the coastal road. He could not afford to take any risks on this portion of his front. So I went along to discuss the problem with Bill Williams (G-1 Intelligence) and found that he shared my views. Fortunately the latest intelligence reports showed that 90th Light Division had been moved to the northern sector, no doubt due to successes achieved by the 9th Australian Division. It became obvious therefore that the Axis front farther south had been weakened. I decided to take Williams along to see the Army Commander, and appraise him of the changing situation. Montgomery had previously been much impressed by Williams' explanation of how Rommel had distributed his German troops in order to 'corset' the Italian units, and he was quick to see that the present situation gave an excellent chance of attacking where the enemy was weakest — where most of the defenders were Italian or at least at the junction of the two Axis allies.

Montgomery was never slow in making up his mind — provided, of course, that he had the necessary facts — and in this case he immediately decided to change the axis of the forthcoming attack. I well remember leaving the map lorry in high spirits, and later on that day I rang up McCreery who was quite delighted at hearing the news. This decision, as I'm sure, a decisive contribution to victory.

The Australians continued their attack on the night of 30/31, crossed the coast road, and at one time it looked as if the bulk of the Germans inside the salient would be cut off and destroyed. They managed, however, to get away with the help of tank reinforcements, but this attack to the north had paid a big dividend, for it kept the enemy's attention focused on the coastal area, besides causing great damage among the Germans themselves.

On November 1 we heard that XXI Panzer Division had moved even farther north, so everything was set for the final phase. After a delay of 24 hours [to rest the troops, and give more time for reorganisation] Supercharge was launched, helped by a creeping barrage at 0100 hours on the morning of November 2. Some 300 25-pounders and the corps medium artillery supported the attack.

The frontage of attack was 4,000 yards, and the depth of the advance 6,000 yards. The infantry (151st and 152nd Infantry Brigades) attacked, and everything went wonderfully well, so on reaching their objective the armour moved through and formed a bridgehead, through which it was proposed to pass the armoured divisions of 10th Corps. The objectives were reached, but the 9th Armoured Brigade suffered heavy casualties from enemy anti-tank weapons. Then the 1st Armoured Division came through to assist, and an armoured battle was fought.

On November 3 we knew that the enemy was beaten, as air reports came in showing that the retreat had started, and we knew that Rommel had insufficient transport or petrol to get back more than a portion of his force.

Yet November 3 still did not see us right out into the open country, for the enemy were still plugging the hole with anti-tank guns, but on the night of the 3/4 a clean break-through was made by the 51st and 4th Indian Divisions, after mounting a sudden attack with the greatest skill.

The battle had been won in 11 days, which was just about the Army Commander's estimate of how long the heavy fighting would last. The enemy was defeated and in full retreat, and our armour and armoured cars were now operating in open country.

When on November 3 all information showed that the enemy was in full retreat, it was hoped that the Desert Air Force would cause havoc among his transport; for reports described a scene of vehicles, head to tail, four and sometimes eight deep, moving westwards either on or just off the road. Indeed we had visions of the retreat being turned into a complete rout, bearing in mind the fact that we enjoyed virtual air superiority. In the event, the results were very disappointing. When setting out along the road between the Alamein battlefield and Daba, I had expected to see a trail of devastation, but the visible signs of destroyed vehicles were few and far between. The fact is that at this period of the war we had not learned the technique of low strafing, for our fighter bombers had been employed in air fighting and bombing. I believe the attacks on the retreating columns were made mostly with bombs, and that the aircraft were not allowed to come down low; no doubt because our pilots had not been trained in low-flying attacks with cannon. I feel, however, that an opportunity was lost, and that it should have been possible to have produced a form of paralysis in the enemy's rearward movement.

It was also a great disappointment that we were unable to cut off completely Rommel's surviving forces and so save the long and arduous series of operations that took us to Tripoli and beyond. Montgomery, however, knew that it was only a matter of time, and in any case he was very unlucky, for the forces which he had ordered to cut off the enemy at the bottlenecks of Fuka and Matrûh were deprived of fulfilling their object through the interference caused by some most unusually heavy rain storms, which 'bogged' them down within a stone's throw of the retreating enemy.

An Italian machine-gun in action: Italian troops formed the main static element in the Axis line

The Hinge of Fate

1942 October 6: General Montgomery issues his final plan for 8th Army's offensive.
October 23: 2125 hours; artillery bombardment begins in the 13th Corps sector. 2140; 30th Corps bombardment begins. 2200 hours; 30th Corps with four divisions and 13th Corps launch two attacks — on Himeimat and Gebel Kalakh.
October 24: 0200 hours; leading elements of 1st and 10th Armoured Divisions begin to move through the corridors. By dawn most units of 30th Corps have reached their 'Oxalic' line objectives, but 10th Corps has been unable to clear the bridgehead and reach 'Pierson'. After a successful start, 13th Corps is held up between the minefields, but is successful in keeping XXI Panzer Division in its sector. By the evening, 1st Armoured Division has got some units out of the minefields, but 10th Armoured Division's attack at 2200 hours makes little progress.
October 25: 0200 hours; congestion in the southern corridor reaches a dangerous level, but after a conference at 0330 hours, Montgomery confirms that the attempt to break out must continue. 0800; the leading brigade moves clear. The New Zealand Division and 8th Armoured Brigade also clear the main minefield and turn to advance southwestward, fighting off counterattacks by XV Panzer. 1200 hours; Montgomery decides to switch the axis of the attack to the north — 9th Australian Division is to strike northward and 1st Armoured Division westward behind the coastal salient.
October 26: The 9th Australian Division gains ground, but all other attacks are held; Montgomery decides to regroup — the New Zealand Division moves back into reserve, and is replaced by the 1st South African and 4th Indian Divisions. Two German tankers — the *Proserpina* and the *Tergesta* — are sunk; Panzerarmee's fuel problem becomes acute.
October 27: XXI Panzer moves northward; the British redeployment continues with 7th Armoured Division being withdrawn from 13th Corps and brought north. A series of German attacks on 1st Armoured Division are thrown back with losses of 50 tanks.
October 28/29: Further attacks by 9th Australian Division in the northern sector drive a wedge into the enemy position.
October 29: Montgomery decides to launch the break-out (Supercharge) as far north as possible, but revises his decision (on hearing that the German 90th Light Division has also moved north) in order to strike Italian not German troops.
October 30/31: The Australian attack continues in an attempt to cut off the enemy forces in the coastal salient.
November 2: 151st and 152nd Brigades launch Operation Supercharge, they reach their objectives successfully, and at 0615 9th Armoured Brigade advances, but is held up by heavy anti-tank fire. The 1st Armoured Division moves through to eliminate the opposition. At 2015 hours, after a conference with General von Thoma, Rommel decides to begin the retreat to the Fuka position.
November 3: Confused fighting, but during the night the break-through is achieved by the 51st and 4th Indian Divisions in the south.
November 4: After further fighting, Axis troops begin to retreat, followed by 1st, 7th and 10th Armoured Divisions.

Operation Torch was notable for the long approach voyages – troops came straight from the US and the UK to the beaches

TORCH AND THE TUNISIAN BRIDGEHEAD

On the morning of November 8, 1942, a force of over 100,000 American and British soldiers went ashore on the coast of Vichy French North-West Africa, and a period of close Anglo-American co-operation began. Altogether over 500 ships had carried and guarded the assault force: 102 of them crossing the Atlantic from America; the remainder sailing in two convoys – one fast and one slow – from Britain. They all arrived at their destinations within a few hours of each other and a pattern of smooth timing and organisation had been set.

Once on North African soil, however, the reactions and responses of a third nationality were soon to complicate events, adding to them at the same time a purely Latin flavour of tragicomedy. The American belief that they were so beloved by the French while the British were so hated as to make the essential difference between welcome and resistance in North Africa had already caused unnecessary complications in the tactical planning (in that the landings had to appear to be all-American). But the French desire, on the one hand to avoid retribution at the hands of the Germans if the landings proved a failure, and on the other

Imperial War Museum   Imperial War Museum   US Army

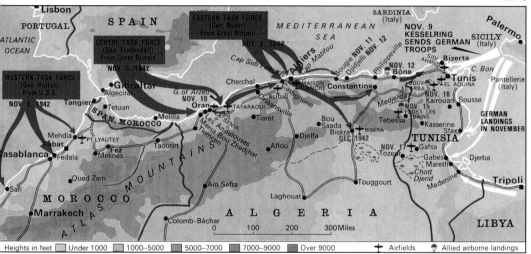

Heights in feet ▢ Under 1000 ▢ 1000–5000 ▢ 5000–7000 ▢ 7000–9000 ▢ Over 9000   ✚ Airfields   ⬤ Allied airborne landings

Top left: **Air-raid practice during the voyage.** *Centre:* **British troops of the eastern Task Force.** *Right:* **American troops**

An American soldier carrying his rifle – the famous Garand ·30 M1, described as 'the best battle implement ever devised'

to play an important part in their own liberation should they succeed, complicated the situation immeasurably more. However, by one of history's oddest twists, the Gordian Knot was cut by the very man who had most reason to hate the British, and good reason to suspect the Americans. Admiral Darlan, the Vichy C-in-C who was visiting the area at that time for purely personal reasons, was one of the few French leaders with the authority to order the French forces to stop their desultory resistance and join the Allies. After some hesitation he ordered a ceasefire and the Allies could at last turn their energies to the more important military objectives – the ports of Tunis and Bizerta.

The Oran landings were followed by smooth disembarkation

Shortly after the main landings in Algeria and Morocco, th
British 1st Army drove into Tunisia to clear the coastline and lin
up with the 8th Army, now advancing from El Alamein. But the swif
liberation of Algeria and Morocco had been untypical; in Tunisi
the Germans reacted with speed and efficiency, and rapidly built u
their forces. Within three days of the Allied landings, German air
lifts were bringing troops and equipment into Tunis, and by the en
of the month 15,000 well-armed and experienced German soldier
and 9,000 Italians were expertly deployed to block Allied plans. B
pouring troops into this 'Tunisian Bridgehead' Hitler was hoping t
prevent or at least delay an Allied attack on southern Europe. B
the end of January the Axis had over 100,000 troops in Tunisia an
had brought the Allied advance to a halt.

Meanwhile at the other end of the Mediterranean Rommel wa
also heading for Tunisia. Four days before the Torch landings too
place, the Axis defences at El Alamein had finally given way an
the 8th Army began the last pursuit of the Afrika Korps — who wit
typical efficiency succeeded in fighting repeated and stubborn rea
guard actions despite their exhaustion and lack of supplies.

A Sherman tank of the 1st Army: neatness was their hallmark

Commander's hatch
Gunner's shield
Radio aerial socket
30-inch machine-gun
(hidden by breech)
Radiator
Left fuel filler-cap
Chrysler 5-bank 30-cylinder
445-hp engine (1,253 cu in)
Cooling fan

50-inch machine-gun
75-mm gun
Gun elevating gear
Turret traverse me
Machine-gunne
hatch (open)
Ventilator
Machine-gunn
(driver on left
17 75-mm
(each sid
14 75-mm rounds
Turret floor/walls
drum
Turret gunner's seat
Machine-gun ammunition
and grenades
15 75-mm rounds
12 75-mm rounds

The Allied Juggernaut

After the earlier designs of the Grant and Lee
tanks — which had themselves performed
invaluable services with 8th Army in early 1942
— the main American and Allied battle tank
came to be the Sherman. Its mass delivery to
the Allied armies in North Africa and
southern Europe was the result of an un-

precedented feat of production. In 1941,
American factories turned out 14,000 Shermans;
in 1943, this rose to 21,000. And these numbers
alone, matched by the virtues of mechanical
reliability, gave the Sherman a very
significant counter to the German gun and
armour superiority. Solidly armoured, formidably
armed, this model's most extraordinary feature

was its Chrysler engine, built up from five
25-hp truck engines. *Max speed:* 23 mph.
Range: 80 miles in average conditions.
Crew: five. *Weight:* 71,900 lb. *Engine:*
Chrysler model A57 (30-cylinder, 460-BHP).
Armament: one 75-mm M3 gun, one ·50-inch
machine-gun in hull, one ·30-inch machine-gu
on flexible mounting

Map legend:

→ Lines of 1st Army advance
⋯ Airborne landings
◄ Lines of German advance
━ ━ Front line Jan. 1, 1943

Heights in feet
- over 3,000
- 2,000-3,000
- 1,000-2,000
- under 1,000

✝ Airfields

**Map labels:**

NOV. 9 GERMAN ADVANCE PARTIES LAND (from Sicily)

Bizerta
Sidi Ahmed
Tindja
Mateur

NOV. 10 GERMANS ESTABLISH FIRST BRIDGEHEAD

Gulf of Tunis

NOV. 30 36th BDE. ATTACKS REPULSED
NOV. 27
Sedjenane
36th BDE.
NOV. 26 Tamera
Djebel Azzag (Green Hill)
Djebel Agred (Bald Hill)

NOV. 18 BRITISH REPULSE GERMAN COLUMN
Djebel Abiod
NOV. 16 HART FORCE
NOV. 17 36th BDE.
NOV. 18 1st PARA. BN.
NOV. 26 ALLIES RAID AIRFIELD
NOV. 27 1st PARA. BN.
Sidi Nsir
NOV. 17

Tabarka

BRITISH ADVANCE FROM BÔNE

Bône 80 miles

Djedeida
El Aouina
Tebourba
NOV. 27, 29/30 1st E. SURREY REGT. 5th NORTHAMPTON REGT.
Tunis

Longstop Hill
Medjerda
St. Cyprien

Béja
NOV. 25 11th INF. BDE.
Medjez el Bab
DEC. 2nd PARA. REGT. RETIRES
Oudna
DEC. 1
Prise NOV. 30 l'eau

NOV. 16 BRITISH PARATROOPS FLOWN FROM ALGIERS
Souk el Khemis
NOV. 25 Slouchia
NOV. 26 GERMANS WITHDRAW
NOV. 29 GERMAN ROAD BLOCK

Souk el Arba
NOV. 16 1st PARA. BN.
NOV. 18 BLADE FORCE
Teboursouk
Le Kef 40 miles
Bou Arada
NOV. 29 2nd PARA. BN.
Depienne
56th RECCE. REGT.
Pont du Fahs

One of the weaknesses of the Torch planning was that no provision had been made to neutralize Tunisia during the initial stages. German reaction was faster than Allied planners had thought possible, and a race developed between the 1st Army and the German advance parties—first to seize certain vital airfields with airborne troops, and then to occupy the passes leading into the Tunisian plain with orthodox forces. The Allies won the first lap, but their advance towards Tunis and Bizerta was stopped by the Germans on a line running from Oudna through Tebourba towards Mateur. By this time, the 1st Army had outrun its supply lines and lacked the impetus to break through the German defences. Meanwhile, the Germans and Italians continued their build-up, pouring in troops and aircraft. The prime German deficiency was in artillery: guns of all types numbered less than 40, but operations were in fact hardly hampered—the Stukas provided intense fire-support by day and the mortars were a deadly supplement. It was the mountainous terrain, however, which most aided the Axis defence.

Once Admiral Darlan had agreed to support the Allies, French resistance in Algeria and Morocco came to an end and the Allied forces were able to move out from the main cities and complete the occupation of the country swiftly and easily

United Press

New Tide from the Atlantic

1942 July 24/25: The combined British and American Chiefs-of-Staff decide to adopt the 'Super-Gymnast' plan – a major Anglo-American invasion of north-west Africa. Churchill renames the operation Torch; General Eisenhower is given overall command.
October 22/23: American General Mark Clark makes a secret landing on the Algerian coast for talks with key French officials. The first assault forces for Oran and Algiers sail from Britain.
November 2: Rommel gives Afrika Korps orders to withdraw from El Alamein.
November 3: On receiving Hitler's refusal of permission to withdraw, Rommel orders his units to take up new defensive positions.
November 3/4: 8th Army breaches the German defence line, Afrika Korps loses about 200 tanks and armoured vehicles.
November 5: Rommel establishes a new halt-line at Fuka, where his units can reorganise, but it is penetrated by the 8th Army.
November 6: Heavy rain slows up the 8th Army's pursuit.
November 7: French General Giraud, principal candidate to lead the French in Africa, is picked up on the south coast of France by a British submarine, and taken to Gibraltar to await the results of the landing.
November 8: The Allied assault forces land near Casablanca, Oran, and Algiers. At Casablanca, landing troubles delay the invaders, but the other forces are not opposed until they begin to move toward their objectives.
November 9: Following discussions with General Clark in Algiers, Admiral Darlan issues an order to cease fire. After pressure from the Germans this is countermanded by the Vichy government, but the French forces in North Africa obey. On hearing of Torch, Rommel decides to retreat in one bound to El Agheila. Sidi Barrani is evacuated.
November 11: German forces overrun the unoccupied part of France, and begin to pour into Tunisia, as the British 1st Army begins to advance towards Tunis and Bizerta. Afrika Korps evacuates Halfaya Pass. 36th Brigade lands at Bougie.
November 12: Paratroops of British 1st Parachute Brigade occupy Bône Airfield.
November 13: Advance guard of the 8th Army enters Tobruk.
November 16: Souk el Arba airfield is captured by the 1st Parachute Battalion; it begins to advance towards Tunis. The headquarters of 78th Division is established at Bône.
November 20: 8th Army reaches Benghazi.
November 23: Afrika Korps falls back from Agedabia; Montgomery slows up the pursuit in order to reorganise his fighting forces and supply lines.
November 26/30: Medjez is evacuated by the Germans and occupied by 11th Brigade. 36th Brigade reaches Tamera, and continues to probe towards Mateur. It meets strong resistance, and 1st Army's advance is held up on a line Mateur/Medjez. Djedeida is occupied for a short time, but the Germans recapture it.
November 29: The 2nd Parachute Battalion lands at Depienne airfield, and marches to Oudna, but it has to withdraw when 1st Army fails to break through at Djedeida and link up with it.
December 12/13: 8th Army attacks the German line at Mersa Brega, the Afrika Korps withdraws to avoid a major struggle.
December 14/18: Rommel evades an attempt to surround his forces at El Agheila.
December 24: Admiral Darlan is assassinated.

Debut of the Parachute Regiment. By the time of the Torch landings, the British had recruited a small force of airborne troops which was to prove vital during the opening stages of the race into Tunisia. The operations to capture the airfields at Bône and Souk el Arba were among the first occasions in which the new parachute battalions were used in action, and since at this stage they had not acquired a new badge, the men wore the distinctive red beret with the badges of their old regiments. A parachute battalion at this time consisted of about 538 men of all ranks – a headquarters company and three rifle companies – and would be accompanied into action by a variety of specialists: troops from the Royal Engineers, Royal Signals, and Royal Army Medical Corps. The operations in Tunisia were also the first time that the airborne troops used the aircraft which was to become their standard mount for the rest of the war – and the workhorse of almost all the Allied forces in every theatre.

Douglas C-47 Dakota. A military version of the DC-3 airliner, the Dakota had a strengthened floor and larger cargo-handling door on the port side. Rugged and extremely reliable, over 10,000 Dakotas had been produced by the end of the war – 1,200 of them being supplied to the RAF – and many were still in use 20 years after the war ended. **Speed:** 230 mph (maximum), 167 mph (cruising). **Range:** 1,300 miles. **Crew:** Three. **Load:** 9,028 lb of cargo, or 18/24 paratroops

(Below) Dakotas in flight during the advance into Tunisia
(Below right) British paratroops inside a Dakota en route to Bône airfield

Dakota: Workhorse for the Allies

Imperial War Museum

THE CHASE TO MARETH

At the opening of the battle, Rommel had been away sick in Austria, but flew back at once. Weighing up the situation, he planned to withdraw his army to the Fuka position, 60 miles west of El Alamein. That step would have thrown Montgomery's battle-machine out of gear. But Rommel's intention was overruled by Hitler's insistence that no ground must be yielded. So retreat was deferred until after defeat. Then Rommel executed it with his usual celerity and ruthless calculation – abandoning his less mobile and less expert troops, including the bulk of the Italians, in order to bring away his picked troops in the motor transport available.

The chance of cutting him off was lost because the pursuit was not sufficiently indirect or extensive in its circling sweep. In the first place, it turned in too soon to catch the bulk of the forces retreating along the coastal road. Then a longer-range turn-in at 'Charing Cross', near Marsa Matrûh (120 miles west of El Alamein), failed to cut them off through running short of petrol after being impeded by heavy rain. A wider move through the desert, farther inland, would have avoided the rainy belt.

Once Rommel had slipped through the jaws of his armoured pursuers, he did not pause until he had reached his favourite backstop position near El Agheila at the far end of Cyrenaica – 700 miles back from El Alamein. In a fortnight's swift retreat he had outstripped the pursuit, and left few prisoners or supplies behind.

If after El Alamein Rommel had any hopes of once again turning the tables on the 8th Army they were quickly dashed by the Allied landings in Morocco and Algeria. His only chance of survival from then on lay in a successful, defensive withdrawal to the 'Tunisian Bridgehead'.

The crew of one of Rommel's Panzers surrenders at Alamein

Imperial War Museum

Rommel's forces were so weak that he could not even hope to hold a defensive line for long, let alone mount a counterattack. Instead he fought a masterly withdrawal, causing the 8th Army the maximum of trouble while keeping Panzerarmee in being and its morale high.

The 8th Army in pursuit of the Afrika Korps at Alamein

But this time the odds against him were too heavy to permit any riposte, or even a long-sustained stand at El Agheila. A pause of three weeks occurred before the 8th Army could bring up its strength and mount an offensive against the El Agheila position. Just as the offensive developed, Rommel began to slip off. Rommel halted again on the Buerat position, a further 200 miles back. He stayed there three weeks, but when the 8th Army closed up and launched its next offensive, in the middle of January 1943, he fell back again.

This time he made an almost continuous withdrawal for 350 miles, past Tripoli, to the Mareth Line inside the frontier of Tunisia. His decision was the consequence not merely of his weakness of force and the sinking of the majority of his supply-ships, but of the new situation produced by the Anglo-American invasion of Morocco and Algeria – Operation Torch – in November 1942. That move had closely followed the El Alamein offensive, some 2,500 miles away at the other end of North Africa.

As originally conceived, the Allied landings were to have taken place only on the Atlantic coast of Morocco. This would have meant a purely frontal advance, giving the French forces the fullest chance of effective resistance. The advance would have started 1,200 miles away from Bizerta, the key to the whole North African theatre of war, so that the Germans would have had time and opportunity to stiffen the French resistance to the Allied invasion. Fortunately for the Allied prospects, landings on the Mediterranean coast, near Oran and Algiers, were added to the plan. American diplomacy smoothed the path of these landings by securing the acquiescence or quiescence of numerous Frenchmen in authority. Once lodgements were achieved at these points they created a decisive leverage on the backs of the French forces on the west coast, where the initial resistance threatened to be more stubborn.

The landings near Algiers reduced the distance from Bizerta to barely 400 miles. At that moment, a mere handful of motorised troops could have run through to Bizerta and Tunis without hindrance except from the mountain roads. Alternatively, either seaborne or airborne landings nearby would have met scarcely any opposition. But the naval authorities were chary of attempting even small-scale landings so far ahead of air cover, and the overland advance was too cautious.

Meantime, the Germans' reaction was swift, though the landings had taken them by surprise. From the third day onwards they began to rush troops to Tunis in all available troop-carrying aircraft

A field gun of Rommel's Army Group Africa in action as the Germans and Italians make their final retreat into Tunisia after the defeat at El Alamein

s well as in small coasting vessels. Although the total was still small, it was just sufficient to check the leading troops of the Allied 1st Army when these reached the immediate approaches to Tunis two-and-a-half weeks after the initial landings. The result of this check was a five-month deadlock in the mountainous arc covering Bizerta and Tunis.

Nevertheless, this failure worked out to the Allies' advantage in the long run. For it encouraged the enemy to continue pouring reinforcements across the sea to Tunisia, where the Allies could cut off their supplies through developing the stranglehold of superior sea-power, and then cut off their retreat. Ironically, Hitler was led to stake larger forces on the retention of Tunisia than he had ever devoted to the capture of Egypt. By drawing so many of the German and Italian reserves across the Mediterranean and putting them in the bag' there, the way was eased for the Allies' subsequent invasion of Europe. North Africa thus became as fatal a strategic bait to Hitler as Spain had been to Napoleon, in conjunction with their respective invasions of Russia.

German transports head for the front past a burning US truck

BATTLE OF KASSERINE

The 1943 campaign in Tunisia opened, however, with a German counterstroke that gave the Allies a bad shock. It came just when their two armies – the 1st from the west, and the 8th from the east – seemed about to crush the Axis forces between their jaws. The Axis command aimed to forestall that danger by dislocating both jaws, and for such an aim the conditions had become more favourable than was apparent on the surface of the situation. By now the reinforce-

ments sent to Tunis had been built up into an army, under General von Arnim, while at the same time the remnant of Rommel's army was acquiring fresh strength, and equipment, as it came nearer to the supply ports in its westward retreat. Profiting by this temporarily favourable turn in the situation, Rommel's design was to exploit his central position between the two converging Allied armies to strike, and cripple, them separately and successively. The design had brilliant promise, but its execution suffered a heavy handicap in being largely dependent on forces which were not under Rommel's control. For when the operation was launched Arnim's army was independent, and even the veteran XXI Panzer Division, which was to deliver the main thrust, had passed to Arnim's command when it had been sent back to help in holding open Rommel's line of retreat and supply.

The American 2nd Corps (which included a French division) was the immediate target of the counterstroke. Its front covered 90 miles, but was focused on the three routes through the mountains to the sea, with spearheads at the passes near Gafsa, Faid, and Fondouk. These passage-ways were so narrow that the occupiers felt secure. But at the end of January, the XXI Panzer Division made a sudden spring at the Faid Pass, overwhelmed the French garrison

The small map shows the ultimate targets of Frühlingswind – the German offensive in southern Tunisia. To break through the mass of Allied men and material between the Tunisian front and the Allied bases of Bône and Constantine was a formidable task – but the confusion which was caused by the first attacks (below) seemed to promise fulfilment of all Rommel's hopes. The Axis troops in the Mareth Line were saved from the threat of an American attack from the west – but Commando Supremo failed to appoint a unified command and thus concentrate the Axis strike forces for a further advance. By the afternoon of February 22, Rommel had lost faith in the attack and had begun to withdraw; and the badly-shaken Allied armies recovered themselves

113

'NEBELWERFER' 150-MM ROCKET-LAUNCHER: The most widely used of the family of launchers developed by the Germans, the six-barrelled Nebelwerfer ('fog-thrower') was used to lay down extremely heavy short range bombardments or smoke screens. As compared with conventional artillery, the Nebelwerfer fired a heavy projectile (below) from a light carriage, and was thus very manoeuvrable, but it was far less accurate. The six barrels had to be fired separately (this took 10 seconds) to prevent the carriage overturning; the tubes could be reloaded in 90 seconds. *Weight of launcher:* 1,195 lb. *Range:* 7,330 yards with high explosive, 7,750 yards with smoke shells. *Weight of rocket:* 75·3 lb (high explosive), 78 lb (smoke)

before American support arrived, and thus gained a sally-port.

On February 14 the real blow came, starting with a fresh spring forward from the Faid Pass. Arnim's deputy, Ziegler, was in charge here. Rommel urged Ziegler to drive on during the night and exploit the success to the full, but Ziegler waited for 48 hours until he received Arnim's authorisation before pushing on 25 miles to Sbeitla, where the Americans had rallied. Even then he was able to throw them back again, although the fight was harder and they rallied again at the Kasserine Pass.

Alexander, who had just been placed in charge of both the Allied armies, and now arrived on the scene, said in his dispatch: 'I found the position even more critical than I had expected, and a visit to the Kasserine area showed that in the confusion of the retreat American, French and British troops had been inextricably mingled, there was no co-ordinated plan of defence and definite uncertainty as to command.'

Rommel wanted to exploit the confusion and panic by a combined drive with all available mechanised forces through Tebéssa towards the Allies' main communications with their Algerian bases. But it was not until early on the 19th that a signal came from Rome authorising a continuation of the thrust, and Rommel to conduct it – but ordering that it should be made due *northward* to Thala, instead of *north-westward* to Tebéssa as Rommel had proposed.

Thus the thrust came along the line which Alexander had expected, and where he was best prepared to meet it. He had ordered the army commander to 'concentrate his armour for the defence of Thala', and British reserves from the north were being rushed down to that sector. The Americans, too, had collected in strength on the line of approach to Thala, and held on so stubbornly to the Kasserine Pass that the Germans did not break through it until the evening of the 20th. Next day they drove into Thala, exhausted, and were pushed

out by the British reserves that had now arrived there.

This too-direct approach not only proved an expensive failur itself but caused delay in releasing the divisions needed for Rom mel's intended second stroke – against Montgomery. By March when Rommel struck, Montgomery had quadrupled his strength besides 400 tanks he had now over 500 anti-tank guns in positio Thus in the interval Rommel's chance of striking with superi force had vanished. The attack was brought to a standstill by t afternoon and the Germans' loss of 50 tanks was a serious han cap in the next phase of the campaign. By then they had also lo Rommel, who had gone back to Europe sick, and frustrated.

For their ultimate victory, the Allies owed more to the enem misjudged offensive efforts than to the effect of their own assaul The Allies' chance to turn the tables only came after the Germa had overstretched themselves in the offensive.

MARETH LINE

The 8th Army's attack on the Mareth Line was launched on th night of March 20. The main blow was a frontal one, intended break through the defence near the sea and make a gap throu which the armoured divisions could sweep. At the same time, t New Zealand Corps made a wide outflanking march towards Hamma in the enemy's rear, with the aim of pinning down t enemy's reserves that were placed there. The frontal attack fail to make an adequate breach. So, after three days' effort, Montgome changed his plan, side-stepping inland and sending the 1st A moured Division to the enemy's rear.

**Left map labels:**

MAR. 21/22
XV PZ. DIV. COUNTERATTACKS
AND CONTAINS BRIDGEHEAD

MAR. 20/21
50th DIV. ESTABLISHES
BRIDGEHEAD

ITALIAN
YOUNG FASCISTS

XV PZ. DIV.

Zarat

Marshes

ITALIAN
XX CORPS

TRIESTE
DIV.

Mareth

4th IND.
DIV.

90th LT.
DIV.

1st DIV.

10th
CORPS

SPEZIA DIV.

7th ARMD.
DIV.

10th
CORPS

Horseshoe

1st
ARMD.
DIV.

ITALIAN
XXI CORPS

Toujane

PISTOIA
DIV.

Matmata
Hills

■▢ Corps headquarters
�P▢ Divisional headquarters
── Axis minefields

0   Miles   8

164th
LT. DIV.

**Right map labels:**

To Gafsa   To Sfax

W. Akarit

Chott el Fedjadj

MEDITERRANEAN
SEA

El Hamma

MAR. 22 XXI PZ. DIV.

Gabès

MAR. 27
AXIS FORCES AT
MARETH LINE ESCAPE

MAR. 26/27
BREAKTHROUGH
BY 1st ARMD. DIV. &
N.Z. CORPS

El Hamma Plain

Djerba

MAR. 28

MAR. 22
164th LT. DIV.

Djebel Tebaga

NIGHT MAR. 21/22
ITALIAN SAHARAN
GROUP

Tebaga Gap

Matmata

Bene Zelten

MARETH
LINE

Mareth

MAR. 20/22
50th DIV. HELD AT
BRIDGEHEAD

MAR. 20
N.Z. CORPS

Toujane

MAR. 23/26
1st ARMD. DIV.

TRAFFIC JAMS

MAR. 24/25
4th IND. DIV.

Medenine

Bir Soltane

Ksar el Hallouf

MAR. 23
10th CORPS
INCL. 1st ARMD. DIV.
MOVES UP TO TEBAGA GAP

4th IND. DIV.

N.Z. CORPS
INCL. 8th ARMD. BDE.

Ksar Rhilane

Foum Tatahouine

NIGHT
MAR. 19/20

MAR. 11/19
N.Z. CORPS
ASSEMBLES

Wilder's Gap

To Ben Gardane

Legend (top right):
Axis forces
N.Z. Corps
1st Armd. Division
Axis front Mar. 21

0   Miles   20

Legend (bottom right):
Heights in feet
over 1600
1200–1600
900–1200
300–900
0–300

The main defences of the Mareth Line ran along the formidable natural barrier of the Wadi Zigzaou. The 50th Division succeeded in forcing a bridgehead across the Wadi after bitter fighting, but it was contained and almost destroyed in a well-timed counterattack by XV Panzer Division. To outflank the Mareth Line, stretching from the sea to the foothills of the Matmata Hills, troops of the 8th Army were sent through Wilder's Gap and across the waterless Dahar to Tebaga Gap to eventually emerge on the El Hamma Plain. Montgomery saw this outflanking move purely as a diversion, while the main thrust would be through the Mareth Line. When the first attack was pinned down, however, he rapidly transformed the 'left hook' into the main offensive

British troops using ladders to climb the sides of Wadi Zigzaou, the most formidable obstacle along the Mareth Line

Even then, the British attacks were checked by the German backstop defences at El Hamma. Thus, although the threatened cut-off led the enemy to abandon the Mareth Line, he was able to hold the gate open and draw off his forces without much loss.

He stopped again barely 10 miles behind El Hamma, along the Wadi Akarit which spanned the Gabes Gap—a very narrow-fronted position between the sea and the hills. The Americans had already tried to forestall the enemy on this position and to pounce on his back while he was gripped by the 8th Army, but they had again been checked before they could debouch from the hills. Then, in the early hours of April 6, the 8th Army attacked the Wadi Akarit under cover of pitch darkness. That tactical innovation resulted in a penetration, though the exploitation was checked by the Germans when daylight came. On the next night they broke away and retired rapidly up the coast towards Tunis.

Within a few days the enemy's two armies had joined hands, to offer a united defence along the mountain arc covering Tunis, and it looked as though they might there maintain a prolonged resistance. Alternatively, they might utilise the breathing space gained, by the swift withdrawal, to evacuate their forces to Sicily.

The German Supreme Command, however, was led to attempt a prolongation of the campaign in Africa, rather than draw in its horns and base its defence of Europe upon the southern shores of Europe. Even in Tunisia it tried to hold too extensive a front for its resources – a 100-mile perimeter – in the endeavour to preserve both Tunis and Bizerta.

On April 20 the offensive was opened by the 8th Army with an attack on the enemy's left flank. But the coastal corridor became very narrow beyond Enfidaville, and the advance soon slowed down, coming to a halt on the 23rd. On April 21 the 5th Corps attacked from the left centre, through the hills leading to Tunis. Next day the 9th Corps struck from the right centre near Goubellat, with the aim of achieving an armoured break-through. But the effort failed to pierce the enemy's defences, though it strained them severely and further weakened the enemy's remaining tank strength. A pause of nearly a fortnight followed on most of the front, but in the north the Americans brought up from the south and a corps of French African troops continued to make a gradual penetration, which brought them within 20 miles of Bizerta.

Infantry advance through smoke in an attack on Longstop Hill

MEDJERDA: THE END IN AFRICA

Meantime Alexander again reshuffled his hand. Leaving only a screening force in the right centre near Goubellat, he moved the bulk of the 9th Corps over to the left centre, concentrated it behind the 5th Corps, and reinforced it with two picked divisions from the 8th Army – the 7th Armoured and 4th Indian. The effect of the deception-plan was reinforced by the reputation of the 8th Army, and of Montgomery, so that General von Arnim kept a disproportionate part of his strength in the south. But Arnim had little chance

After the abortive attempts by 8th Army to break through the Axis defences in the south and thus earn the glory of ending the Tunisian campaign, the rest of the battle to liquidate the bridgehead fell into two distinct parts. In a series of attacks on April 26/30, 1st Army attempted to seize the last Axis strongpoints barring the way to the plain; but it met such stubborn resistance that the offensive halted, having threatened to lose all momentum. It was then that Alexander stepped in and, taking advantage of Montgomery's offer of help, shifted several of 8th Army's units north to prepare for the final breakthrough

Auster AOP-1. AOPs (airborne observation posts) played an important role in the desert, spotting for the fire of artillery and ferrying commanders to important sectors of the battlefield.
Operating speed: 102 mph
Operating range: 375 miles. No armament; two seats

of perceiving the deception, or of re-adjusting his dispositions after the blow fell, because of the Allies' command of the air.

The assault of the 9th Corps, now under General Horrocks, was launched in the starlit but moonless early hours of May 6. It was preceded and covered by an intensive artillery bombardment from over 600 guns, upon a sector less than 2 miles wide, in the Medjerda valley leading to Tunis. After daylight, the air force extended the blast with a terrific storm of bombs. The stunned defenders of the gateway were soon overrun by the infantry of the 4th Indian and 4th British Divisions. Then the concentrated tanks of the 6th and 7th Armoured Divisions drove through the breach. But they lost time in dealing with various small pockets of German resistance. By nightfall they were still some 15 miles from Tunis.

In the morning, however, it became clear that the opposing army as a whole was still paralysed by the combined air shock and strate-

gic shock to such an extent that it could not develop any tactical countermeasures. By the afternoon the leading troops of the British armoured divisions had swept into Tunis. Almost simultaneously the Americans and French poured into Bizerta.

The enemy command had been caught off its balance, and then its machine was thrown out of gear by the combination of air pressure overhead and tank impact on its back. Dislocation of control was the primary cause of collapse, while the breakdown of communications accentuated the demoralising effect of lack of reserves and disruption of supplies. Another factor was the closeness of the enemy's bases to the broken front. The rapid penetration into the bases was as dislocating to morale as it was to the administrative system. The loss of their bases deepened the depressing sensation of fighting with their backs to the sea – a sea now dominated by the Allies' sea power and air power.

Although disappointing as an interceptor, the Curtiss Kittyhawk — which had been widely supplied to the RAF under lend-lease — came into its own during the North African campaign. Its ruggedness made it one of the most widely used aircraft for the new close-support techniques the RAF was developing there.
Maximum speed: 362 mph at 15,000 feet **Range:** 700 miles
Armament: Six .50-inch machine-guns and two 250-lb bombs

117

D-DAY
INVASION OF HITLER'S EUROPE

British and Canadian troops wade up 'Juno' beach to Bernières
against only sporadic German resistance, as high tide comes in

United Press

Operation Overlord

THE PLANS TAKE SHAPE

With the coming of summer 1944 the Allies prepared for their greatest trial – 'Overlord', the invasion of Occupied Europe. Previous attacks on German-held coasts – Dieppe, Salerno, and Anzio were the most notorious – had taught some bloody lessons: if Overlord were to succeed, the Allies would have to amass huge air and sea armadas which could land the armies and supply them in an unbroken chain of operations. In this article, Major-General R. H. Barry explains how it all began

Churchill had been the first to foresee the necessity for an Allied re-entry of the continent of Europe. Only shortly after Dunkirk, when British fortunes were apparently at their lowest ebb, he had directed that planning should be initiated with this ultimate end in view.

The Russians had been pressing for the opening of the Second Front ever since the end of 1941, and as the Americans began to gather strength in the European theatre, their eyes turned naturally to the direct assault on 'Fortress Europe' as the major and decisive operation of the war. Owing to the vicissitudes of the war, however, and the calls of other theatres, particularly the Far East, no major concrete steps were taken to start planning for what subsequently became known as 'Overlord', until the Casablanca Conference of 1943. There it was decided to set up an Allied Staff to plan the operation under a 'Chief-of-Staff to the Supreme Allied Commander (Designate)' – COSSAC – and a British officer, Lieutenant-General F. E. Morgan, was appointed to the post in March. At the Washington Conference in May 1943 absolute priority was allotted to Overlord and the target date for the operation was laid down as May 1944.

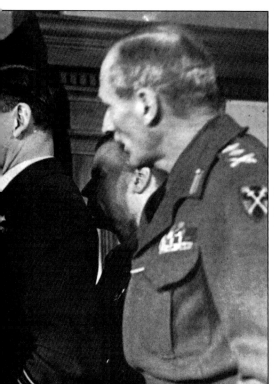

Left to right: **General Eisenhower, Supreme Commander of Overlord; Air Chief-Marshal Leigh-Mallory, commanding Allied Expeditionary Air Force; Air Chief-Marshal Tedder, Deputy Supreme Commander; General Montgomery, commanding 21st Army Group**

By the time the Quebec Conference assembled in August 1943, COSSAC had produced an outline plan. His first problem naturally had been to select the area of the assault. The choice was rapidly narrowed down to two alternatives – the Pas de Calais and the Normandy coast east of the Cherbourg peninsula and its port. The advantages of the Pas de Calais were obvious: it offered the shortest sea crossing and the most direct route to Germany, the ultimate objective; it would allow the Allied air forces to produce the maximum weight of support. Unfortunately these advantages were equally obvious to the Germans, and it was here that the bulk of the German forces were concentrated and the coastal defences at their most effective.

There was a further and decisive disadvantage – lack of mounting ports. The entire operation would have to be mounted from the comparatively restricted areas of Dover and Newhaven with Portsmouth and Southampton as somewhat distant adjuncts; an assault further west would allow the main body of the operation to be mounted from the great port complex, Portsmouth, Southampton, Poole, Portland. The choice, therefore, fell on Normandy, where the Cherbourg peninsula would protect the landing beaches from the Atlantic weather and where the German defences were thinner; the price, a longer sea crossing and increased dead flying time for the air forces (particularly the fighters), had to be accepted.

Eisenhower selects his team
In November 1943 Roosevelt and Churchill met again in Cairo. Here the main outlines of the plan were settled and – more important still at this stage – the command structure was agreed and the key appointments made. General Eisenhower was nominated Supreme Allied Commander with Air Chief-Marshal Tedder as his Deputy. Eisenhower chose as his Chief-of-Staff, responsible for forming his headquarters, General Walter Bedell Smith, who had served him so well in North Africa. Subordinate to this headquarters were to

be two army groups, a US army group under General Omar Bradley and a British army group under General Montgomery; the latter was to be in command of all the land forces during the assault phase and until the area captured was sufficient to permit the deployment of the two army groups. A British officer, Admiral Ramsay, was appointed to command the naval forces; under him the US naval forces were commanded by Admiral Kirk and the British by Admiral Vian. Another British officer, Air Chief-Marshal Leigh-Mallory, commanded the Allied air forces, of which the British and Canadian component was under Air Marshal Coningham, and the American under General Brereton.

Choosing the target
The final presentation of the combined D-Day plans took place under the supervision of SHAEF (Supreme HQ, Allied Expeditionary Force) at a conference held at St Paul's School on May 15, 1944, before a distinguished gathering, which included the British Monarch, the Prime Minister, the Chiefs-of-Staff, the Supreme Commander, and his senior commanders.

The plan in its final shape belonged to General Sir Bernard Montgomery, the Ground Force Commander; Admiral Sir Bertram Ramsay, Commander-in-Chief Allied Naval Expeditionary Force; and Air Chief-Marshal Sir Trafford Leigh-Mallory, Commander-in-Chief Allied Expeditionary Air Force. For five months the headquarters of these three had built upon the solid foundations laid by COSSAC and his Allied staff. The final work bore many 'signatures', owing its existence to the constant planning of Naval and Combined Operations Headquarters, and the original 'Combined Commanders'.

By May 15, the plan had expanded west of the Vire estuary to the beaches of the Cotentin peninsula, and eastward to the Orne (see map). Its three divisions in the assault lift had become five, supplemented by 14 tank regiments, Commandos, and special service troops. The airborne lift had grown from two-thirds of a division for which COSSAC had not been granted sufficient air transport, to three airborne divisions. The naval tasks had expanded steadily in proportion. Nevertheless, the plan remained fundamentally the creation of COSSAC. He had been forced to build with shadows, spinning invisible webs, and sustained by drive and faith.

The target date – Y-Day – was June 1. The day – D-Day – would follow at the earliest possible moment thereafter. The earliest possible moment was Y+4. The conditions essential for the assault had been agreed between the Supreme Commander and Admiral Sir Bertram Ramsay on May 1. The extensive mine-laying operations of the enemy, coupled with the great mass of mined obstacles sprouting from the beaches and planted far out beyond the low water mark, called for a landing on a rising tide as soon after low tide as possible, and in daylight as near to dawn as possible. A moon was desirable by night. These considerations fixed the possible dates as June 5, 6, and 7. The 5th and 6th were both good, the 7th not so good. After that, no further opportunity would occur until June 19, and without the moon.

The possibility of a forced delay of two weeks, dire in its inferences, had been planned for in all its stark detail. It involved the halting of an avalanche of men and supplies, and all that must go with them, already on shipboard, and half of them at sea. About 1,000,000 more men, armour, artillery, transport, and 1,000,000 tons of supplies were in the pipe lines, converging on the embarkation points; 1,000,000 more behind them, reaching back across the Atlantic.

The thought made men shudder. 'The problems arising out of a postponement of 12-14 days to the next suitable period are too appalling even to contemplate,' wrote Admiral Ramsay. Nevertheless, the problems were fully contemplated, and the implications faced.

On May 8, the Supreme Commander tentatively agreed D-Day with his commanders on land, sea, and air, as June 5. The navy and air forces had been laying mines for three weeks to protect the convoys; the far more complex task of mine-sweeping lay ahead. Ten channels to Normandy must be swept from the assembly point known to the Royal Navy as 'Piccadilly Circus', and officially as 'Area Z' just south of the Isle of Wight. The state of the tide for the landing meant that the mine-sweeping would have to be done across the tide setting strongly to the east in the opening stages, and setting westward at about the half-way mark. Mine-sweeping had never before been carried out in such conditions, and great difficulties in timing were involved; 12 mine-sweeping flotillas were assembled for the job.

By the end of the first week of April, Montgomery, with the commanders of the naval and air forces, was able to announce his full plans to his general officers, and hammer out the possibilities with his senior field officers. His intention, as he expressed it, was:

'To assault, simultaneously, beaches on the Normandy coast immediately north of the Carentan Estuary and between the Carentan Estuary and the Orne river, with the object of securing as a base for further operations a lodgement area.'

The lodgement area must include, at the earliest possible moment, airfield sites south-east of the important road centre of Caen, and the port of Cherbourg. He expounded his plan to develop a major threat to break out on the eastern flank, thus to draw the main weight of the enemy reserves and strength against the British and Canadians. Having established a firm hinge pivoting upon Caen, and drawn the enemy to full commitment in the east he would break out with Bradley's US armies to cut a wide swathe 'to cut off all the enemy forces south of the Seine, over which river the bridges were to be destroyed by air action.'

The US 1st Army, with three regimental combat teams, would assault astride the Carentan Estuary, to capture Cherbourg and develop their attack southward upon St Lô to conform to the British 2nd Army.

The British 2nd Army, with five brigades, would assault between Asnelles and Ouistreham, with the Canadians in the centre, to develop a bridgehead south of a line St Lô, Caen, and south-east of Caen to secure airfield sites and to protect the eastern flank of the US 1st Army.

Both armies would be supported by specialised engineer troops, armour, Commandos and US Rangers.

The US 82nd and 101st Airborne Divisions would land south-east and west of St Mère Eglise, astride the flooded Merderet river, to capture crossings and to secure the line of the Douve river, thereby to assist the seaborne assault on Utah beach and prevent the movement of enemy reserves into the Cotentin.

The British 6th Airborne Division would land east of Caen to seize crossings over the Orne river at Bénouville and Ranville.

It was hoped to land 1,500 tanks, 5,000 tracked fighting vehicles, 3,000 guns, and 10,500 vehicles ranging from jeeps to bulldozers on D-Day. Such in broad outline was the land force task, and it gave the senior officers present plenty to talk about all through the day following the opening of the conference. There would be little room for manoeuvre, no opportunity 'to feel a way in'. Supported from the sea and sky by a colossal weight of fire most skilfully devised, the assault troops had to gain their footholds by direct, uncompromising assault, and force their ways in. There would be no way back, only forward.

The US forces were on the right, the western flank, for reasons of supply. As soon as Cherbourg and the Brittany ports could be opened they would be supplied direct from the United States. The British would finally rely upon the Channel ports and Antwerp.

The enemy were expected to hold some 60 divisions in the west under Field-Marshal von Rundstedt. Montgomery's immediate opponent would be Field-Marshal Rommel, commanding Army Group B, consisting of the German VII Army in Normandy and Brittany, the XV Army in the Pas de Calais and Flanders, and the 88th Corps in Holland. The greatest concentration of enemy strength behind the most powerful fortifications lay in the Pas de Calais. It had been the business of the Allies throughout many months, by feints, rumours, diversions, to keep them there, and to bolster the natural enemy fears based on the simple proposition that a straight line is the shortest distance between two points.

Air Chief-Marshal Sir Trafford Leigh-Mallory explained the main tasks of the British 2nd and the US 9th Tactical Air Forces in close support. He feared greatly the results of the airborne attack on the right flank, and expressed his fears up to the final hour. The attacks sustained against railways, roads, and bridges were well known. The extent of the success was not remotely realised. On 'The Day' the air forces would maintain a sustained density of ten fighter squadrons over the beaches, five British and five American. Six squadrons would be alerted to support the beach cover. Five squadrons would cover the main naval approaches, and a striking force of 33 fighter squadrons would be in reserve.

Following the fulfilment of escort duties for the airborne troops a total of 171 squadrons would be apportioned, 54 squadrons to beach cover, 15 squadrons to shipping cover, 36 squadrons to direct support, 33 squadrons to offensive operations and bomber escort, and 33 squadrons as a striking force.

On paper, the Luftwaffe still maintained impressive figures. In the air it could do nothing to counter the immense weight of Allied air power, and little even to harry it.

In round figures, some 5,000 ships and 4,000 ship-to-shore craft would be at the service of the assault. Their fire power, from the heavy armament of the battleships and cruisers down to the destroyers, the rocket ships, the armour and artillery firing from their craft on the run-in, was truly colossal.

Operation 'Neptune' would launch Operation 'Overlord'.

1. Normandy or Calais?

The Allied planners knew that the Germans expected an invasion across the Narrows of the Channel, where the distance was short both for shipping and air cover. But this would mean long distances along the south coast for all ships based on the western ports. If Normandy was the target, however, all convoys would converge on an assembly area equidistant from all the major ports

2. The COSSAC plan

In drawing up the preliminary plans for the invasion of Europe, COSSAC had to cut his coat according to his cloth. He was only able to lift two airborne brigades to cover the flanks — and only envisaged landing three assault divisions on the sector between the Vire and the Orne

3. Montgomery's amendment

Montgomery's first reactions to the Overlord plan were highly unfavourable. He wanted five divisions, not three; separate sectors for US and British forces, each corps to have its own landing-beach — and at least two full-strength airborne divisions

4. The final plan

Eisenhower's staff backed Montgomery's broadening of the assault plans and added a third airborne division. Build-up preparations, too, were intensified: it was now intended to get 18 divisions ashore by D + 10

NEPTUNE'S INVASION FLEET

To carry the overall total of 40-50,000 men with their vehicles and equipment, an armada of over 4,000 landing ships, landing-craft, and barges of varying types was required; only about half of these were capable of crossing the Channel under their own power, the remainder having either to be towed or carried aboard the larger ships. When it is remembered that every man and every vehicle had to be allotted to a specific ship or landing-craft, that every vehicle before embarkation had to be waterproofed, that men and vehicles had to arrive at the right time at the 'hards' (improvised landing places) at which their particular landing-craft was beached – the complications of planning and organisation can easily be imagined. Only when all this had been done, did the huge task of the Royal Navy in assembling, marshalling, and shepherding this heterogeneous collection of vessels across the Channel into paths swept through the enemy minefields, in landing them on the correct beaches, and providing the necessary fire support begin.

Apart from the non-combatant ships and landing-craft carrying men, vehicles, and stores, the US Navy and Royal Navy assembled for the escort and support of the operation a fleet of over 1,500 vessels, ranging from battleships to armed landing-craft. They were divided into two 'task forces', the Western Task Force from the US Navy supporting the US landing, and the Eastern Task Force, provided primarily by the Royal Navy, supporting the British/Canadian landing. Each task force was further sub-divided into 'forces', one to each beach, responsible for escorting the assaulting force concerned, positioning it correctly, and providing fire support for the landing. The assault looked primarily to naval gunfire to silence the German coastal batteries and strongpoints.

The magnitude of the naval effort can be judged by the fact that the forces included seven battleships, 23 cruisers, 148 destroyers, as well as a swarm of smaller vessels – sloops, frigates, trawlers, corvettes, patrol craft and minesweepers. In addition, a fleet of 350 specially designed landing-craft carrying guns, rockets, anti-aircraft guns, and machine-guns was assembled for the close support of the actual assault.

The air effort in direct support of the assault was on a similar immense scale. It comprised the most modern types of aircraft available at the period, primarily the Spitfire, Mustang, Typhoon, Lightning, and Thunderbolt.

The exact timing of the assault proved a most complex problem which had its repercussions upon the dates on which the operation could be launched.

Although from the point of view of the assaulting troops there was much to be said for an assault in darkness, both the navies and air forces had to have daylight to carry out their bombardment tasks, and darkness would dangerously increase the likelihood of troops being landed in the wrong place. To assist navigation and for the airborne landings, moonlight was essential. Finally, the German underwater beach obstacles meant that landing must begin three to four hours before high tide. The only suitable periods for the operation therefore were those when there was four to five hours' daylight between dawn and high tide and at the same time good moonlight was available. All these conditions could only be satisfied on approximately three days in each lunar month.

However powerful and successful the assault, it would clearly be valueless unless the forces ashore could be built up more rapidly than those of the enemy and properly maintained when there. This involved three problems: the planning, escorting, and routing of the follow-up convoys; ensuring that those convoys contained the right personnel, vehicles, and equipment arriving in the right order; and finally ensuring that they could be rapidly unloaded on arrival.

Fifteen personnel ships, 74 ocean-going merchant ships, and more than 200 coasters were loaded before D-Day and these were to form the first wave of the build-up; the requirement thereafter was for eight convoys a day. Once having got the assault force across, however, movement of these convoys was not likely to present any particular problem for the Allied navies.

The question of what they should contain after the initial pre-planned flight was more difficult, and a special organisation known as 'Build-Up Control' (BUCO) was set up in Southampton to ensure that what was shipped across the Channel was geared to the requirements of the battle.

The question of rapid unloading initially appeared the most difficult of all; it could clearly not be done across the beaches as a long-term measure and the likelihood of capturing port facilities intact appeared small, at any rate in the early stages. The problem was solved by perhaps the most famous devices of the entire operation – the artificial harbours known as 'Mulberries'. They owed their existence primarily to the foresight of Churchill himself, who had directed their development as early as 1942, with his oft-quoted minute: 'They *must* float up and down with the tide.... Don't argue the matter. The difficulties will argue for themselves.' They consisted of an outer breakwater formed partly of sunken blockships and partly of concrete 'caissons', 200 feet long, which had to be towed across the Channel; in the area of sheltered water so created were floating piers adapted to take coasters, landing ships or barges; unloading was further assisted by a fleet of amphibious lorries known as DUKWs. The success of the system may be judged by the fact that shortly after the assault, an average of 6,500 vehicles and nearly 40,000 tons of stores was being landed weekly.

The supply of motor and aircraft fuel presented a particular problem. Initially tankers were moored offshore and the fuel fed by buoyed pipeline into depots on land. Preparations were made, however, for an underwater pipeline direct from England to the

***Bangor*-Class Minesweeper** (reciprocating engine)
A wide minesweeper class – it formed a large part of the Neptune minesweeper strength of 287. *Bangor*-class 'sweepers were built in three versions – diesel, turbine, and reciprocating engines. Displacement: 672 tons. Crew: 60. Speed: 16 knots. Armament: 1 × 3-in, 1 × 40-mm. 4 × .303-in mg

French coast – PLUTO, or 'Pipe-Line-Under-the-Ocean' – and eventually, though not in the early stages, fuel supply was in effect drawn direct from England.

The impression so far given may well be that this was an exclusively British/American/Canadian operation, but the contributions of the other Allies must not be forgotten. The French, for instance, provided two cruisers, one destroyer, one armoured division, and four squadrons of aircraft; the Belgians one brigade and two squadrons; the Dutch two gunboats, one brigade, and two squadrons; the Poles one cruiser, two destroyers, one armoured division, and nine squadrons; the Norwegians three destroyers and four squadrons; the Czechs three squadrons; the Australians five squadrons; and the New Zealanders five squadrons. Practically every occupied country of Europe was represented in one way or another.

Finally, it must not be forgotten that the invading forces could expect assistance from an ally inside France. In this context the French resisters deserve to be included in the catalogue of forces available to the Allies. SOE had been doing its best to organise

RAF Air/Sea Rescue Launch
These boats saved about 13,000 airmen during the war, and were the natural seaborne counterpart to the huge Allied air umbrella which would cover the Neptune operations. Length: 68 feet. Speed: 38 knots. Armament: 3 × .303 Lewis mg

and arm them and from early 1943 German demands for labour had assisted recruiting; by 1944 some 100,000 young men had taken to the 'Maquis'. The vast majority of the resisters' plans were, of course, geared to the great day when the Allies would land in France once more; in 1943 they had put forward a series of seven ambitious plans to deal with railways, road movement, telecommunications, ammunition dumps, oil fuel installations, headquarters, and railway turntables. By the beginning of 1944, however, many resistance networks had been broken up by the Gestapo and only the railway demolition plan appeared to be capable of any certain implementation. Nevertheless both numbers available and arms supplied were considerable: by May 1944 80,000 Sten-guns, 30,000 pistols, 17,000 rifles, and nearly 3,500 Bren-guns had been parachuted into France; overall there were probably some 100,000 men plus another 35-40,000 in the Maquis who had a weapon of some sort.

To assist the Resistance and ensure that as far as possible its operations were co-ordinated with those of the Allies, SOE prepared

Armed Salvage Tug
Quite apart from the job of moving the huge Mulberry units to the Normandy coast, the fleets of tug-boats had to cope with about half the landing-craft – those unable to cross the Channel under their own power, and which could not be carried on the decks of transports. Displacement: 700 tons. Speed: 13 knots. Crew: 30. Armament: 1 × 3-in, 2 × 20-mm, 2 × .303-in mg

a number of three-man teams (American/British/French) to be parachuted – in uniform – into areas where resistance was expected to flourish, so as to act as liaison between the resisters and the regular forces. In addition the British Special Air Service and the American Operational Groups were entrusted with various raiding and harassing operations for which it was hoped that they could obtain the assistance and support of the Resistance.

Finally, preparations had to be made to take over and run civil affairs in the liberated areas of France pending recognition of a French government. Here also assistance from the Resistance organisation was hoped for.

So the balance sheet of this immense operation shows the following staggering figures:

- 50,000 men in the assault drawn from five divisions;
- Over 2,000,000 men to be shipped to France overall, comprising a total of 39 divisions;
- 138 major warships used in the assault, together with 221 smaller combat vessels (destroyer category and below);
- Over 1,000 minesweepers and auxiliary vessels;
- 4,000 landing ships or craft;
- 805 merchant ships;
- 59 blockships;
- 300 miscellaneous small craft;
- 11,000 aircraft, including fighters, bombers, transports, and gliders;
- Over 100,000 partially armed men of the Resistance ready to lend such support as they could.

With such a weight of numbers and material it might well be thought that the assault would be practically irresistible, but two factors must be remembered: first, the hazards and extreme complexity of an amphibious operation of this magnitude, for which there was no precedent; all the most meticulous arrangements could be upset and the utmost confusion caused by some chance occurrence or unpredicted change in the weather: second, the great inherent superiority of the defence over the attack in an amphibious operation, especially against prepared coastal defences; however great the Allied superiority, there could be no certainty that the force would succeed even in securing a foothold. Surprise and deception were the essence of the operation – and complete surprise there could not be, for the Germans knew that the invasion was coming; all they did not know was when and where.

Finally, it was clear to both sides that this was the decisive operation of the war. If the landing succeeded, Germany must eventually be crushed sooner or later between the advancing forces of the Russians and the Allies. Should the landing fail, the Allies might well take years to recover from their losses in men, material, and morale; the peoples of Occupied Europe would give up hope and Germany would be left free to turn and square the account with the Russians.

The broad shoulders of General Eisenhower carried an immense burden.

Armed Trawler
Trawlers – with the minesweepers and other light flotilla craft – were to perform invaluable services as convoy escorts shepherding and marshalling the transports. Hundreds of them were pressed into service for this role. Typical specifications were: Displacement: 378 tons. Speed: 11½ knots. Crew: 30. Armament: 1 × 4-in, 3 × 20-mm, 2 × .303 mg; about 20 depth-charges

From the Liverpool docks a tug hauls a Mulberry Harbour section on the first stage of its journey to the Normandy beachhead

Hitler's Atlantic Wall

THE GREATEST FORT OF ALL TIME?

'I am the greatest fortress builder of all time' boasted Hitler; 'I built the West Wall; I built the Atlantic Wall . . .' But the much-vaunted Atlantic Wall, against which the invading Allies were intended to dash themselves into ruin, was only a figment of Hitler's imagination. He had never visited the invasion coast; and despite Rommel's frantic efforts to create a strong defence system, it was only in the Pas de Calais that the 'Wall' existed in anything like its intended form. And the Pas de Calais was not the Allied target area . . .

From the moment of Germany's offensive against Russia her forces had been totally inadequate for the defence of the 3,000 miles of western coastline she controlled. Field-Marshal von Rundstedt, transferred from his command in the West in April 1941, to command Army Group South in the attack against Russia, confessed that the bareness at his back gave him a feeling of chill. He expected Britain to walk in. This is not only illustrative of the Nazi weakness in the West, but of German ignorance of the true condition of the almost unarmed remnants of the British army that had survived Dunkirk. Such thinking helped to save Britain from invasion.

Returning to command in the West in 1942, Rundstedt found the situation little more to his liking. Throughout that year France had been used as a rest area for divisions badly mauled on the Eastern Front. The 50 or 60 divisions available at all material times on paper seldom mustered 25 field divisions of reasonable quality, and seldom at full strength. A Nazi decision that it would be more profitable to use prisoners of war as soldiers rather than to exterminate them, or induce them to rot in their 'Belsens' led to a complex situation, but it relieved the growing strain on German manpower. In 1942, foreign battalions were being drafted into German divisions, and in one German regiment no fewer than eight different kinds of 'Pay Book' were in use, covering at least a score of Eastern 'tribes'. A hotch-potch of races under German officers made up at least 10% of the strength of many divisions, and up to 25% of the strength of a few.

It can be seen at a glance – and it was seen at a glance by Rundstedt – that 50 or 60 divisions, even of the highest quality, would 'go' at least ten times too many into 3,000 miles of coastline. One division to 3 miles was not excessive in defence; one division in 50 or 60 miles was hopeless. One of the main enemy problems, therefore, was to decide where as well as when a major assault from the West might be expected. Whatever decision is made, wide areas must be left bare. The problem of reserves becomes insoluble.

The appreciation of Field-Marshal von Rundstedt, which remained constant, was that the Western Allies would assault against the Pas de Calais area, probably astride the Somme, not only because it was the shortest route from shore to shore, simplifying sea and air cover and a quick turn-round, but because it offered the shortest route to the Rhine, and on into the heart of the Reich. The fact that it was obvious could not exclude it, and the view from France was very different from the view from Britain. While the Allies saw the strength of the enemy positions, Rundstedt was acutely aware of the weaknesses. If the 'Atlantic Wall' was more than the 'propaganda structure' Rundstedt considered it, it was also much less than Hitler had led himself or the Allies to imagine. The materials and labour were never available to carry out his dreams, and even had the dreams been practical the fate of the immensely powerful Maginot Line had proved that defences were no stronger

than their weakest links, or their defenders. The 'Atlantic Wall' existed in something like its 'propaganda strength' in the Pas de Calais, and nowhere else.

Throughout 1943, as the Nazi armies were bled white in the East, and the Allied strategic bombing offensive moved steadily towards its terrible crescendo, Rundstedt strove to reorganise the meagre and poor quality troops at his disposal. Static coastal divisions were formed, carrying a high proportion of second grade troops, but with the virtue of gaining familiarity with their allotted areas.

The Allied landings in North Africa in the late autumn of 1942 put Hitler 'constantly on the jump', in the words of General Blumentritt. He expected landings anywhere and everywhere. His anxieties included Holland, Portugal, Spain, and the Adriatic. The fall of Tunis led him to believe that the south of France was immediately threatened. At the same time his fears for the vulnerability of Norway matched Churchill's recurrent desire to make these fears come true. It was an impossible situation for his generals, almost all of whom were kept in ignorance of the progress of war outside their immediate command areas. In April 1943, Geyr von Schweppenburg, then commanding the 86th Corps, was ordered to prepare Operation 'Gisela' in which five mechanised divisions would fan-out through Spain, four divisions making a 'dash' for Madrid while the fifth anchored on Bilbao. It is not to be wondered at that Geyr described the project as 'This folly'.

But although the generals did not share the wide range of their Führer's haunting apprehensions they were compelled to act upon his hunches, especially when they pointed to the region of the Somme and Normandy.

In September 1943, the elaborate exercise carried out in Britain, partly as a rehearsal of the massive and complex troop movements and loadings problems for Overlord, and partly to mislead the enemy, failed in its second purpose. The bluff, Rundstedt thought, was 'too obvious', and it seems that the Germans were misled and alarmed more by the natural rumours abounding in the occupied countries than by the stories planted by the Allies.

The autumn of 1943, bringing with it the first heavy seas and the promise of winter, limited the areas of possible Allied attack, and a respite to the enemy. All was probably secure until the spring of 1944. All that could be done was to strengthen the 'Atlantic Wall', increase the minefields guarding the approaches, and improve the training and rather miscellaneous weapon strength of the available troops. The placing and use of the armoured reserve was always looming as a difficult matter, and one which the suspicions of Hitler and the air power of the Allies, would make impossible.

Through the year the quality of the French Resistance had greatly improved, the quarrels of the various groups had abated, and the whole movement had responded well to British aid and organisation. By the winter of 1943/44 the Resistance had become a serious problem for the Germans, sabotaging railways and transport, and undermining morale with the fears that there might always be a bomb under the bed or in the wardrobe, that trains might leave the rails, or mysteriously blow up. And these things happened with growing frequency. The signs that the moment of crisis in the West was approaching could not be misread. 1944 would be the year, Western Europe the place, the spring or summer would bring the hour.

The snout of a German coastal gun emerges from its bunker

Information reaching the Axis through a German Foreign Office report dated January 8, 1944, by way of Ankara, gave the code name of 'Overlock' to the Allied plans, and provided 'conclusive evidence that the Anglo-Saxons are determined to force a show-down by opening a "Second Front" in 1944. However, this Second Front will not be in the Balkans.'

An Intelligence analysis by the Chief of Western Military Intelligence followed a month later:

For 1944 an operation is planned outside the Mediterranean *that will seek to force a decision and, therefore, will be carried out with all available forces. This operation is probably being prepared under the code name of OVERLORD. The intention of committing large forces becomes clear from the fact that the operation is expected to produce the final military decision within a comparatively short period of time.*

The exact area to be attacked eluded the enemy, but an Intelligence report dated February 21 re-affirmed that:

The frequently expressed determination to bring the war to an end in 1944 *is to be considered* the keynote of the enemy's operational planning. *It is also repeatedly mentioned as a definite fact that the decision will be sought by a* large-scale attack in Western Europe.

The Germans expected the attack either in the first or the third quarter of the year. Their Balkan fears were at an end. Time had narrowed down to May-August, 1944; place could be narrowed perhaps to the Pas de Calais . . . or Normandy.

Rommel faces the facts

The appointment of Field-Marshal Rommel in November 1943, to inspect and improve the defences of the Western coastline from Denmark to the Spanish border complicated an already difficult command situation. Possibly General Blumentritt exaggerated when he said that 'soon the armies did not know whether they were under command of Rundstedt or Rommel'. Rommel's direct line through to Hitler certainly invested him with great influence, but equally there is no doubt that he respected Rundstedt, C-in-C West, and observed the proper etiquette. Rundstedt, while holding a poor opinion of Rommel as a strategist, has paid tributes to his courage and loyalty. In the hands of one of the Nazi upstarts the appointment would have rendered the position of the C-in-C intolerable.

It was, inevitably, an uneasy situation, eased over the months by Rommel's appointment to command Army Group B, with responsibility under Rundstedt for the vital sectors of the Channel coast from the Dutch-German border to the Loire. Later, the appointment of Colonel-General Blaskowitz to command Army Group G covering the Biscay and Mediterranean coasts of France, clearly, if unsatisfactorily, clarified the 'Ground Force Command'.

But the Ground Force Command, even in isolation, and it was virtually in isolation, remained subject to powerful influences, arising not only out of the divergencies of opinion between the C-in-C West and the Commander of Army Group B, but also from General Guderian, Inspector General of Armour since March 1943, and from General Geyr von Schweppenburg, commanding Panzer Group West, and controlling the armoured reserve.

Rommel, sharing Hitler's view that Normandy would be the main Allied target, and believing that the enemy must be annihilated, if possible on and in the sea, and certainly on the beaches, wanted the armour close up under his hand ready to deliver an immediate and massive counterstroke. He had had painful experience of Allied air supremacy in the Western Desert, and knew well the fate of armoured columns attempting to move by daylight under 'open bomb sights'. If the armour was not 'there' he doubted its ability to get there, and certainly not in time. It was, in any case, virtually impossible to move armour on the stricken roads by day.

None doubted the magnitude of the Allied air threat, of which they were having daily and nightly experience, but at the same time neither Rundstedt nor the Panzer generals agreed with Rommel's tactics, or shared his beliefs about the site of operations. First, Rundstedt visualised delivering massive counterstrokes after the Allies had broken through the outer crust of the sea defences; second, he did not share Rommel's views on Normandy; third, he could not agree to the commitment of the armoured reserve close up before the event. The air argument which rendered the armour difficult to move might easily trap it and destroy it if Rommel had his way, and the main assault should come in against the Pas de Calais, or elsewhere.

Guderian, greatly worried about the situation in both the East and West, breakfasted alone with Hitler in early January 1944, and urged upon him the necessity to strengthen the Eastern defences

Hitler boasted of his Atlantic Wall as the greatest rampart in history. But Rommel saw its weaknesses, which only effort and time could amend – but time was running out

Alfredo Zennaro

Whole forests were cut down to make beach obstacles, designed to rip open a landing craft – but there were 3,000 miles of coast

and release much needed reserves to the West. This touched off a typical Hitler outburst:

'Believe me! I am the greatest builder of fortifications of all time,' Hitler ranted. 'I built the West Wall; I built the Atlantic Wall . . .' He then began to deluge Guderian's ears with 'tons of concrete' and a mass of statistics. In fact, Hitler had never visited the 'Atlantic Wall', and it existed, like the Emperor's clothes, largely in his imagination.

Guderian then toured the West, and was at once alarmed by Rommel's intended dispositions, and his intention to commit the Panzer divisions close up before the 'Day'. 'Disposed thus,' he wrote, 'they could not be withdrawn and committed elsewhere with sufficient rapidity.'

Back at Supreme Headquarters, Guderian took the opportunity to point out 'this error' in conference. Hitler refused to countermand the orders of the 'man on the spot', and advised Guderian to 'go to France and discuss the matter once more with Rommel'.

Guderian and Schweppenburg then visited Rommel at his Headquarters at La Roche Guyon. The Field-Marshal explained his views fully, but was not disposed to argue. Apart from his belief that Normandy would be the sector of assault, he was convinced that the enemy must be destroyed without gaining a foothold. Given his own way he might deliver such a blow to the enemy in the shallows and on the beaches that it would be impossible to mount a further assault, at least in that year. And if he were right in these beliefs, which he shared with Hitler, then he must be right about the disposition of the armour close up. The risk, admittedly was great, but there was no escape from that. Clearly Rommel did not share Rundstedt's view that a battle of mobility might be won.

Disastrous compromise

Hitler, meanwhile, clung to his intuitions, reinforced by his reasonable deductions from Allied troop placings, especially in the south-west of England, that Normandy would be the main target, and that Cherbourg would be the natural port for the Allies to aim at. But the nagging possibility of a second assault – even a major effort – elsewhere, began to divide his mind, disposing him far more than the commanders on the spot to the ultimate disasters of compromise.

Guderian had made a third attempt to convince Hitler of the dangers of Rommel's armoured dispositions, but early in May, Schweppenburg, fearing that Rundstedt was moving closer to Rommel's views, appealed to Hitler on his own account. He wanted to hold the bulk of his armour north and south of Paris, and at last Hitler dithered. The result was a disastrous compromise whereby four Panzer divisions were held as an assault reserve under the command of OKW, Supreme Headquarters. This weakened Rundstedt's command, for the old Field-Marshal, already thwarted in his attempts to organise an infantry reserve in Normandy by with-

drawing strength from south of the Loire, now found himself deprived of the means to deliver an effective counterstroke against the beaches, or later, without seeking permission from OKW.

Thus Schweppenburg had unwittingly brought about a situation which was to prove fatal.

These worries were enough, but they were but one expression of a general weakness based on suspicion and decay at the top.

Whereas Rommel, in his natural desire to have full control of the battle his armies must fight, was in a position comparable with Montgomery's, Rundstedt's position was not in any way comparable with Eisenhower's. Not only was Rundstedt deprived of full control of his ground forces, but he was also forced to 'request' air and naval support when he might need them. There was no machinery for combined planning between the services. Worse, the German navy controlled the coastal batteries which must play a major part in repelling an assault. The fact that naval and air strength had been reduced to very small, almost negligible proportions, strengthened rather than weakened the need to co-operate and co-ordinate all available defences.

Admiral Theodor Krancke, C-in-C, German Naval Group West, had his small fleet of some 60 miscellaneous craft, hemmed into port under incessant Allied air attack. Clashes in the Channel reduced his destroyer flotilla to two operational vessels. For the rest he could muster two torpedo boats, 31 motor torpedo-boats, and a handful of patrol vessels and mine-sweepers. In addition 15 of the smaller U-boats in Atlantic ports were to be made available, but were not under his command.

In the event, even this small 'fleet' was virtually unable to put to sea.

The German Luftflotte III, commanded by General Hugo Sperrle, was equally a broken reed. Compelled to use half-trained pilots its effectiveness, even with its dwindling numbers, was poor, and it was harried constantly on the ground as well as in the air. At the beginning of June 1944, Luftflotte III mustered some 400 aircraft operational 'on paper'. Again on paper these were divided between Jagdgeschwader IV and V under II Fliegerkorps. Those of Jagdgeschwader IV had the priority task of intercepting Allied bombers bound for the Reich, but could be diverted in the event of Allied assault landings. In the event none of the units of II Fliegerkorps had aircraft available to make their presence felt on the 'Day'. The promised fighter 'wings' on the way from Germany mostly failed to arrive. Few pilots knew France; few could read maps. The Chief-of-Staff of II Fliegerkorps estimated that he had no more than 50 aircraft under command.

Thus, the Western Allies could not be challenged at sea or in the air, and Rommel had few illusions about his task. It was, in a sense, simple: the German armies in the West, battered incessantly from the air, short of training, short of essential transport, and of poor quality, deprived by the disruption of their radar installations of

Beneath millions of tons of concrete the Germans set their long-range guns – but they were prime targets for Allied gunners

the full use of their 'eyes' and 'ears', stood alone, waiting.

For nearly six months Field-Marshal Rommel devoted his tremendous energies to the task of making the coastal defences impregnable from Cherbourg to the Somme, giving as much attention as was permitted to the problems of Normandy. Moved by a profound pessimism, untrammelled by the limitations of the orthodox military thinking which patterned the minds of Rundstedt and the older school, perhaps even sub-consciously aware that there could be no compromise for Germany while Germany was Hitler, he knew that the enemy must be beaten on the beaches. Perhaps he knew also that it was a forlorn hope: there was no other.

There is no evidence to suggest that Rommel would have disliked a battle of manoeuvre. It was simply that he knew it would be too late, and lost. There was no room, therefore, for Rundstedt's belief that the Allies were bound to gain a foothold, and that the battle for Normandy would then be fought.

To Rommel such optimism was another name for despair, and Hitler, with the shadow of disaster already darkening his door, knew it also. Blumentritt remarked that messages from OKW at

this time invariably began: 'The Führer fears . . .' He was full of fears, centring on Normandy where the Valkyrie rode the skies. But whereas Rommel was a realist concerned with men and materials, concrete and mines, guns and ammunition, Hitler was a visionary, seeing figures in a glass darkly. His support for Rommel was split too many ways, and never effective. He stated clearly, to Warlimont and others: 'If we do not stop the invasion and do not drive the enemy back into the sea, the war will be lost.' He had the greatest faith in Rommel, yet apart from ordering a few anti-tank and anti-aircraft units to reinforce Western Normandy, he did almost nothing about it. US troop concentrations and assault landing exercises in south-west England pointed ever more clearly to Normandy, and to Cherbourg, but Hitler vacillated. Neither he, nor anyone else, had conceived the possibility of the harbours the Allies planned to tow in their wake.

A powerful factor in the indecision in regard to the armoured reserve was the haunting fear that Normandy might not be the place, or only one place. The extreme lack of mobility of the German armies in the West haunted the minds of the Commanders.

155-mm Coastal Gun
Along the invasion coast these guns were dug in in batteries of three or four. Set back from the cliff edge, and protected by a carapace of ferro-concrete, their main purpose was to break up an Allied invasion fleet before it reached the inshore approaches. But they were large and the natural first target for Allied bombardment. Crew: 12. Max range: 12 miles. Ammunition: 200 rounds

1. 155-mm gun
2. Reinforced concrete carapace, capable of withstanding a 500-lb bomb without shattering
3. Entrance, protected against rear fire
4. Magazine (shell room other side)

The Allied air forces would not only be able, in Rommel's considered opinion, to prevent troop movement in battle, but they had already knocked the wheels from under the ground troops, condemning them to static rôles.

It was impossible to make the best of it. In spite of repeated demands Rommel did not receive the command control essential to the carrying out of his basic plans even on a minimum basis. His demands for labour and materials could not be 'orders', but merely 'requests' through the normal channels. Denied the help of the Todt Organisation, fully extended on fortress work mainly in the Pas de Calais, and unable to cope with the sustained Allied air attacks which were wrecking the transport services, Rommel used his troops as labourers to the detriment of their essential training. Some units were employed for three full days a week on labouring tasks, and much of the remainder of their time was taken up with special guard duties.

In February, Rommel issued a directive to his army commanders, and repeated it again towards the end of April:

In the short time left before the great offensive starts, we must succeed in bringing all defences to such a standard that they will hold up against the strongest attacks. Never in history was there a defence of such an extent with such an obstacle as the sea. The enemy must be annihilated before he reaches our main battlefield. We must stop him in the water, not only delaying him but destroying all his equipment while it is still afloat.

Repeatedly he emphasised to his commanders and staff that the first 24 hours would be decisive. He conceived an elaborate system of obstacles between high and low water marks covering the beaches, which would make the passage even of flat-bottomed boats perilous in the extreme, if not impossible. Rommel planned to lay over 50 million mines as the first line of sea defence, and sow minefields over the beaches. The mines were never available, and when at last inadequate deliveries were made, the minelayers were immobilised by Allied air attack and unable to put to sea. In the event not more than 6 million mines were laid, little more than one-tenth of the minimum programme.

Regarding Rundstedt's 'Zweite Stellung', or second line of defence as 'a waste of time', Rommel ordered all work upon it to cease, and the entire effort concentrated upon strengthening the forward positions. Innumerable 'hedgehogs' and anti-tank obstacles were moved forward to reinforce the massive concoctions of angle iron, the 'Tetrahydra' and 'Belgian Gates', which with thousands of mined stakes slanted seaward, mazed the approaches to the beaches. So grave was the shortage of labour that the 352nd Division, covering the vital stretch of beach from Grandcamp to Arromanches, had to cut and haul its own stakes from the Cerisy forest, 11 miles inland, and drive each stake by hand into position.

In the areas behind the Cotentin, Rommel had planned an extensive network of poles linked by wires and mined as a defence in depth against airborne landings. When the work should have been completed in the middle of May he visited the site and found that the task was only in its opening stages. The 13,000 shells necessary to set off explosions were not available.

Luftwaffe jealousy

The acute shortage of labour, mines and materials of all kinds, and the reduction of transport to the horse and cart and the bicycle, made the carrying out of a massive defensive plan impossible. Of 10 million mines needed for the 30-mile front of the 352nd Division only 10,000 were forthcoming, and these did not include any Teller mines. The situation of the 716th and 711th Divisions covering the vital frontage behind the Normandy beaches was no better. Not more than two-thirds of the coastal guns covering the army group front had been casemated by the end of May. A system of strongpoints spaced from 800 to 1,300 yards apart were in the main unprotected. 'Of the installations in the sector of the 352nd Division only 15 were bombproof; the remainder were virtually unprotected from air attack.' The 716th Division regarded its situation as even worse.

The minimum daily need of the VII Army in Normandy to fulfil its construction tasks was for 240 carloads of cement alone. In one typical three-day period the records show that it received 47 carloads. The forced closure of the Cherbourg cement works for lack of coal aggravated the extreme shortage. This was, above all, due to the Allied attacks on road and rail transport.

These desperate shortages sharpened the edge of Rommel's bitter criticism of the Luftwaffe. He pointed out that the Luftwaffe employed 50,000 men to maintain its communications, and engaged a further 300,000 on ground services. This worked out at 100 men on the ground to every man in the air. That Hugo Sperrle, commanding Luftflotte III, largely shared his views availed nothing. The situation existed to feed the grandiose dreams of Göring.

Rommel's repeated attempts to gain the services of the III Flak Corps in Normandy were thwarted, and it remained under the Luftflotte III, subject to the whims of Göring, and useless in defence. It might have done much to counter the overwhelming air strength of the Allies, and would have given some comfort and a sense of 'hitting back' to the battered troops in their dug-outs. Even the II Parachute Corps, tactically under VII Army, remained administratively and for training under the Luftwaffe. Göring refused to permit these troops to be used to help in defence works.

Thus, as June opened, the gaps in the defences were frightful, and each new device had been observed by the Allies, and often tested through the courage of the small teams of men who explored the shallows by night. By abandoning the 'Zweite Stellung' the defences had been deprived of depth, and reduced to an outer crust too fragile to withstand the immense weight of assault in store for it. Nevertheless, the fault was not Rommel's. He had attempted the impossible, and had achieved much. He had inherited a myth, and had given it 'teeth' to inflict a dangerous, if not deadly bite. He had also greatly improved the dispositions of his troops.

On the eve of 'D-Day', Field-Marshal von Rundstedt's command in the West numbered 60 divisions, one of them, the XIX Panzer Division, refitting after a severe hammering on the Eastern Front, another in the Channel Islands, reducing the effective total to 58 divisions (see map).

Of these, 31 divisions were in static rôles, and 27, including 10 armoured divisions, were as mobile as the suspicions of the Führer and the available resources allowed. They were disposed from Holland to the Atlantic and Mediterranean coasts, five divisions in Holland in the 88th Corps, including the 'lame' XIX Panzer, 19 in the Pas de Calais between the Scheldt and the Seine, 18 between the Seine and the Loire. The remainder were south of the Loire.

Some 43 divisions out of the grand total of 60 were grouped under Field-Marshal Rommel's Army Group B, the 88th Corps in Holland, the powerful XV Army in the Pas de Calais, the VII Army in Normandy. The XV Army, commanded by Salmuth, was virtually anchored in its positions mainly by the incapability of the German military mind to disengage itself from a pre-conceived idea. The Western Allies did their best to nurture the illusion.

By the eve of D-Day, Field-Marshal Rommel had succeeded in improving and strengthening the dispositions of the VII Army under Dollmann which he believed, must fight the decisive battle on the beaches. The 352nd and 716th Infantry Divisions lay in their dug-outs and resistance 'nests' along the coast of Calvados from the Vire river to the Orne. On the German left flank the 91st Division, with the VI Parachute Regiment under command, covered the left flank of the 352nd in the area of Carentan. The 709th Division covered the eastern coastline of the Cherbourg Peninsula.

Behind its right flank positions, known to the Allies by the code name 'Utah' beach, the extensive marshes and the flooded areas following the courses of the rivers Dives and Merderet from Carentan to le Port Brehay, were regarded as safeguarding the rear, and blocking the exits from the beaches. The 243rd Division faced west in the Peninsula.

On the German right flank the 711th Division with one regiment of the 346th Division under command covered the coast from the River Orne to the Seine Estuary opposite Le Havre.

The 709th, the 352nd, and the 716th Infantry Divisions would, therefore, meet the Allied assaults on the beaches codes named 'Utah', 'Omaha', 'Gold', 'Juno', 'Sword'. Against the will of Rundstedt, Rommel had succeeded in bringing up the XXI Panzer Division to the Caen area, poised to strike against the Allied left flank. The three armoured divisions, the XII and 116th Panzer, and the Panzer Lehr, the Army Group B reserve, capable of delivering a massive punch, lay in the rectangle Mantes-Gassicourt, Chartres, Bernay, Gacé, the 116th forward. But the fears of Rundstedt, Guderian, and Schweppenburg had placed the force under OKW, subject to the will of Hitler. Thus, the outcome of the day of decision lay with the coastal batteries and with the three divisions entrenched along the Normandy coast, the 91st Division and its parachute regiment on the left, and the XXI Panzer Division on the right.

The Allied assault had been expected in the middle of May, and in spite of warnings from the German Naval Command in the West, the military view was that the assault would be at high tide. When the middle of May had safely passed there was a tendency to relax, in the belief that the attempt would be delayed until August. Enemy appreciations continued to be governed by the belief that the Allies must gain the use of a port or ports, and naval opinion

moved away from the Pas de Calais, hardening in the belief that Le Havre and Cherbourg would be the main objectives. Allied troops and shipping concentrations in the south and south-west of England strongly supported this view, as also did the comparative freedom of the two ports from air attack, and the general pattern of Allied bombing at the end of May. The navy also believed that the rocky shallows covering the eastern sector of the Normandy coast would rule out landings, and expected that a major effort would come in against the Cotentin, together with airborne landings.

By the end of May, Admiral Krancke, Navy Group West, had lulled himself into an optimism, the more remarkable in view of the almost total immobilisation of his naval force. He believed that his coastal batteries could blow the Allied armada out of the water, and noted that Allied air attacks on the batteries had accounted for only eight guns, five of them between Le Havre and Le Treport, and three in Normandy. The Admiral began to believe that the massed shipping in British ports, the immense activities, the assault exercises, of which the enemy had some knowledge from isolated air reconnaissance and the reports of agents, were all part of a bluff.

The rapid deterioration of the weather in the first days of June ruled out the possibility of invasion in the mind of the enemy. The interceptions of warning messages broadcast to the Resistance and handed to Admiral Dönitz, failed to weigh against the high winds and rising seas in the Channel. On June 4, while General Eisenhower met with his admirals, air marshals, generals, and weather forecasters at Portsmouth, and the approaches to the Channel already seethed with the ships of the spearhead troops, Admiral Krancke in Normandy reached the view that no attack was or could be imminent. General Blumentritt, Chief of Staff, OB West agreed with him.

Right: Rommel could not believe that the Allies would ignore the Pas de Calais, and therefore he did not try to diminish the German forces already massed there. But he knew that if the Allied beachheads were to be smashed before they could be built up into secure jumping-off points, the Panzer divisions would have to be stationed near the beaches; for Allied air superiority would prevent all large-scale reinforcement from moving up to the front. And he had lost his battle to put the Panzers where he wanted them: OKW insisted on retaining the armour inland, as an inner ring of strategic defence – the classic pattern of mobile reserve. Rommel lamented: At one time they (OKW) looked on mobile warfare as something to keep clear of at all costs, but now that our freedom of movement in the West has gone, they're all crazy after it . . . thanks to the Allied air forces we will have nothing there in time. The day of the dashing cut-and-thrust tank attack of the early war years is past and gone . . .

Left: By June 1944 the Germans knew that the launching of the Allied Second Front could not be long delayed, and that the main blow would be a cross-Channel invasion. But Hitler expected supplementary invasions everywhere – and even Rommel came to believe that the Allies would follow up their first landings with other operations in France. And so the West was allocated some 58 divisions – but they had to be spread from the Netherlands to the Italian frontier, and divided between two separate army groups

Map legend:
- Infantry divisions
- Training divisions
- Paratroop divisions
- Panzer divisions
- Army Group boundary
- Army boundaries

0   100 Miles
0   200 Kms.

NETHERLANDS
NORTH SEA
Rotterdam
BRITAIN
London
Calais
Boulogne
ENGLISH CHANNEL
Dieppe
Cherbourg
Le Havre
Brest
St. Nazaire
BAY OF BISCAY
Bordeaux
SPAIN
GERMANY
Antwerp I SS PZ
Brussels
BELGIUM
LUX
II PZ.
XV ARMY
116th PZ.
XXI PZ. XII SS PZ.
Paris
PZ. LEHR.
VII ARMY
ARMY GROUP B
SWITZ
XVII SS PZ. GR.
ARMY GROUP G
I ARMY
XI PZ.
XIX ARMY
IX PZ.
II SS PZ.
Marseilles
Toulon
FRANCE
ITALY
MEDITERRANEAN SEA

The Waiting is Over
THE GREAT GAMBLE BEGINS

They had trained on remote beaches. They had been shuttled and shunted in darkened trains. The Allied armies were like a gigantic coil spring winding and waiting in grey limbo – aware that a moment would come when they would be disgorged upon an enemy shore, bristling with devices of death, swept by withering fire. All they were waiting for was the weather.

By June 4 the weather was so bad that the invasion had to be delayed for one day. On the 5th, though conditions were still terrible, there was some slight chance of improvement. Appalled by the chaos which must ensue if there was any more delay, Eisenhower decided that the great gamble must be taken: D-Day, the assault on Hitler's Europe, would be June 6

287,000 men and a host of armoured fighting vehicles were pre-loaded into ships, as early as the first of the month

△ Grim-faced American troops file aboard a landing ship.
▽ British soldiers pass the time learning about their target.

135

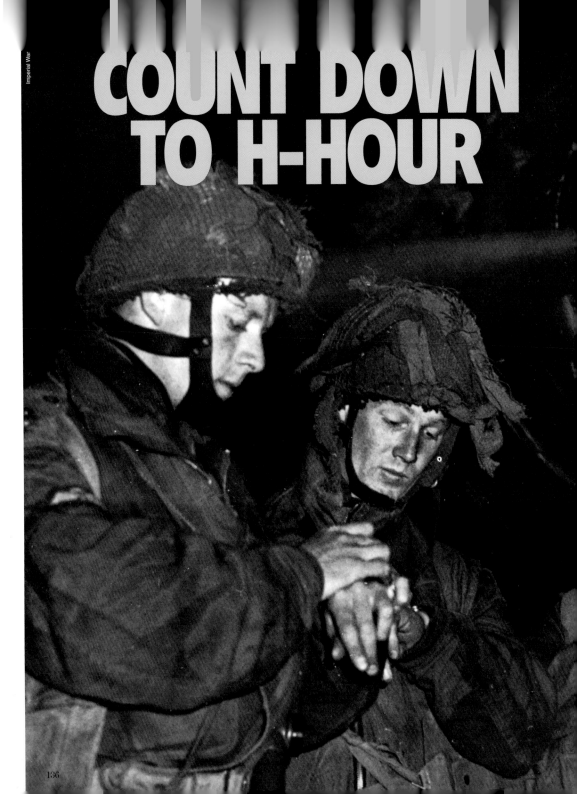

COUNT DOWN TO H-HOUR

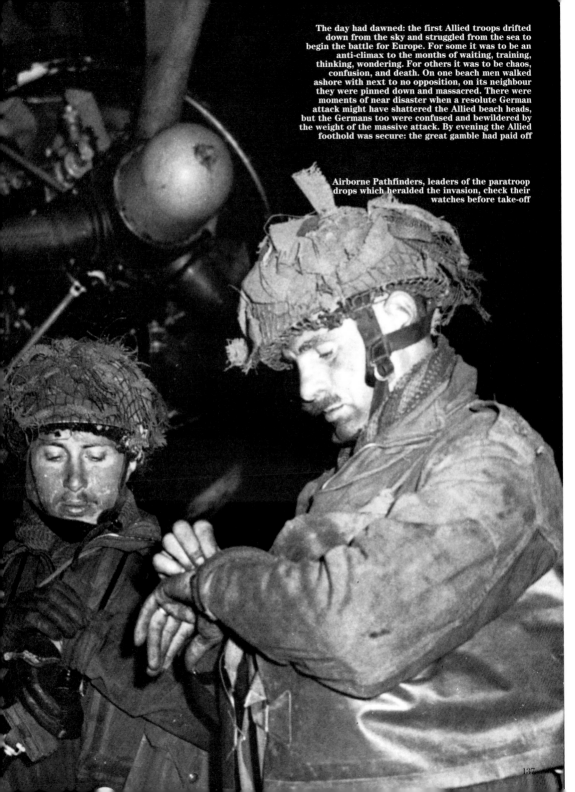

The day had dawned: the first Allied troops drifted
down from the sky and struggled from the sea to
begin the battle for Europe. For some it was to be an
anti-climax to the months of waiting, training,
thinking, wondering. For others it was to be chaos,
confusion, and death. On one beach men walked
ashore with next to no opposition, on its neighbour
they were pinned down and massacred. There were
moments of near disaster when a resolute German
attack might have shattered the Allied beach heads,
but the Germans too were confused and bewildered by
the weight of the massive attack. By evening the Allied
foothold was secure: the great gamble had paid off

Airborne Pathfinders, leaders of the paratroop
drops which heralded the invasion, check their
watches before take-off

Lieutenant-Colonel Hoffmann had just glanced at his watch. The time was forty minutes past midnight. June 6 was less than three-quarters of an hour old. For the past hour there had been a continuous drone of aircraft above the battle headquarters of III Battalion, 919th Grenadier Regiment, east of Montebourg.

Another wave was approaching. The roar grew louder.

Hoffmann stepped outside the bunker. He gave a start. Six giant birds were making straight for his battle headquarters. They were clearly visible, for the moon had just broken through the clouds. 'They're bailing out.' For an instant Hoffmann thought the aircraft had been damaged and its crew was going to jump. But then he understood. This was an airborne landing by paratroops. The white mushrooms were floating down—straight at his bunker.

'Alarm! Enemy paratroops!' The men at III Battalion headquarters had never pulled on their trousers so fast before.

'Alarm! Alarm!'

The sentries' carbines were barking. They were firing at the parachutes floating down from the sky. Then the moon hid itself. Darkness enveloped the descending enemy. Hoffmann grabbed a rifle. Then the darkness was rent by the first burst of fire from an American submachine-gun.

The battle for Normandy was on.

Fifty miles south-east of the battle headquarters of III Battalion, 919th Grenadier Regiment, on the far side of the Orne, things were also fairly noisy. The German sentry on the eastern end of the bridge over the Caen canal at Bénouville jumped as some 50 yards in front of his concrete sentry-box a spectral aircraft swooped towards the ground without any engine noise. A moment later there was a crash and a splintering sound, then quiet.

The sentry snatched his carbine from his shoulder and loaded. He held his breath, listening. 'A crashed bomber,' was his first thought. After all, enemy bomber formations had been roaring overhead in from the coast for well over an hour. From the Caen direction came the noise of explosions. Anti-aircraft guns were barking from the neighbourhood of Troarn.

'They've had it,' thought Private Wilhelm Furtner. Then a searing flash blinded his eyes. He no longer heard the burst of the phosphorus grenade.

His comrades in the dugout by the approach to the bridge leapt up. They raced to their machine-gun. They fired a burst at random. They saw nothing. Suddenly they heard voices calling: 'Able-Able.' They did not know that this was the recognition signal of A Detail of a combat team of the British 6th Airborne Division, one of whose gliders had just crash-landed there in front of them. The lance-corporal of the guard was about to lift up the telephone to give the alarm to his platoon commander on the far side of the bridge. But there was no time. Two hand-grenades came sailing in through the aperture of the pill-box. Finished.

There was no point now in keeping quiet. The hand-grenades were bound to have roused the guard on the far side. With shouts of 'Able-Able' the Tommies galloped across the bridge.

They heard other gliders crashing. They also heard the rallying cries of B Detail: 'Baker-Baker.' And a moment later they could hear C Detail as well: 'Charlie-Charlie.'

The German machine-gun was blazing away over the bridge. The first Tommies were falling. But the bulk of them got through. A short skirmish. The guard on the bridge was overwhelmed. The crossing of the Caen canal at Bénouville was in British hands. Only Lance-Corporal Weber got away. He tore through the village to the commandant. 'British paratroops have seized the canal bridge.' What he did not know was that the nearby bridge over the Orne at Ranville had also been seized by men of the British 5th Parachute Brigade in a surprise attack. At 2nd Battalion, 192nd Panzer

artillery, much of it in the floods of the Merderet and Douve rivers.
Neither division was able to prepare adequately for the arrival of its glider-borne follow-up, the losses were severe and tragic.

Yet the remarkable fact is that so great a confusion was created in the enemy by this incoherent scattering of men in their midst that there was no possibility of reserves supporting the beach defenders.

No coherent pattern has ever emerged from the struggles of the isolated remnants of the airborne divisions on that day; nor will such a pattern ever emerge. The individual contributions of many men who fought bravely alone or in twos and threes will never be assessed. Even those who gave up without a fight added to rather than subtracted from enemy bewilderment. The Pathfinders of the airborne divisions did not do well. Many failed to find and to mark the dropping zones; some beacons were missing entirely, especially west of the Merderet in country infested by enemy; others were wrongly placed.

Major-General Maxwell Taylor, commanding the 101st, dropped with a nucleus of his divisional HQ, and struggled all through the day to make contact and to bring some sort of order out of chaos. He felt 'alone on the Cotentin'. In the upshot the pattern may be seen dimly in the struggles of half-a-dozen colonels, each managing to group between 75 and 200 men round him, aided by the tell-tale click-clack of the toy 'crickets' with which every man was provided.

By a stroke of remarkable fortune a small band of men ambushed and killed the commander of the German 91st Division, returning from an 'exercise' conference to his headquarters. Thus the 91st Division, trained in the role of defence against airborne attack, and forming almost the sole available reserve behind the defenders of the Cotentin coast, was deprived of its commander and severely handicapped.

While many German officers were sure that this must be the beginning of the main Allied assault – so long awaited and expected – and that the battlefield was Normandy, others, including Lieutenant-General Speidel, Rommel's Chief-of-Staff, and Lieutenant-General Blumentritt, Chief-of-Staff to Rundstedt, were doubtful. Thus the German military machine remained hesitant and palsied, its slender reserves uncommitted, its armour waiting, Rommel out of touch, Hitler sleeping. These things gave the airborne troops on the western flank an initial advantage of which, perforce, they were unaware, and saved them from the possibility of annihilation.

Throughout the whole day and night the 101st Airborne Division, reduced to much less than the effective strength of a single regiment, was not only isolated from its own widely scattered units, but also in complete ignorance of the fate of the 82nd Airborne Division. Ironically, it may have achieved at least as much in its confusion as it could have hoped for in coherence, for chaos bred chaos.

The story of the 82nd Airborne Division is simple. Two of its regiments with the tasks of clearing the area west of the Merderet

river and in the angle of the Douve, were not in the fight. It fell to one regiment to save the day, and to fight the one clear-cut battle fought by the US airborne forces on D-Day. While scores of men struggled in the swamps of the Merderet, dragging themselves towards the dry land of the railway embankment, concerned in the main with the problem of survival, the third regiment had dropped in a fairly tight group to the north-west of Ste Mère-Église. This was not due to chance, but to the determination of the pilots to find their targets. Long before the dawn, Lieutenant-Colonel Krause, finding himself on the outskirts of Ste Mère-Église with roughly a quarter of his battalion, bounced the town without waiting for more, and taking the enemy completely by surprise began to establish a solid base and by the afternoon the town was securely held.

The 82nd Airborne had dropped on the fringe of the assembly area of the German 91st Division, and its position from the outset was much more precarious than that of the 101st. All troops, however fragmentary, were at once in the midst of the enemy, and fighting for their lives within minutes of finding their feet. Some small groups up to 50 or 60 strong fought all day in the ditches and hedgerows within 1,000 yards of others with whom it was impossible to make contact. Often they were unaware of their nearness.

The performance of the 101st and 82nd Airborne Divisions on D-Day may only be seen in fragmentary terms. At the end of the day the divisions had not made contact. Each believed it had lost some two-thirds of its troops. Neither one had cause for satisfaction, or the haziest idea of what was happening. All that they could do was to wait for the morning.

Fortunately, the enemy's confusion was equivalent to almost total breakdown. Hammered savagely and incessantly from the air, handicapped by the chance of a conference at Rennes of their senior commanders coinciding with the assault, their communications disrupted, and with, as it seems, a premonition of inevitable doom, their resistance was as fragmentary as that of the airborne troops infesting their imaginations as well as their fields. Many surrendered almost without a fight. Major von der Heydte, commanding the German VI Parachute Regiment, probably the finest enemy troops available in the Carentan area, has told of his difficulties in getting orders from his senior commanders. From the church steeple of St Come-du-Mont he had a personal view of the seaborne armada on the western flank. It seemed to him curiously detached from reality, almost peaceful. At noon the sun was shining, and the whole scene reminded him 'of a summer's day on the Wannsee'. The immense bustle of landing craft, and the warships fading into the horizon, lacked to his ears the orchestration of battle.

Von der Heydte sent his three battalions into battle, one to the north to attack Ste Mère-Église, another to the north-east to protect the seaward flank in the area Ste Marie-du-Mont, the third back on Carentan. Von der Heydte almost at once lost contact. Organised defence on the western flank had crumbled.

-HOUR DRAWS NEAR

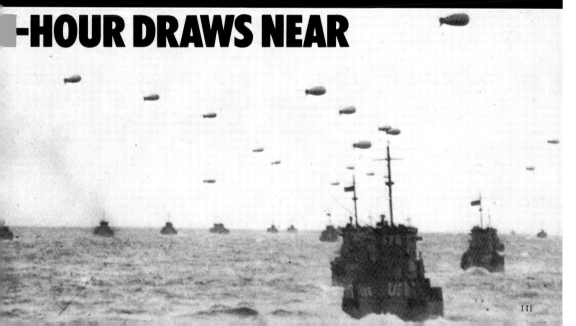

H-HOUR AND THE RAMPS ARE DOWN

At 0200 hours on June 6, the leading ships of Force U, organised in 12 convoys comprising 865 vessels commanded by Rear-Admiral Moon, USN, moved into their assembly area 12 miles off the western coast of the Cotentin Peninsula, opposite the dunes of Varreville – Utah Beach. The assault upon Utah Beach on the extreme western flank was virtually an isolated operation. If all else failed it might have been reinforced to establish a bridgehead, to cut off the Cotentin Peninsula, gaining Cherbourg as a major port from which to mount some subsequent effort. In that event Overlord would be no more.

Field Order 1 states: '7th Corps assaults Utah Beach on D-Day at H-Hour and captures Cherbourg with minimum delay.'

Steadily into the hours before dawn the orders to 7th Corps reduced down to those few who would debouch into the shallows of the unfriendly sea. The 4th Infantry Division would establish the bridge-head; the 8th Infantry Regiment leading – the 1st Battalion on the right, 'Green beach'; the 2nd Battalion on the left, 'Red beach'; two companies of each battalion forward; 30 men to each landing craft; five landing craft to each company, 20 landing craft carrying 600 men in the van, with two companies of the 70th Tank Battalion in the first wave. Behind them, wave upon wave of their fellows and the waves of the sea, H + 5, H + 15, H + 17, H + 30, on and on through all the day and night, and beyond; infantry, armour, engineers, into the shallows, through the obstacles, the mine-fields, over the beaches, the sea wall, the causeways, the floods, inland to the villages and fields; 27 miles across the neck of the peninsula, Carentan to Lessay; north to Cherbourg.

H-Hour on the western flank was 0630 hours, but along the invasion beaches tidal-variations decreed four different H-Hours from right to left, from Utah Beach to Sword Beach, a span of one hour and 25 minutes. But the men on the right were in their own cocoons of loneliness. Now, in the bitter morning, they were being buffeted in the shallow draft vessels, the dark sky above them wild with the roar of aircraft, the crescendo rising, the blasting roar of the main armament, the scream of shells, and all around a turbulence of men and craft.

To the left, for nearly 50 miles, variations on the theme were un-folding over the waters, Omaha, Gold, Juno, Sword, and over the dark shoreline from end to end the dust was rising, blasted in towering columns by shells and bombs to hang, an opaque and ominous curtain, above the stage.

Enemy shells air-bursting over the water, the spasmodic explosions of mines, the shouts of men floundering, arms flung out, weighed down by equipment, created an uproar in the mind and senses in which the last cries of the lost, the total personal tragedies, were no more than the plaintive squeakings of mice in a cage of lions. The 60 men of Battery B, 29th Field Artillery Battalion, became a statistic on the debit side, dark shadows threshing in the water, under the water, part of the pattern at the bottom of the sea.

But the pattern advanced, untroubled by calamity, the second wave, the bulldozers on their craft, the special engineer units, all in position, the heavy armament of the bombarding squadron blasting the grey dawn to crimson shreds, 40 minutes to go. Some 276 aircraft of the US 9th Air Force roaring in over the beach defences, delivering their bombs, 4,404 bombs each of 250 pounds upon seven targets, 'according to the book'.

Seventeen of the 33 supporting craft seemed to tear the crackling scalp off the universe in an unbearable rasping agony as their mattresses of rockets shuddered inshore. Other craft were machine-gunning, perhaps in the hope of detonating mines, perhaps simply to boost morale, but all 'drenching the beaches with fire'.

About 700 yards to go, and on time, ten assault craft, 300 men on the left, ten assault craft, 300 men on the right; in their wakes 28 DD tanks, swimming, slopping the choppy water across their grey backs, the long muzzles of their guns like snouts, a seeming miracle thanks to the bold initiative and swift decision of their commander to launch close in at 3,000 yards, 'not according to the book'.

US Coast Guard

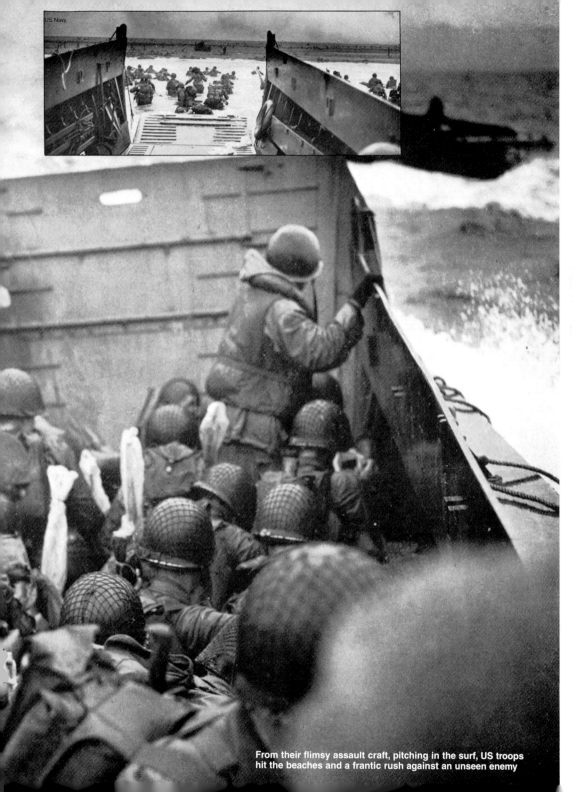

US Navy.

From their flimsy assault craft, pitching in the surf, US troops hit the beaches and a frantic rush against an unseen enemy

The beach was almost invisible behind the sand pall, blasted by gunfire and bombs, joining it to the sky, and in it, under it, the enemy – if there could be an enemy!

Some 67 of the bombers had failed to release their bombs, one-third of the remainder had fallen between high and low water mark, the bulk of the rest on the fortifications of La Madeleine.

A swift, painless landing

Out of the leading wave of the assault craft smoke projectiles hurtled to the sky, demanding silence from the gunners of the bombarding force. About 300 yards to go, and the ramps down, 300 men of the 2nd Battalion, waist deep in water, floundering, finding their feet, wading in, rifles held high, to the dry sand, and the sudden upsurge of spirit. Normandy, the first men ashore, and not a shot out of the haze of battle, the grey shapes of the tanks crawling up out of the sea in their 'skirts', striking terror to the few who still lifted up their heads in the defences and dared to fire, a few wavering shots, 'desultory fire'.

These few men, and their comrades in the van, landing within minutes on their right, did not know that the south-easterly set of the tide had carried them more than a mile south of their target. It was a fortunate chance. Two hours later the leading troops were off the beach. The enemy strongpoints yielded to mopping-up operations in company strength, and the sea wall did not demand assault. Six battalions of infantry had begun to move off the beach by 1000 hours, and little more than an occasional air burst hampered the engineers at their toil, or reminded them of their extreme vulnerability as they placed their charges by hand. By noon the beach had been cleared at a cost of six men killed and 39 wounded out of the 400 involved in static roles, all of them sitting ducks without cover, and without armour.

Shortly after midday three battalions of the 22nd Infantry Regiment were moving north to open the northerly exit, the 3rd Battalion along the coast road to anchor a flank on Hamel-de-Cruttes, the 1st and 2nd Battalions wading diagonally, and miserably, waist deep, and often armpit and neck deep, across the floods all the way to St Germain-de-Varreville.

The 12th Infantry Regiment found the going worse, wading from the Grand Dune position immediately backing the beach, and crossing the line of march as they reached dry land, many of them soaked to the ears.

In all that day, the 8th and 22nd Infantry Regiments lost 12 men killed. Twenty times the number would have been counted fortunate; 100 times the number a misfortune to be looked for. A single resolute man armed with a flint lock could have accounted for more than 12 men on the beach in the first half-an-hour, including a brigadier-general and a colonel. The struggle of the 4th Infantry Division was mainly against the forces of nature, which were considerable. Eastwards it was different.

OMAHA BEACH: THE BLOODBATH

The beach of Omaha lies between the outcropping rocks of Pointe de la Percée in the west, and Port-en-Bessin in the east, a shallow arc of sand enclosed inland by bluffs rising in a gentle slope 150 feet to a plateau of tiny hedge-enclosed fields, deep lanes, and scattered hamlets built solidly of stone. It is a thinly populated region, the largest village, Trévières, 3 or 4 miles inland on the south side of the Aure river, counting not more than 800 inhabitants.

Three coastal villages, Vierville, St Laurent, and Colleville lie behind the beach at regular intervals a mile and a half apart, and linked by a narrow lane from 500 to 1,000 yards in from the shore line. A stretch of paved promenade along the 'front', and with a score or more of good houses between Vierville and St Laurent, backs a low sea wall of masonry and wood. Gullies opening from the beach give access up narrow lanes to the villages.

At low tide the sands slope gradually to the sea wall, and in places to a heavy shingle bank of stones 3 inches in diameter, a barrier 8 to 10 feet high between the beach and the reedy grasses of the bluffs. Seaward the stresses of the sea and the strong currents carve runnels in the wet ribbed sands.

The rocky shoulders of the bluffs of Omaha, flanking the crescent of the beach, provided concealed gun positions to enfilade the fore shore and the sea approaches, and behind the obstacle of the heavy shingle bank and the wall, the enemy defended entrenchments linking strongpoints, pillboxes, and concrete gun emplacements

French Canadians land on Juno Beach. Waiting until the tide had risen meant that theirs was the last assault to go in

sited to bring devastating cross-fire to bear upon the beach. Theoretically, at least, light and heavy machine-guns, 75- and 88-mm artillery pieces, would make a beaten zone of the entire beach area from end to end. And behind the forward defensive positions the terraced slopes of the bluffs gave cover to further trench systems, machine-gun nests, and minefields.

The beach itself was moderately mined, especially in the areas between the gullies, and from low to high water mark an elaborate system of staggered lethal obstacles seemed to defy the passage of any craft larger than a matchbox. But all these things had been studied in some detail by small parties visiting the beaches by night, and from countless air photographs.

Omaha Beach held no mystery and no surprises. Even the bringing in of a new and vastly superior division – 352nd – had been observed by British Intelligence, and passed on to US 1st Army. Unhappily, this piece of information had seemed suspect to the 1st Army Command, and the assault troops were not informed. Yet it is inconceivable that they had been briefed to expect less than the worst the enemy could be expected to perform. To attack this superb defensive position General Bradley had rejected Hobart's magnificent array of assault armour, and had accepted DD tanks only with reluctance.

A terrible confusion
At 0300 hours on June 6, Force O, commanded by Rear-Admiral Hall, USN, and carrying 34,000 men and 3,300 vehicles and with a follow-up force, almost its equal, a few hours astern, began to put its assault craft into the water 12 miles off shore. There followed four hours of a macabre Dantesque confusion, through which men struggled blindly with the sea, a prey to despair, knowing the dregs of misery. While the larger vessels moved forward, finding difficulty in maintaining their stations in the heavy sea, the smaller craft were exposed to the full force of the north westerly, fighting seas up to 6 feet high, unstable and making water too fast for the pumps.

Some of the larger ships had put their assault craft into the water fully loaded, but others had put their men over the side into craft pitching and rolling wildly, an ordeal for men wracked with sea sickness. The sea, unfriendly through all the hours of the long passage, became in minutes a dark heaving formless jungle upon which men and boats wrestled like the damned in a labyrinthine maze of driven spume.

Almost at once ten small craft foundered, and upwards of 300 men struggled for their lives in a darkness which seemed to contain a kind of uproar in its relentless impersonal violence. Rudderless, foundering small craft and the sodden wreckage of equipment added to the menace, buffeting the men in their life jackets.

In nearly 200 assault craft, the crews and troops who must presently assault the enemy across open beaches in the face of withering fire, baled with their tin hats for their lives, in some boats 100% sea-sick, in all boats sodden, cramped, and cold. At last on the verge of nervous and physical exhaustion the assault troops neared the shore, and their craft strove to manoeuvre for the final run-in.

These men in the vanguard were more naked than they knew or greatly cared. Behind them the seas had stripped them steadily of guns and armour, and the teams of combat engineers had suffered no less than they. With a reckless irresponsibility the commander of the tank landing-craft carrying 32 DD tanks due to land at H−5 launched his massive vehicles into the steep seas 6,000 yards off shore. Even with well-trained crews there would have been small hopes for the tanks; as it was 27 were swamped within minutes and sank. Two, by brilliant seamanship and chance, managed to reach the shore. Three others were saved the ordeal by the jamming of the ramp of the landing craft, and were carried in. Thus the 96 tanks planned to provide vital close support for the 1,450 men of eight companies, and the first wave of the engineer teams, in the moment of assault had dwindled by almost a third of their number.

Disaster had also met the attempts to ferry the supporting artillery ashore in DUKWs. The small overloaded craft, almost unmanageable, quickly foundered. The 111th Field Artillery Battalion lost all its 105-mm howitzers save one. The 16th Infantry Cannon Company shared the same fate, and the 7th Field Artillery was very little better. The engineer teams, off-loading their heavy equipment from LCTs to LCMs, also had their troubles and losses.

It was a battle of material, of landing craft and armour, but it was men who had to walk up the beaches – and pay a price

Imperial War Museum

Commandos go ashore in the British sector, their specialised armour already at work flailing a path across the beaches

US 1st ARMY
(Bradley)

US 7th CORPS
(Collins)

US 5th CO
(Gerow)

US 4th INF. DIV.

US 1st INF

To Barfleur 10 miles

Cotentin Peninsula

Valognes

Quineville

Montebourg

St Marcouf
709th INF. DIV.
Ravenoville

PLANNED
ASSAULT AREA

St Germain
de Varreville

Dunes of
Varreville

91st INF.
DIV.

Ste Mère-
Eglise

La Madeleine

US 82nd
ABN. DIV.

Chef du
Pont

la Galle

Ste Marie-du-Mont

US 2nd RANGER
BTN.

Pointe
du Hoe

Grandcamps
les Bains

Vierville

St Laurent

Colleville

Pont l'Abbé

Vierville

US 101st
ABN. DIV.

914th INF. DIV.

Formigny

St Come-du-Mont

VI PARA. REGT.

Isigny

Trévières

Colombières

352nd INF. DIV.

St Jores

Carentan

Blay

115th RCT
116th RCT

Littry-la-Mine

Forêt
de
Cerisy

Balleroy

UTAH

OMAHA

CHARLIE DOG EASY FO

Legend:

Planned airborne dropping and landing zones

Areas held by German troops
at 2400 Hrs on D-Day

UTAH Assault areas

Green Beach, Red Beach

Major German gun batteries

First Allied assault waves

XXI Panzer Corps counterattacks

Attacks by Allied Commando
and airborne units

Railways

Roads

Areas held by Allies at 2400 Hrs on D-Day

Flooded areas (Prairies Marécageuses)

Line of planned Allied beach-head
at 2400 Hrs on D-Day

0   5   10 Miles

0   10   15 Kms

RCT   Regimental Combat Team

Nevertheless, in the last hour a great concourse of men, guns, and armour approached the lethal regions of the shallows, their initial losses far less than must have been inflicted by an enemy capable of even a moderate challenge on the sea and in the air. But the sea and air belonged to the Allies. With 40 minutes still to go the powerful bombarding squadron opened fire on the coastal defences with a great armament from the 16-inch guns of the battleships to the 5-inch guns of the destroyers, deluging the line of the bluffs with fire and smoke. At the same time 329 out of the 446 Liberators sent to do the job attacked 13 targets on and about the beaches with more than 1,000 tons of bombs.

The leading assault craft were some 800 yards out when the barrage behind them lifted and the vast uproar muted to the violent staccato sounds of the guns in the close support craft in their wakes. The crash of bursting mortar bombs, of shells, and the smash of machine-gun bullets against the ramps warned the assault troops that the enemy held them in his sights. The cries of men in the water, the sudden searing sheets of flame, the thunderous explosions as craft were hit by enemy shell and mortar fire, caught them up and splintered their isolation to fragments, and the ramps went down.

There is a devastating simplicity about disaster. There were no dry landings. The assault craft, and the larger LCVPs and LCMs grounded on the sandbanks, slewed in the sand runnels, and cast scores of men knee, waist, and neck deep into seas lashed not only by the

wind, but by mortar bombs, shells, and machine-gun bullets. While isolated groups waded to the shore, dazed and bewildered by their loneliness on that 5-mile-long wilderness of sand, blinded by the smoke of many fires raging on the bluffs, uncertain what to do, others, the great majority, were in the midst of infernos of exploding ammunition and engineer charges set off by direct hits. Here and there craft blew up in ferocious ovens of flame.

The LCTs of the 743rd Tank Battalion leading in the van on the right flank surged on with men diving from stricken craft on either side, seeking the shelter of the waves, while others fought for footholds, clawing their ways to the beach, weighed down with equipment, some on hands and knees, others dragging forward on their bellies, with their wounded and their wounds. But it was safer in the sea.

A direct hit on the leading LCT killed all the company officers, save one, but eight of the DD tanks landed on the rim of the sea to open fire on the Vierville strongpoint: range 200 yards. The tanks of the 743rd were getting in further east, but the men without armour had little chance. When the ramps of the leading assault craft went down the enemy machine-guns tore through living flesh so that the front cavities of the vessels became in seconds raw wounds, thick with blood. Dozens leaped this way and that for their lives.

Within half-an-hour of H-Hour there were at least 1,000 assault infantry and engineers alive on the beach and in the shallows, but they were not fighting the enemy; they were fighting quite simply for

146

survival, many exhausted, all too weary to drag their equipment across the beach, very few among them able to run, to assault, head-on, the enemy strongpoints.

Some went back to the water, and came in with the tide until at last it brought them, like flotsam, to the meagre shelter of the sea wall or the shingle bank. Very few of those scattered, almost at random, along the length of that beach, and all trained for the specific tasks with which, it was planned, they would be faced, knew where they were. Very few had come in on those 'stages' for which they had rehearsed. Boat teams, organised as fighting units, were miserably scrambled, and often alone, a detachment here, another 200, 300, even 1,000 yards away. For all many of them knew they were alone on the beach known as Omaha. The sea was behind them, and the blinding smoke, saving them from enemy fire in the lucky places, dazed them. The few officers were often slow to get their bearings, or to make up their minds what to do. Few found the leadership in that first hour which alone could have got them off the beach. Above all they were exhausted, and there was no refuge. The engineer combat teams, coming in on the heels of the assault infantry, had suffered severely on the run-in, losing much of their vital equipment. Direct hits had blown some of their craft to pieces. Of 16 teams, each trained for its special role in its sector, only five came near to their assignments, and of these, three were utterly alone, unprotected by man or gun, naked to the enemy. Within minutes only three bulldozers out of 16 survived for the work of

Overlord began with the airdrops: in the west to isolate the Cotentin Peninsula, in the east to hold the left flank on the Orne. Despite widely scattered landings, both objectives were achieved. Opposition to the seaborne landings varied. On Utah Beach US troops were off the beaches by 1200 hours. On Omaha lack of special armour pinned the infantry down in a deadly firefight. On Gold and Juno the 'Funnies' carried the British and Canadians towards Caen, and on Sword Commandos were linking with the paratroops by 1400 hours, turning the counterattack of XXI Pz Div from behind

heaving aside the heavy barriers of angle iron and obstacles, and these lost their ability to manoeuvre as men took cover behind them.

Yet despite their crippling losses, and their exposure to the full force of enemy fire, the engineers salvaged what gear they could and strove to clear lanes through which the follow-on forces hoped to pass. Heavy mortar and shell fire detonated chains of fuses painfully laid by hand, and blew up whole detachments of engineers before they could get clear. The swiftly rising tide foamed round their feet, their waists, submerging the outer obstacles, and forcing the survivors to the sea wall and the shingle before their tasks were a tenth-part done. On the whole sector of the 116th RCT they had cleared two gaps. Far to the east, where scarcely a man had landed, they had cleared four gaps, but of them only one was marked. The effort had cost more than 40% of the engineer strength.

147

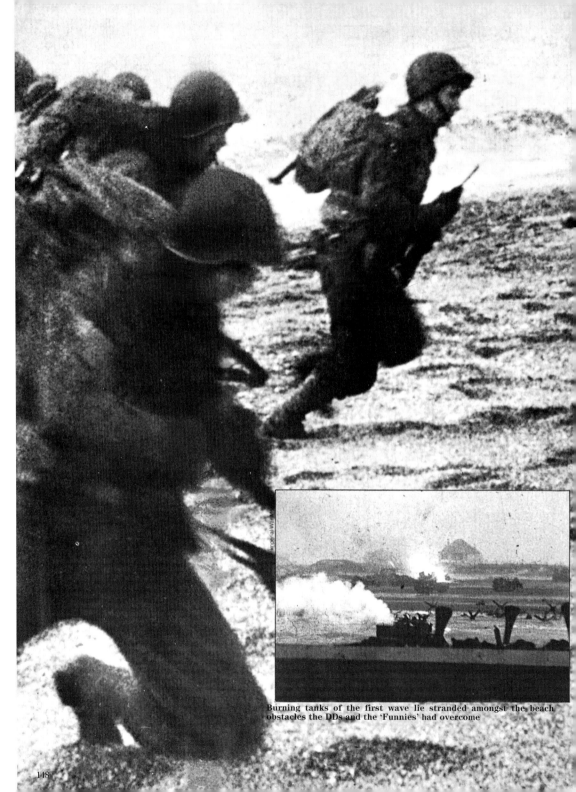

Burning tanks of the first wave lie stranded amongst the beach
obstacles the DDs and the 'Funnies' had overcome

But always behind the engineers, not only the rising tide, but the tremendous tide of men and vehicles pressed on, steadily wave upon wave, building up on the beaches, in the shallows, demanding an outlet. After three terrible hours the foreshore was a wilderness of wreckage, of burning vehicles, of shattered craft, and shattered men. Not one of the exits from the beach was open, not one of the defensive positions had been stormed, and a message went back to the sea to land no more vehicles, but only men.

Nevertheless, long before the destroyers of the naval force came close inshore to blaze away at the enemy strongpoints at little more than 1,000 yards, a desperate beginning of order was growing out of chaos, and men, tried to the limits of endurance, regained their feet, lifted up their heads, and began to fight for more than their lives. They had paid a terrible price for General Bradley's rejection of the specialised armoured fighting vehicles Montgomery had offered him, for these were the 'tin openers' to Normandy.

AIR DROP IN THE EAST: ALMOST OVERWHELMED

The task of the British 6th Airborne Division was to establish a bridgehead across the Orne river and the Caen Canal, midway between the city of Caen and the Normandy coast, and to protect the eastern flank of the seaborne landings. In its initial stages the task was both complex and of a desperate simplicity; complex because the pieces in the pattern were many, simple because there was no room for finesse, no time. A number of *coups de main* must succeed, and become one simple *tour de force*.

Two parachute brigades would land in the very midst of the enemy, on the boundary of the German VII and XV Armies, seize the vital objectives, and at all costs prevent reinforcements from reaching the main battlefields.

Powerful elements of the German 711th and 716th Divisions defended every village, strongpoint, and bridge; the XXI Panzer Division poised and ready to strike was on their right flank, and behind them the whole weight of the German armoured reserve lay within striking distance. Unless, therefore, the two leading brigades of paratroops could strike their blows like lightning out of the sky, and consolidate, unless they could clear landing places for the glider-borne brigade, and could have with them anti-tank guns, mortars, and the bulk of their heavy equipment, their task would be beyond hope. Whatever might be won by lightning strokes must inevitably be lost, even before the sun was up, and assuredly before the sun was down.

The 5th Parachute Brigade would seize the bridges across the Orne and the Caen Canal north of Ranville, clear and protect landing zones for their gliders, and establish a firm bridgehead.

The 3rd Parachute Brigade would demolish the bridges across the flooded Dives river at Troarn, Bures, Robehomme, and Varaville. They would block and hold all routes leading in from the south-east. They would destroy the powerful Merville battery of 155-mm guns and its garrison before it could enfilade the left flank of the seaborne attack with devastating fire. For this latter task there would be a maximum time of one hour.

It was 2330 hours on the night of the 5th when the first of six Albemarle aircraft of the Pathfinder force took off from their English field with 60 men who must light the beacons to lead the way. At the same hour, six gliders bore a small force of the 2nd Battalion, the Oxford and Bucks Light Infantry, and Royal Engineers to seize crossings of the Caen Canal and the Orne. It was a night of drizzling rain and gusty winds, and lit by tattered patches of moonlight; a night filled with the roar of aircraft, the bombers, the transports, the tugs and their gliders in their thousands teeming through the Channel sky from Le Havre to Cherbourg. Below them the wakes of 5,000 ships cleaving the gun-metal sea into greenish-white trails of foam.

At 0030 hours, the first of the Pathfinders touched down on the soil of France, two-thirds blown awry by the winds, beacons lost, equipment damaged, but enough on their targets to do the vital minimum as best they might. Within minutes the leading glider of the first of the *coup de main* parties crash-landed 47 yards from its objective, overwhelmed the enemy with the sleep still in their eyes, and seized intact the bridges over the Caen Canal and the Orne. Already the enemy tracer looped the sky, and the flak streaming up into the cloud-banks exacted a price in gliders and transports over the coast. A hot reception met the men of the 7th, 12th, and 13th Battalions of the 5th Brigade tumbling out of the cloud-banks. While many landed fighting, at once at grips with the enemy, others hung suspended in the trees, sitting ducks, few to survive.

A flare lighting up the medieval tower of Ranville Church pinpointed the position, and nearly half of the 7th Battalion was able to move swiftly to reinforce the bridgeheads. Civilians, possessed of an awful optimism, both hindered and inspired the British. By

0230 hours, the 7th Battalion was engaged desperately on both banks of the Orne against units of the German 716th Division and two battalions of Feuchtinger's XXI Panzer Division, which had been committed soon after 0100 hours. One company of the 7th, hard pressed at Bénouville, held on, fighting against time, knowing that relief could not reach them until early afternoon, but the colossal detonations of the naval bombardment preceding the seaborne landings brought inspiration.

The 12th Battalion, having seized Le Bas de Ranville, found itself in need of luck as well as inspiration. Its forward platoons, outnumbered twenty to one, faced 88-mm guns firing point blank at 70 yards, and with the breech block of their solitary 6-pounder smashed on landing, their only hope lay in the uncertainty of the enemy, and fortunately this was great. While Blumentritt strove to arouse an adequate sense of urgency in the German High Command, and

Horsa gliders and parachutes litter the fields of Normandy. It took the airborne troops hours to link up as a coherent force

obtain the release of the armoured reserve, Speidel was advising Rommel of the situation with equal urgency, and receiving orders for the employment of the XXI Panzer Division.

But Feuchtinger had committed a battle group of the XXI Panzer Division on his own initiative soon after 0600 hours. Had this battle group pressed its attack it must have overwhelmed the defenders of Le Bas de Ranville, and greatly restricted the bridgehead. As it was, the confusion in the enemy command, the widespread threats developing over the entire Normandy coast, was the luck the paratroops needed. At about mid-morning the German armour turned its back upon Le Bas de Ranville leaving the battered defenders in possession.

The effects of the struggle in the early hours on the extreme left flank were to have a vital significance in the crises developing on Omaha Beach, for when Feuchtinger was ordered to move his infantry battalions to counterattack the Americans, he was unable to extricate them from their fight with the 5th Parachute Brigade. His anti-tank battalion was also deeply committed in an attempt to save the 716th Infantry Division from the seaborne infantry and armour. Thus no reserves were available to move against 'Omaha' at the vital hour.

When the first of the Commandos fought through from the beach at Ouistreham, reaching the Orne bridgehead only two-and-a-half minutes behind schedule, the small force of the Oxford and Bucks

Light Infantry, with the help of the 7th Battalion, had held for 12 hours against powerful counterattacks supported by artillery and mortars. One company, with all its officers killed or wounded, held on without relief for 17 hours. It was 1400 hours when No. 6 Commando crossed the Orne bridge on its way to reinforce the 9th Battalion of the 3rd Parachute Brigade. The Commando had then fought its way through enemy strongpoints, destroyed a battery in full blast against the beaches, and marched 9 miles.

Daring of a high order

It seemed impossible that a coherent pattern could emerge from the complex missions of the 3rd Parachute Brigade, or that seven major tasks, covering a 7-mile front from the town of Troarn, due east of Caen, to the coast at Merville, could be successfully fulfilled. Each demanded daring of a high order, meticulous planning, impeccable timing, and above all the ability to improvise if, as was almost certain, things went wrong.

The Albemarles carrying advance parties with the urgent role of clearing a way for a small glider-borne force with anti-tank guns, dropped their cargoes reasonably near their objective, but the brigadier, wounded and wallowing in the flooded Dives with his HQ, and elements of the 1st and 9th Battalions, did not regain the main body of the brigade before dusk. The 3rd Brigade had a bad drop. The smoke and dust from the heavy bombing of the Merville battery position obscured dropping zones on which many beacons were damaged, and failed to show up. Flak and the strong wind gusts played their parts; gliders parted from their tugs, many were hit, but above all, perhaps, 46 Group in particular had lacked the time for training. Now, on the day, on sea and land, the miserable and bitter battles waged by the Overlord planners for air and sea landing-craft, always denied until the last moment, were reaping a harvest in lives from end to end of the Peninsula.

On the left the Canadians of the 1st Battalion found sufficient strength to press home immediate attacks on their objectives at Varaville and Robehomme. While all kinds and conditions of civilian men, women, and children, including a boy of eleven and a Cockney woman of 55, a native of Camberwell, helped stragglers to rejoin their battalion, the solid nucleus of one company attacked Varaville, destroyed the bridge, and at once became too heavily engaged to extricate itself until late in the morning. Meanwhile a captain of Royal Engineers, with elements of the battalion, blew the Robehomme bridge.

These exploits, performed with satisfactory speed in spite of the chaos predicted by the brigadier, were outshone by a deed of a different order. This was the assault on the Merville Battery position.

The 150-mm guns of Merville were housed in concrete emplacements 6 feet 6 inches thick, reinforced by 12 feet of earthworks, and protected by steel doors. The perimeter fence, lined with a concertina barbed wire barrier 15 feet wide and 5 feet high, enclosed an area of some 400 square yards defended by a garrison of 130 men. At least 20 weapon pits and machine-gun positions were sited to protect every possible avenue of approach through surrounding minefields, and with no cover from fire for attackers over the open fields and orchards. At least one 20-mm dual-purpose gun completed the known armament of a battery which threatened the left flank of the seaborne assault at close range. It was imperative that the Merville guns should be destroyed. Direct hits by heavy bombs had failed to penetrate the casemates, and the naval gunfire, to be directed against the battery if all else failed, could only hope to put the guns out of action by direct hits through the embrasures or up the 'spouts'. Such hits occur by mere chance, and are not to be looked for.

A force of 1,000 Lancasters unloading a deluge of 4,000-pound bombs shortly after midnight failed to hit the target, but killed a number of cattle and provided some deep craters which might be useful cover for the attackers.

In the last four or five minutes of the flight from England, enemy flak forced pilots to take evasive action, and tumbled the battalion commander of the assault force into the garden of a German headquarters. The rest of the force lay scattered over an area ten times as large as it should have been. Yet at 0250 hours the battalion commander had assembled 150 men, one Vickers heavy machine-gun, a bare minimum of signals equipment, and 20 lengths of bangalore torpedo. Jeeps, 6-pounders, mortars, sappers, mine detectors, had all gone astray. With this force, organised in groups 30 strong, each with a special mission, the commander attacked. Within a minute or two of 0430 hours the assault went in. Half an hour later, after a hand to hand mêlée of a desperate and deadly intensity, the success signal blazed out. It had been a fight of gaunt shadow shapes against a spasmodic background of smoke, flame, and violent explosion. One of the battery guns had been destroyed by firing two shells simultaneously, and the other three by gammon bombs. A lieutenant, dying of his wounds, checked the destruction and was

added to 66 British dead. Some 30 men were wounded, 20 of them seriously. Not a man of the party was over twenty-one years of age, and few had fought before.

By early evening, the two brigades of the British 6th Airborne Division, anxiously awaiting their glider and seaborne reinforcements, had carried out their tasks, and established bridgeheads across the Caen Canal and the Orne. They had been strengthened by the arrival of the 1st Commando Brigade, and had blocked all roads from the east. Their future – if they were to have a future – must depend on the success or failure of the British 3rd Infantry Division, spearheading the left flank assault on the beaches.

By evening it had become clear that the advance out of the beachhead was too slow. Infantry had dug in too soon, when they should have pressed on. Traffic jams building up on the beach prevented the British from shaking loose until early afternoon, and Feuchtinger's armour, at last with its orders, was driving down, nearly 90 tanks strong, to the sea at Lion-sur-Mer. Nevertheless, the diversion of the German armour to meet the major threat of the British landing had saved the airborne from being overwhelmed.

SWORD BEACH: HITLER WAKES UP

The battle for the Orne bridgehead was already six hours old when Hobart's armour led the British and Canadian seaborne assaults to the rock-enclosed strips of beach fronting Ouistreham and Lion-sur-Mer, Langrune and Courseulles, la Rivière and le Hamel. Far away on the right, beyond the outcropping rocks of Port-en-Bessin, the Americans had suffered for a full hour under the guns of the long bare stretch of Omaha. The hopes of surprise in the east had seeped away, but it appeared to make no difference to an enemy hammered from the sea and sky.

A smoke screen veiled the whole British left flank from the powerful guns of the Le Havre batteries, which had withstood a hundred batterings from the air, and were a graver menace than the rough sea to the convoys assembling 7½ miles offshore, and putting their hordes of small craft into the water. Enemy E-boats, choosing their moment to venture out of Le Havre, emerged momentarily from the smoke to discharge four torpedoes, one to sink a Norwegian destroyer, another to force the command ship, HMS *Largs*, full astern in evasive action, the remaining two to pass harmlessly between the warships.

Torrents of bombardment from the air soon after dawn were followed by greater bombardments from the sea, concentrating an enormous weight of metal and explosive upon the narrow coastal strips, the grey lines of buildings protruding like desolate crusts out of the mists of smoke and flame which tore the amphitheatres to shreds. The helmsman of an assault craft was seen to be hanging out over the stern acting as a human rudder. Men floundered to death by drowning; the assault and landing craft surged on, as if borne on the screaming, crashing ferocity of their own gun craft, which blazed away with 4·7s, rockets, Oerlikons, and machine-guns, while the armour and field artillery went into action from their carrying craft. Mines, mortar bombs, and shells erupted small craft out of the water to fill air and sea with falling wreckage; explosions tore the entrails out of larger vessels, and leapt into furnaces in which, miraculously, men survived.

The high wind was piling the rising tide above the outer belts of obstacles, and there was nothing for it but to ride in, attempting to navigate the lethal forest of angle iron, stakes, and steel, and crash down in the foam of waves breaking on the shore.

H-Hour was 0730 hours, with the armour leading in at H−5. Force S for Sword had put its DD tanks into the water 3 miles out, and it was clear that only fine seamanship on the part of their crews, the 13/18th Hussars, would bring them in on time, or at all. Low in the water, beaten by waves 4 feet high, the grey upper works were almost invisible, and a line of tank landing craft cutting across their bows sank two, and might have swamped a score but for a mattress of rockets falling short, and forcing the tank landing craft

to alter course away from the fragile DDs swimming in the water.

When the bombardment of the warships began to lift, the shore approaches were a turmoil of weaving craft and wreckage, and almost to the minute the flail tanks crawled on shore in the lead, eight assault teams, beating up towards the beach exits, engaging enemy guns point blank, followed by the whole strange 'menagerie' of armoured monsters, the bridging tanks, the bobbins, the petards, and 33 out of 40 DD tanks crawling out of the water in time to shoot the infantry over the hazardous stretch of beach.

Within minutes, the wreckage of armour added a grotesque dimension to the inferno. A flail, losing its tracks, continued to engage an enemy 88, another brewed, a bridging tank lost its bridge, and somewhere a DD tank foundered in a bewildering mass of steel. Sappers leaving their armoured vehicles pressed on, clearing by hand. Men leapt from blazing craft in the shallows, and struggled towards the beach through the crumpled ruins of men and equipment.

On the right, the 1st Battalion of the South Lancashire Regiment, spearheading the 8th Infantry Brigade, quickly cleared the beach in the wake of the armour, and began to assault the strongpoints. The 2nd Battalion, the East Yorkshire Regiment, their brothers-in-arms on the left, fought their way more slowly to a foothold. Over all the beach, left and right, enemy mortar and small-arms fire was intense, thickened by the anti-tank guns sited on Périers Ridge, and the divisional artillery ranging on the barrage balloons.

Order out of chaos
Out of the seeming chaos and confusion, and the increasing wreckage on the beach, the threads of order began to emerge. By 0930 hours, Hobart's armour − manned by the 22nd Dragoons, the Westminster Dragoons, and two squadrons of the 5th Assault Regiment, Royal

British assault troops run for cover, the beach behind them crowded with an ever-growing arsenal of heavy equipment. Inset: A bespectacled RM Commando lands on Juno Beach

Engineers—had cleared seven out of the eight lanes through the exits. At La Riva Farm, the squadrons were rallying, some to aid Commando troops fighting for possession of the Ouistreham Locks, and for Lion-sur-Mer, others making ready to spearhead the infantry on the road to Caen.

The South Lancashires reached Hermanville in good time, one-and-a-half miles inland, confronting the vital Périers Ridge, bristling with Feuchtinger's anti-tank guns and defended by infantry of the 716th Division. But the 8th Infantry Brigade had lost its vital momentum. Enemy guns broke up armoured sorties, and the infantry dug in at Hermanville.

Meanwhile, by 1100, the 185th Brigade was assembling its three battalions in the orchards beyond Hermanville, and an immediate attack should have been pressed home against the Périers Ridge, not only to open the road to Caen, but for the urgent relief of the Orne bridgehead. Where Commando troops had marched boldly through, the infantry, dourly led, performed its slow set-piece gyrations.

A contributory cause of the slowness in front was, however, the growing mass of men and armour, striving to break loose from the beaches, and the impossible tangles of traffic in the narrow streets, the laterals, and leads out of the exits. The tanks of the Staffordshire Yeomanry, with the role of carrying the men of the King's Shropshire Light Infantry on the road to Caen, could not be prised loose from the mêlée. It was late when the guns of the Périers Ridge were silenced, and the Shropshires took the road alone.

The infantry of the line did all that its leaders demanded of it, but it was not enough. The East Yorkshires had taken a severe hammering, losing five officers and 60 men killed, and more than 140 wounded, in gaining their objectives. The Shropshires on the lonely road out of Hermanville were marching boldly into the midst of the enemy, their flanks bare. At 1600 hours, the battalion, joined by the self-propelled guns and armour of the Staffordshire Yeomanry, reached Biéville, barely 3½ miles short of Caen.

It was, in fact, a position of extreme difficulty, for at last Feuchtinger had his clear orders, Rommel was speeding on his way to his command, Hitler had awakened from the effects of his sleeping pills, and the German armour was on the move. At Biéville 24 tanks leading a powerful battle group of the XXI Panzer Division, probing for a crevice in the British assault, clashed head-on with the Shropshires and their armour. Self-propelled guns accounted for five enemy tanks, and the enemy withdrew. In spite of the armoured threats the Shropshires strove to press on, only to be halted by intense fire from the thickly wooded Lébisey Ridge. Casualties were growing steadily; a renewed armoured attack might develop at any moment, and the flanking battalions of the 185th Brigade were making very slow progress. Caen was a fading dream.

But Feuchtinger's armour was not coming that way again. The British, now in command of the Périers Ridge, had pushed the battle group further west, and the spearhead, bouncing off the Shropshires, and again off the British guns, was pounding northward down the wide gap between the British and Canadian landings, 90 tanks strong. There was nothing to stop them.

Imperial War Museum

GOLD BEACH
HOBART'S TIN-OPENERS WORK

The main weight of the British seaborne assault fell on the right, on the beach code-named Gold, a shallow arc streaked with treacherous strands of soft clay, and behind that to the west the powerful strongpoints and fortified villages of Arromanches and le Hamel, and to the east, la Rivière.

It was 0725 hours when the leading flotillas carrying the flail tanks and armoured fighting vehicles of the Westminster Dragoons and the 81st and 82nd Assault Squadrons, Royal Engineers, closed the beaches of le Hamel and la Rivière. It was at once clear that the heavy air and naval bombardment had failed to silence the enemy guns, especially on the right. Only one of the flails serving the 231st Brigade's right flank succeeded in beating a lane up and off the beach, while in its wake others foundered, losing their tracks to mines and heavy machine-gun fire. On-coming craft, driven like surf boats by the strong wind and heavy seas, fouled obstacles and armour, creating a sense of chaos on the edge of the sea.

The squadron commander of the right flanking teams was killed at the outset in the turret of his AVRE, but many armoured vehicles, temporarily unable to crawl, engaged the enemy with their main armament, and were a valuable cover. But further to the east, beyond the immediate beaten zone of fire from the le Hamel strongpoints, the three assault teams serving the left flank of the brigade made good progress. While flails lashed the beach, lumbering on in the midst of eruptions of mines, mud, and sand, to gain the coast road, the bobbins laid mattresses over patches of soft blue clay, and fascine bridging tanks crawled over the beach with their huge unwieldy burdens, finally to fill craters, to make anti-tank barriers crossable, to pave the way for infantry, armour, and the great mass of vehicles bearing down, with a pressure impossible to deny, upon the beaches.

The DD tanks, finding the sea passage to the beach hopeless under their own power in the rough conditions, had been held back, later to beach dry shod, and add greatly to the early armoured firepower. Meanwhile, the spearhead role belonged to the flails and their supporting AVREs.

Well within the hour Hobart's armour had emerged from the turmoil of the water's edge and cleared four safe lanes out of six over the le Hamel beaches, and spearheaded the leading battalions of the 231st Brigade on to their objectives. Petard tanks all along the line were dealing out murderous treatment to fortified houses and strongpoints which would have tied up infantry platoons and companies, perhaps for hours, and taken a steady toll in dead.

On the 69th Brigade front facing la Rivière the flails and AVREs of the assault teams fought their way with infantry across the beaches in the face of intense mortar, anti-tank, and machine-gun fire directed from well-sited pillboxes, and houses linked together in systems of strongpoints. Three clear lanes were opened out of six from the edge of the sea to the edge of the marshland beyond the coast road. While petard tanks supporting the infantry blasted the coastal crust of strongpoints with their giant mortars, like ancient cannon, AVREs filled craters and anti-tank ditches with fascines, provided soft landings for armour behind walls, bridged culverts, and bulldozed tracks for the host of vehicles and men coming in fast on the rising tide. Within the hour armour and infantry were more than a mile inland, and the hard outer crust of the defence was broken.

Saved by the 'specials'
On the right flank of le Hamel there might have been a 'little Omaha' but for Hobart's armour. The 1st Battalion of the Hampshire Regiment, leading on the right flank, had had an uneasy passage. For them the sea-sick pills had not worked. They debouched from their assault craft 30 yards out into waves beating about their thighs and dragging at their feet as they struggled to dry sand. If they were grateful for anything it was simply that the

A Churchill AVRE bridgelayer goes into action. Against the defenders' ingenuity the British set their specialised tanks

152

1

3

2

4

Chris Harrison

movement of the sea had stilled, no longer to rack their guts with sickness. They had come in supported by self-propelled guns and field artillery firing from their carrying craft, aware of mortar and machine-gun fire from the enemy over the last half-mile. It had been uncomfortable rather than deadly. Smoke and flame obscured the beaches, but it seemed that the terrific bombing, followed by the naval bombardment, had failed to silence the enemy.

On the beach, in their first moments of comparative immunity before they came within the traverse of the le Hamel guns, they saw only the confusion of disabled armour, and swiftly discovered that for two-thirds of their numbers there were no safe lanes across the shambles of the beach. An immense weight of fire stopped them in their tracks as they strove to move up the beach, and no gunfire from the sea could bring them aid. With their battalion commander twice wounded and forced out of action, their second-in-command soon killed, there was nothing for it but to abandon the direct approach. Moving east the left flanking companies of the battalion gained les Roquettes, an objective of the 1st Dorsets on their left, and then swung right handed, seized Asnelles-sur-mer, and prepared to assault the le Hamel sanatorium. But it was afternoon before the sanatorium, resisting all infantry attacks, finally caved in to the devastating 'dustbins' of a petard, not the least of Hobart's 'specials'.

Meanwhile the 1st Dorsets, out of reach of the le Hamel guns, had stormed over the beach, covered by the guns of the 'specials', and swung right handed to gain the slight rise of Arromanches.

On the beach of la Rivière the 5th Battalion of the East Yorkshire Regiment and the 6th Battalion the Green Howards, leading the assault of the 69th Brigade, were in no doubt about the value of the armour. From the first, infantry and armour, greatly aided by close-support fire from gun craft, stormed the beach defences in complete co-ordination, and fought a tight battle through the streets, eliminating 88s and pillboxes, cutting out the enemy like a canker, and moving inland. Things had been bad, but not bad enough to curb their momentum on landing, and if men could hurl themselves over the first obstacle of the beach they must win. There was no other place to stop them but in the shallows and on the beaches.

By 1100 hours, seven lanes had been cleared on Gold Beach, the DD tanks were moving fast inland, and with them the 56th and 151st Brigades, carving out the centre, keeping the enemy off balance at all costs. Long before the le Hamel sanatorium had fallen the bridgehead was 3 miles in depth, the 56th Brigade was going well astride the la Rivière-Bayeux road, the 151st, on its left, racing for the high ground, and beyond into the Seulles valley, while left again the 69th pressed on for Creully. Even the right flank, delayed at le Hamel, had cut the Arromanches-Bayeux road, while the 47th Royal Marine Commando was working round to assault Port-en-Bessin.

The Commando had outstripped them all. Coming in to land west of le Hamel they had come under fire from the cliffs and lost four out of their 14 assault craft. Finally, forced eastward, they had run in east of the le Hamel position, hoping to find the way cleared ahead. It wasn't. They had had to fight their way through the coastal villages, each man humping 88 pounds of equipment, and covering 10 miles by early afternoon. By the time the 231st Brigade began to ease their sense of isolation they were occupying the high ground south of Port-en-Bessin. No men on their feet had done more.

JUNO BEACH: SOLID FOOTHOLD

By the time the Canadians stormed ashore with two brigades up astride the Seulles estuary, and raced for the sea walls, the rising tide had reduced the gauntlet of the beaches to as little as 100 yards at the narrowest point, and the battles of the beaches on the flanks were already from one to two hours old. The Canadians had no intention of being left behind.

The Canadian 7th Brigade, the Royal Winnipeg Regiment and the Regina Rifles leading, came in on the right, west of the Seulles river,

The assault on the invasion coast was spearheaded by the specialised armour of the British 79th Armoured Division. On the day they were highly successful, and where they were not used on Omaha Beach the price was a high toll in casualties. 1: DD Sherman tanks were the first ashore, engaging enemy positions from the water's edge. 2: They are followed by the flail tanks beating overlapping mine-free lanes. 3: To breach the sea wall and any anti-tank ditch, an AVRE would place its SBG bridge, allowing DD gun tanks to close the range. AVRE-dropped fascines would then fill the ditch. By now infantry (red arrows) would be crossing the beach. 4: The flails continued to clear the minefields, widening the beachhead. Petard and flamethrower tanks would mop up any remaining pillboxes.

An American soldier lies dead, still wearing his lifebel

beating the Canadian 8th Brigade to the beach by a minute or two. With them were eight, possibly ten, DD tanks manned by the Canadian 1st Hussars. The tanks had taken to the water 800 yards out, threatened by the turbulent sea, in constant danger of swamping, threading their ways through a maze of scantlings jutting out of the water like the stumps of some petrified forest.

On the left, the Queen's Own Regiment of Canada and the North Shore Regiment led the Canadian 8th Brigade without armour, and raced for the sea wall, the heavy machine-guns of the enemy cutting swathes out of the Queen's Own in the 30 seconds or so it took them to reach the shelter of the wall. The landing craft carrying the assault armour of the engineers were still battling with the heavy seas and obstacles, and the DD tanks were coming in to land dry-shod when the spearhead infantry were well away, blasting the enemy out of Courselles and Bernières, and pressing on. When the Régiment de la Chaudière came in 15 minutes later there was scarcely a shot.

The Canadian battalions were borne in on a rough sea driven by the wind which flung them onto the beaches, and in one bound across them. The dangerous reefs and rocks of that narrow coast forced the assault craft to wait for the tide, and when at last they were clear of the reefs the larger craft had to charge the obstacles, hoping for the best, while the small craft strove to swerve and weave through tangles of angle iron and stakes. At one point 20 out of 24 assault craft blew up, and men struggled for the shore with the splinters of their landing craft falling from the skies about their ears. According to the record, 'chunks of débris rose a hundred feet in the air and troops, now hugging the shelter of a breakwater, were peppered with pieces of wood'.

Driven by the wind, the rapidly rising tide piling up the heavy surf, the helmsmen of the assault craft could only hang on and pray. The first three craft coming in on the Canadian left blew up, but their entire complement, save two killed, struggled out of the débris and water to make the beach and fight.

There were many brave men manning the landing craft all along the line from Sword to Utah, men fighting lone battles against outbreaks of fire and exploding ammunition, one man at least, a man named Jones, saving wounded from drowning in a flooded hold and amputating two horribly mangled legs. He was no doctor, merely a sick-berth attendant, but he did the job. And there were scores of 'Joneses' at sea that day off the beaches, but none had a struggle as grim as that of the men who carried the Canadians ashore on Juno.

The LCOCU (landing craft obstacle clearance units) of the naval demolition teams, and the beach units, striving to sort out the horrible muddle of mined obstacles, machines, and men, were under shell fire from enemy corps and divisional artillery long after the last mortar, machine-gun, and 88 of the beach defences, even the last sniper, had been silenced. Bulldozers not only bulldozed débris out of the way, but bulldozed beached craft back into the sea, giving them a start on the way back.

When the engineer assault armour of the 22nd Dragoons and the 26th Assault Squadron, Royal Engineers, reached the beach on the Canadian 7th Brigade front, the DD tanks which had landed with the infantry had settled the score with the worst of the enemy strongpoints mounting the 75-mm guns and the heavy mortars and machine-guns, but there was plenty of mortar and automatic fire coming in from a bit further back. The flails were urgently needed to carve clear lanes through to the exits for the mass of armour and vehicles building up behind them, to keep the infantry going at high pressure. The petards and bridging tanks lumbered up behind them, to keep the infantry going at high pressure.

East of the Seulles the going was good, and on both sides of the river the flails had opened the exits before 0930 hours, the fascines and bridging tanks had bridged the worst of the craters and culverts, and opened the sluices of the Seulles to drain a crater as large as a village pond, and twice as deep.

On the left at Bernières, flails and petards had smashed exits through the 12-foot-high sea wall, and cleared lanes and laterals well in time to work in with the infantry against the pillboxes and strongpoints. Before noon on the right flank the flails were advancing inland under command of the Canadian 2nd Armoured Brigade.

Twelve lanes were cleared that day on the Juno beaches by Hobart's armour, and the exits linked right through to join the brigade fronts. The DD tanks, beaching dry shod an hour behind the infantry, were swiftly off the beach, adding their firepower to the men storming on inland to keep the enemy off balance and not giving him a chance to form a second line. By late afternoon the Canadian 7th Brigade was challenging the 69th Brigade of '50 Div' for the lead, its armoured patrols probing for the main Bayeux-Caen road at Bretteville, while on the left, the Canadian 9th Brigade, breaking

Left: British Commandos have broken out of the beaches and into a coastal town, hugging the walls as cover against snipers

loose from the chaos and confusion on the beach, was through the 8th Brigade, and going well astride the Courselles road to Caen.

The centre bridgehead from Langrune to Arromanches was solid, 12 miles wide and growing deeper every hour. The bottleneck was behind, in the congestion of the narrow beach, the struggle of armour, vehicles, and men, to break loose from the appalling traffic jams. And on the right, there was the growing awareness of an ominous gap, the dangerous toe-hold of Omaha, the Americans inching slowly off the beach, their progress measured in yards.

Whatever happened the enemy reserves must be prevented from reaching Omaha, and it was this above all which made Dempsey pause, ready to reach out a helping hand, holding back his armour.

AT THE END OF THE DAY

A FOOTHOLD ON THE CONTINENT OF EUROPE

It was late afternoon before the German High Command began to emerge from confusion. The lack of air reconnaissance, the blocking of radar, the dislocation of communications of every kind, had reduced observation almost to the eyes and ears of men. Reports could not be quickly confirmed, or information co-ordinated. Uncertainty inhibited the violent counterblows which alone could have driven the British and Americans back into the sea. And the instrument was lacking. The I Panzer Corps lay west of the Seine, immobilised, awaiting the decision of the Führer.

Field-Marshal Rommel had been right about the first 24 hours: they would be decisive. He had made repeated efforts to move the XII SS Panzer and the Panzer Lehr Divisions on a line St Lô-Carentan. Had these divisions been there, the Omaha beach-head must have been smashed; even had Rommel himself been there on the day, able perhaps to rouse Hitler out of his early morning dreams, it might not have been too late. It was too late when Hitler held his afternoon conference, and released the XII SS Panzer Division.

All that could be done against the Allied air and seaborne assaults had been done by the forces immediately available. Feuchtinger,

From behind the shallow cover of the sea wall US troops begin to move off Utah Beach. By nightfall 20,000 men were ashore

Keystone

British men and vehicles advance through a coastal village. Such bottlenecks delayed the advance from Gold Beach

American combat engineers strive to bring order out of chaos on the beaches – working to keep the advance going

commanding the XXI Panzer Division, the only counterattacking force within reach, had reacted swiftly against the British airborne landings on the Orne, according to his standing orders. But at once there followed a long period of uncertainty, due partly to a breakdown in communications. When at last the division was put under command of the 84th Corps, General Marcks, the corps commander, was right in his appreciation that the British 3rd Division was the more potent threat, and that Caen must be at once powerfully screened. Nevertheless, too much time had been wasted, and he might have done better to commit the division against the airborne bridgehead. Had that been done the great glider-borne force might have arrived to a terrible reception.

As it was, Feuchtinger could not disengage his infantry battalions from the British, nor his anti-tank guns from the German 716th Division. He had been shot away from the Périers Ridge by British guns when he might have shot the British armour out of the way with his own guns – if he had had any.

But XXI Panzer Division did very well in view of its difficulties. Had they not taken fright at the impressive spectacle of 250 air-tugs towing their gliders full of reinforcements for the airborne divisions on their flank, and at the evening sky black with the fighter escorts, the battle group, powerfully and swiftly reinforced, might have disrupted the British right flank on Sword Beach, and driven a dangerous wedge between the British and Canadians, down to the sea. Instead it withdrew to take up a position to the north of Caen. There was no second chance.

But it is unlikely that the XXI Panzer could have prevailed, even the first time. Air power had done its work for the Allies, sealing off the battlefield, holding the ring, denying mobility to the reserves, making of each day a hideous nightmare, and of each night a tortured crawling progress. Of the more than 11,000 sorties flown by the Allied air forces on June 6, not one single aircraft was lost to the Luftwaffe. Air superiority, it has been estimated by some staff authorities, multiplies superiority on the ground by three. On D-Day, Allied air power was overwhelming, and decisive.

The pattern of the Battle for Normandy was beginning to set by the end of the first day, with the British and Canadians thickening a stout shoulder on the left, holding off the entire enemy armoured reserve, while the Americans made ready to exploit the open right flank. If – if that right flank could have been smashed at the outset, vulnerable, almost defenceless, on the long beach of Omaha, then a terrible, nagging battle of attrition might have gone on and on, the British bridgehead virtually sealed off. But the 6th Airborne, and then the British 3rd Division, and then the Canadian 3rd Division, had made that 'if' impossible. General Bradley may have feared a German counterattack, but General Kraiss, commanding the German 352nd Division, knew that counterattack was impossible.

And the maintenance of an 'open right flank' was essential to Allied victory. That was the point and purpose of General Montgomery's strategy, and by the end of the day he knew that he would win; that he would impose his will on the shape of the Battle for

Normandy. He didn't care much for 'phase lines' and estimates of progress. He was concerned with the end result.

Meanwhile, by taking a chance, Rundstedt had dared to move a powerful force of the XII SS Panzer Division to Lisieux, and as soon as the release order came through from the High Command, this group, under Kurt Meyer, was ordered at once to the battlefield. By midnight, constantly harassed and desperately short of fuel, it reached Evrecy, 9 miles south-west of Caen, to find its petrol dumps a burned-out ruin. When it was able to move it had to counter a powerful Canadian threat, for it was opposite the line of advance from Juno Beach. Thereafter, the British and Canadian 3rd Divisions absorbed its offensive power, and sapped its defensive strength.

The Panzer Lehr Division was nowhere near the battlefield on D-Day; or the day after.

'As a result of the D-Day operations a foothold has been gained on the continent of Europe,' General Montgomery was able to report.

For General Bradley, commanding the US 1st Army, it must have been a night of grave anxieties, even – but there is no evidence – of some self-questioning. For General Dempsey, commanding the British 2nd Army, there was cause for some satisfaction, but not for jubilation. Dempsey, of whom very little has ever been written, is a quiet, gentle man, a good strategist and a sound tactician. He confined himself absolutely, and with a remarkable devotion, to his work of soldiering. On that night of June 6, Dempsey knew that his army had done enough. It was a good army, perhaps the last real 'army' Britain would ever produce. The dreams had faded; as they had been almost sure to fade. The vital momentum which might – might – have carried the Canadians and the British into the open country beyond Caen was never there. Beyond the Caen-Bayeux road there was no open country, only the bocage, the close-hedged, deep-ditched fields, the narrow lanes, the steep wooded valleys. The real open country had never been truly 'in the sights'. Perhaps it did not matter. The pattern of the struggle would have been different, but not necessarily more favourable to the Allies.

The first of the landing craft, turning about, had reached the hards of England, the small ports, the estuaries, in the afternoon, swiftly replenishing ammunition, stores, men, cleaning and greasing the guns, setting forth a second time through the great maze of shipping. Through all the day and night the Mulberry tows were breaking loose, the tugs fighting scores of desperate battles with hawsers, winches, and chains, clawing at the huge unwieldy objects they sought to drag through the seas. Some 40% of the 'Whale' units broke away and were lost. But it would go on, and on.

It was a strange day and night on and off the beaches. Men clung marooned to obstacles and debris, on rocks, decks of drowned vehicles, while naval and small craft, DUKWS and outboard motors, buzzed and weaved about their business, impervious to croaking cries for help, and to the full-blooded curses of frustrated, angry, frightened men. Many of those picked up by craft on the 'turn-about' were carried straight back to England whether they liked it or not. There were a good many men wandering about for days.

There was not much chance to rest in the bridgehead. The smoke rose from the burned-out houses lining the battered sea fronts from Ouistreham to Arromanches, and beyond to the desolation of Omaha and the isolation of Utah, the dunes of Varreville. In the midst of the monstrous chaos of the beaches, in the jungles of shattered craft, tank tracks, wheels, and twisted masses of iron and steel, the bodies of men lay under gas capes, awaiting burial.

At Sallenelles on the left, in the 3-mile gap between Sword and Juno, and in the chasm between Gold and Omaha, there was no rest. The airborne and the Commandos were having a rugged time. Yet some lay in the meadows, and wrote home about 'butterflies' and 'bird song', which seemed the oddest things of all in the day.

Morale was high. To most of those not 'in contact', and not 'fighting' – and a minority is 'in contact' doing any 'fighting' – it seemed an anti-climax. One man called it 'a crashing anti-climax'. In a sense it was an anti-climax not to be dead, after so much waiting, training, thinking, and expecting 'God knew what'.

Some thought that the French were warm and friendly, others that they were suspicious and unfriendly, still others that they were indifferent. Many were startled by the extreme youth, or age, of the captured enemy and inclined to believe that it was going to be, what they called in those days, 'a piece of cake'. But the men who had charged the strongpoints, and gone into the cellars behind grenades, knew better. The German 716th Division had been cut to pieces, but its isolated 'bits' fought on.

The men, above all, who felt themselves to be 'out on a limb' that night were the US 82nd Airborne, holding on in Ste Mère-Église and with the 101st in scores of tiny 'pockets', wondering when their small seaborne 'attachment' was going to catch up. They didn't realise that many of their small bits and pieces would presently come together and give a much greater length and depth to the Utah bridgehead than it looked.

But the Utah bridgehead was sound. The entire 4th Division was

American wounded. The day claimed 2,500 killed, 1,000 of them on Omaha Beach where the special armour was not used

The US flag laid out for Allied aircraft recognition on a shattered German bunker as GIs winkle out the defenders on shore well before midnight, and much more besides, 20,000 men and 1,700 vehicles in round figures. The two leading regiments had lost twelve men killed between them. General Collins, the corps commander, was far more worried about the possible actions – or lack of actions – of Admiral Moon, than about the bridgehead. The General wanted to go on shore, but he dared not leave the *Bayfield*. The Admiral, worrying about his losses, wanted to suspend landing operations through the night, and General Collins had 'to hold down Admiral Moon', as Bradley put it.

General Gerow, commanding the US 5th Corps, with no such sea cares, but with plenty on shore, had set up his command post on the bluffs of that desolate stretch of coast. There were 'no rear areas on Omaha' that night, according to the record, no comfort, no feeling of security. Enemy were still firing from beach positions, sniping all night, and all through the next day. Barely 100 tons of supplies had come on shore, and the men were hungry, weary, hanging on grimly, short of ammunition, sleep, short of most things. At the deepest point the penetration on Omaha was not much more than 1,500 yards, and there wasn't a line, not even the planned 'Beach Maintenance Line'. It was a miracle that they had gained a foothold, but they had. Men without armour.

No one may ever know what General Bradley thought about it. Why had he refused the flails, the petards, and all the rest of Hobart's armour? Chester Wilmot believed that it was Bradley's contempt for British 'under confidence and over-insurance'. Captain Sir Basil

Liddell Hart summed up: 'Analysis makes it clear that the American troops paid dearly for their higher commander's hesitation to accept Montgomery's earlier offer to give them a share of Hobart's specialised armour.'

And the Supreme Commander's report states:

Apart from the factor of tactical surprise, the comparatively light casualties which we sustained on all beaches, except 'Omaha', were in large measure due to the success of the novel mechanical contrivances which we employed and to the staggering moral and material effect of the mass of armour landed in the leading waves of the assault. It is doubtful if the assault forces could have firmly established themselves without the assistance of these weapons.

The cost of the day in killed was not more than 2,500 men, 1,000 of them on Omaha Beach. At Towton Field, on 29th March, 1461, 33,000 men perished by the sword and were buried there. Nearly 20,000 British troops were killed on the first day of the Battle of the Somme in 1916. War had become a battle of machines against machines. Tens of thousands of tons of explosive, of copper, tungsten, bronze, iron, steel, bombs, bricks, mortar, concrete, guns, tanks, vehicles, ships, all 'blown to smithereens'. Bridges, railways, dumps, factories, whole towns, flattened to rubble, a war for bulldozers.

And presently the men controlling the bombers sensed their power, making it almost impossible for men on their feet to get through. It will be an unhappy day for the world when men on their feet cannot get through.

After the battle came the liberation. Here, French men and women march across the city square in Rennes, North France waving the 'Stars and Stripes'

US rocket bombardment before the Leyte landings

BATTLE
OF THE
PACIFIC

On map: PACIFIC OCEAN · 1st ATTACK · 2nd ATTACK · 50 HIGH-LEVEL BOMBERS · 51 DIVE-BOMBERS · 43 FIGHTERS · 36 FIGHTERS · 54 HIGH-LEVEL BOMBERS · 80 DIVE-BOMBERS · 70 TORPEDO-BOMBERS · O A H U · WHEELER · KANEOHE · Pearl Harbor · EWA · HICKHAM · Honolulu · ✝ US Airbases

Imperial War Museum

PEARL HARBOR: A BLOW FOR EMPIRE

For years before Pearl Harbor, Japan's military and political leaders had been flexing their Imperial muscles on the mainland of China in an attempt to win territory both along the coast and inland in the productive wastes of Manchuria.

In contemplating an extension of this Imperial war in Asia, those same Japanese leaders had one idea fixed firmly in their minds: that a war involving the United States was quite feasible in the short run, but should that war last more than a year then America's enormous industrial capacity would inevitably become the decisive factor.

Japan's initial war strategy was, as a result, quite simply to direct all her military and naval might southwards against the productive, oil-rich states of South-East Asia – Thailand, Malaya, the Philippines and the Dutch East Indies. Subsequently put into practice and known to historians as the 'Oriental Blitzkrieg', this strategy was intended to rapidly establish a Japanese Empire and a sound industrial base in South-East Asia – an Empire so costly of American lives to eliminate that any negotiated peace settlement would leave it essentially intact.

This strategy was, however, to be dramatically modified before it was ever put into action. Aware that the 'Oriental Blitzkrieg' would, anyhow, bring the United States into the war, Admiral Yamamoto – C-in-C of the Japanese Fleet – reasoned that if war with the USA was inevitable, then it should be provoked to Japan's best advantage.

PEARL HARBOR

Pearl City

Ford Island

CURTISS
RALEIGH
UTAH
SOLACE
NEVADA
ARIZONA / VESTAL
TENNESSEE / WEST VIRGINIA
MARYLAND
CALIFORNIA / OKLAHOMA
HONOLULU / ST LOUIS
OGLALA / HELENA
SHAW
PENNSYLVANIA
CASSIN / DOWNES

The way to do this, he insisted, was to strike a direct blow against America's greatest military asset in the Pacific – her Fleet, whose home base was Pearl Harbor.

As a result – and after Yamamoto's ideas had only weeks before overcome the opposition of the Japanese army and navy Establishment – the morning of November 26th, 1941, saw six Fleet carriers, two battleships, three cruisers and numerous other warships and supply ships of Admiral

L to R: *West Virginia, Tennessee* and *Arizona* after the attack

Nagumo's Fast Carrier Strike Force slip anchor from their staging-post off the Kurile Islands to the north of Japan and, observing strict radio silence, head off 3,000 miles east across the Pacific. Their destination was to be the launch-point for a massive air-strike planned to deal 'a devastating blow against the sea power of the nation standing between Japan and the glorious destiny mapped out by her leaders.'

Meanwhile, despite their knowledge of Japanese diplomatic codes, their monitoring of naval radio communications and the certainty that Japan was, indeed, about to open hostilities against the USA, no one on the American side had any idea of the movement of the Fast Carrier Strike Force . . . nor, on that sunny, early morning of December 7th, 1941, had any particular alert been ordered to protect the warships riding placidly at their Hawaiian moorings around Ford Island, Pearl Harbor.

The great blow was at hand. America was about to be plunged into a World War that would only end some four years later in the holocausts of Hiroshima and Nagasaki . . .

... Pearl Harbor was under air attack.

Since 0615 hours the first wave of Japanese aircraft had been winging their way southwards led by Commander Mitsuo Fuchida, the air group commander, in the leading high-level bomber. A pair of trainee radar operators at the mobile station at Opana, practising with the equipment beyond the normal closing-down hour of 0700 hours, saw them appear on the screen at a range of 137 miles and plotted their approach just as a matter of interest: they were told by the information centre, to which they reported, that the contact could be disregarded as it was probably a flight of Fortresses due to arrive that morning from the mainland.

Fuchida led his swarm of aircraft down the western coast of Oahu, watched with idle curiosity by the many service and civilian families living along the shore, who took them for the air groups returning from the *Lexington* and *Enterprise*. By 0750 hours Fuchida could see across the central plain of the island to Pearl Harbor, its waters glinting in the early sunshine of a peaceful Sunday morning, and through binoculars he was able to count the seven capital ships moored two by two in 'Battleship Row' on the eastern side of Ford Island.

Surprise was complete: he gave the order to attack.

From endlessly repeated practice and meticulous study of maps and models of Oahu and Pearl Harbor, every Japanese pilot knew exactly what he had to do. While the squadrons of dive-bombers split up into sections which were to swoop simultaneously on the several army, navy, and marine airfields, the high-level bombers settled on to their pre-arranged approach course, bomb aimers adjusting their sights, and the torpedo-bombers began the long downward slant to their torpedo launching positions abreast the battleships. A few minutes before 0800 hours, to the scream of vertically plummeting planes, bombs began to burst among the aircraft drawn up, wing-tip to wing-tip in parade-ground perfection on the various airfields. Simultaneously the duty watch aboard the ships in 'Battleship Row', preparing for the eight o'clock ceremony of hoisting the colours, saw the torpedo-bombers dip low to launch their tor-

Sunk at Pearl Harbor, the USS **California. Length:** 624 feet. *Beam:* 97·5 feet. **Draught:** 32 feet. **Displacement:** 32,600 tons. **Speed:** 21·5 knots. **Armour:** *Belt:* 14 inches; *Conning tower:* 16 inches; **Armament:** 1 x 14-inch and 12 x 5-inch guns. **Launched:** 1921

Ford Island and 'Battleship Row' under Japanese attack. Note Japanese aircraft and explosions on far side of Ford Island

edoes and watched, horror-stricken, the thin pencil line of the tracks heading for their helpless, immobile hulls. Not an American gun had yet opened fire. Not an American fighter plane had taken off.

Moored together in the harbour, five of the battleships – West Virginia, Arizona, Nevada, Oklahoma, and California – were in the first few minutes; only the Maryland and Tennessee, occupying inside berths, and the flagship Pennsylvania which was in dry dock, escaped torpedo damage. Other ships torpedoed were the old target battleship Utah, and the light cruisers Raleigh and Helena.

Nevertheless, although to the shudder and shock of underwater explosions was soon added the rising whine of dive-bombers, the shriek and shattering detonation of bombs from them and from the high-flying bombers, the American crews, for the most

part, went into action with speed and efficiency, shooting down several of their attackers. Damage-control parties worked manfully to minimise the consequences of flooded compartments, counter-flooding to keep the foundering ships on an even keel, restoring electric and water power and communications, fighting the fires.

Meanwhile, however, high up above the smoke and confusion, hardly able at first to credit the total absence of any fighter opposition, and little inconvenienced by the sparse gunfire directed at them, Fuchida's high-level bombers were calmly selecting their targets and aiming with cool precision. An armour-piercing bomb sliced through the five inches of armour of a turret in the Tennessee to burst inside it; another plunged down through the several decks to explode in the forward magazine of the Arizona, which blew up. Both the Maryland and the California were hit with devastating effect.

When a lull occurred at 0825 hours, as the first wave of Japanese aircraft retired, almost every US aircraft at the air bases was damaged or destroyed, the West Virginia was sinking and on fire, the Arizona had settled on the bottom with more than a

thousand of her crew fatally trapped below. The Oklahoma had capsized and settled on the bottom with her keel above water; the Tennessee, with a turret destroyed by an armour-piercing bomb, was badly on fire; and the California had received damage that was eventually to sink her, in spite of all efforts of her crew. Elsewhere, all that was visible of the Utah was her upturned keel. The Raleigh, deep in the water from flooding and counter-flooding, was being kept upright only by her mooring wires.

While all this had been taking place, at least one Japanese midget submarine succeeded in penetrating the harbour, passing through the gate in the boom defences which had been carelessly left open after the entry of two minesweepers at 0458 hours. During a lull in the air attacks this submarine was sighted just as it was firing a torpedo at the seaplane tender Curtiss. The torpedo missed and exploded harmlessly against the shore, as did a second one. The submarine was attacked by the destroyer Monaghan and sunk by depth charges. Of the other three midgets launched from their parent submarines, two were lost without trace; the third, after running on to a reef and being fired at by the destroyer Helm, was finally beached and her crew taken prisoner. The parent submarines and the 11 other large boats of the Advanced Expeditionary Force achieved nothing.

The second wave of Japanese aircraft – 54 bombers, 80 dive-bombers, and 36 fighters, led by Lieutenant Commander Shimazaki of the aircraft-carrier Zuikaku – had taken off an hour after the first wave. They were met by a more effective defence and thus achieved much less. In the breathing space between the two attacks, ammunition supply for the US anti-aircraft guns had been replenished, gun crews reorganised, and reinforced; and a number of the Japanese dive-bombers were shot down. Nevertheless, they succeeded in damaging the Pennsylvania, wrecking two destroyers which were sharing the dry-dock with her, blowing up another destroyer in the floating dock, and forcing the Nevada – feeling her way towards the harbour entrance through the billowing clouds of black smoke from burning ships – to beach herself. Meanwhile the high-level bombers were able to make undisturbed practice and wreak further damage on the

already shattered and burning US ships.

At 1000 hours it was suddenly all over. The rumble of retreating aircraft engines died away leaving a strange silence except for the crackle of burning ships, the hissing of water hoses and the desperate shouts of men fighting the fires. For the loss of only nine fighters, 15 dive-bombers, and five torpedo-bombers out of the 384 planes engaged, the Japanese navy had succeeded in putting out of action the entire battleship force of the US Pacific Fleet.

To the anxious Nagumo the success seemed so miraculously complete, and the price paid so small, that when Fuchida and other air squadron commanders urged him to mount a second attack, he felt it would be tempting fate to comply. Against their advice, he gave orders for his force to steer away to the north-west to rendezvous with his replenishment aircraft-carriers, and thence set a course for Japan.

This was a bad mistake – but Nagumo, who was no airman, was not alone at that time in a lack of appreciation of the fact that the massive gun armaments of majestic battleships were no longer the most effective means of exercising sea power. In the vast spaces of the Pacific, only the aircraft-carrier had the long arms with which to feel for and strike at an enemy fleet – and a rich reward would have awaited a second sortie by his exultant airmen. Not only was the Enterprise approaching Pearl Harbor from her mission to Wake, and could hardly have survived a massed aerial attack, but the repair facilities of Pearl Harbor and the huge oil-tank farm, its tanks brimming with fuel, still lay intact and now virtually defenceless. Without them the naval base would have been useless for many months to come, forcing what remained of the US Pacific Fleet to retire to its nearest base on the American west coast, out of range of the coming area of operations in the Pacific.

Thus Yamamoto's daring and well-planned attack failed to reap the fullest possible harvest – though undoubtedly the blow it delivered to the United States navy was heavy indeed. But it had one effect even more decisive than that on sea power, for it brought the American people, united, into the war.

Perhaps only such a shock as that delivered at Pearl Harbor could have achieved such a result.

...WITHIN HOURS OF PEARL HARBOR
THE FIGHT FOR WAKE

Colonel Robert D. Heinl, Jr

Grumman F4F Wildcat was Grumman's first monoplane fighter for the US Navy. Tubby and highly manoeuvrable, it put up heroic resistance to the Japanese onslaught of 1941 and early 1942. The same plane was rushed into British service as the 'Martlet 1'

Max Speed: 330 mph at 21,000 feet. **Range:** 845 miles at cruising speed. **Armament:** 4 × ·5-inch machine-guns

Seven of Wake's 12 Wildcats lie destroyed after a bombing raid on December 8

Admiral Kimmel, the ill-fated commander of the Pacific Fleet at Pearl Harbor, had predicted that one of the first Japanese operations on the outbreak of war would be against Wake; and the first troops had arrived in August 1941. By November, while all weapons had been emplaced, there were still less than 400 Marines to man them. Besides having only one-third of its garrison, Wake suffered from other shortages. Much fire-control equipment had not arrived. Radars intended for Wake were awaiting shipment at Pearl Harbor. There were no mines, no barbed wire, no revetments for aircraft.

On December 4, however, the fighters arrived. Twelve new Grumman Wildcats of Marine Fighting Squadron 211 (VMF-211), flew ashore from USS *Enterprise*. This brought the total of Marines —ground and air—to 449. Commanding the ground defences on Wake was Major James P. S. Devereux; the commander of VMF-211 was Major Paul A. Putnam. The atoll commander, who had relieved Devereux on November 28, was Commander W. S. Cunningham.

At 0650 hours on December 8, 1941, a signal blurted through from Hawaii: Pearl Harbor and Hickham Field were under Japanese attack. Moments later, 'Call to Arms' was blaring for the Marines. Troops piled out with rifles and steel helmets, and trucks jolted over the coral towards the gun-positions.

About noon, rain-squalls masked Wake. While

he Wildcats patrolled north, 36 grey Japanese bombers came in low from the south. The CO of an AA Battery saw them first. Barking the report into a field telephone, he signalled his gunners to commence firing.

Wake's airstrip took the brunt. Seven American fighters were burnt out or blasted. Fires engulfed the squadron's scanty stocks of tools, spares, and manuals. The air-to-ground radio was riddled. Out of 55 officers and men on the ground when the Japanese struck, VMF-211 had 23 killed including three pilots) and 11 wounded.

Methodical to a fault, the bombers returned next day at 1145 hours. Before they could release their bombs, Putnam's four air-worthy fighters slashed in. One bomber faltered and spun down; then the batteries opened fire. Another bomber disintegrated, and others trailed smoke. Battered by flak, the Japanese pounded Wake again, leaving ruin and flame behind them—but this time only 24 bombers limped home.

Even though the flak and the fighters still fought back—three more bombers were shot down on the third day—Admiral Kajioka felt satisfied with the damage inflicted on the Wake defences to date. Structures razed, heavy explosions, large fires, and extensive cratering reported—all presented a picture of destruction. And on December 9 the Japanese fleet set sail

the destroyer *Kisaragi* was bombed by Captain Henry T. Elrod. The depth-charges exploded with a crash—and *Kisaragi* vanished.

Wake's guns and handful of aircraft had stopped an amphibious attack, sunk two warships, damaged seven more, and inflicted about 700 casualties on the Japanese (mostly dead).

For the defenders of Wake, the days following the attack fused into each other. Each day there was at least one heavy air raid, but fighters opposed every attack and the guns shot back even though there was only one serviceable director and one height-finder left.

Wake's resources were wearing thin. On December 17, the atoll commander told Pearl Harbor that over half the vehicles and engineering equipment were destroyed, the petrol mostly consumed, all workshops and warehouses obliterated, and civilian morale poor.

On December 21, Kajioka sailed again from Roi. This time he had additional cruisers and destroyers, and a landing force battalion hastily transferred from Saipan. He also had two fleet aircraft-carriers, *Soryu* and *Hiryu*. Companies of the landing force were aboard two ancient destroyers which, at any cost, were to be rammed ashore on Wake. And, most important, Kajioka knew that Wake's last aircraft had gone: it was lost in desperate combat with Zeros and dive-

to capture Wake. Arriving off Wake before dawn on December 11, the Japanese landing force began to transfer to the boats. As day broke, Kajioka's flagship, two other cruisers, and six destroyers commenced bombardment. Gradually closing in, the Japanese shelled Wake heavily—and received no reply.

At 0615 hours, after a bombardment of 45 minutes' shelling, Major Devereux knew that the moment had come: the Japanese were well inside the range of Wake's guns. He gave the order to open fire. The battery on Peacock Point drew first blood. On the waterline of Kajioka's flagship, two 5-inch projectiles punched through and burst. Steam and smoke belched from the holes, and another salvo hit just aft of the first. Slowing down, *Yubari* turned away while a destroyer made smoke to screen the wounded cruiser.

At the other end of Wake, the Wilkes Island 5-inch battery had been tracking three destroyers. When *Yubari* was hit, these ships closed the beach, firing as they came. Nearing the reef, *Hayate*, leading, turned parallel to the shore. At 4,000 yards, broadside on, she was a tempting target for a battery whose range-finder had been destroyed during the bombing. Estimating range, the battery commander opened fire; and on the third salvo, the *Hayate* was obliterated by a violent explosion. As smoke, spray, and debris cleared away, the American gunners saw that she had been disabled and was sinking rapidly but her crew managed to beach her. She was the first Japanese warship destroyed in the war.

The battery resumed fire on the next ship in column. She too was hit and, like *Yubari*, turned into the smoke. Then the gunners scored hits on another cruiser, on a transport hastily hoisting in boats, and on two more destroyers. Soon after 0700 hours, Kajioka was in retreat.

Now came VMF-211's turn. Putnam had taken off with his four fighters at dawn to intercept any aircraft accompanying the attack—but also armed with bombs in case the Japanese fighters did not intervene. Seeing Kajioka retire, Putnam led his Wildcats in a steep dive through heavy flak and bombed two cruisers. As each pilot dropped his bombs, he swooped back to Wake to re-arm. The second sorties brought even better hunting. Incredibly carrying a deck-load of depth-charges,

bombers from the carriers, on December 22.

Soon after midnight on the 23rd, amid squalls and foul weather, the Japanese formed up off Wake's south shore. Landing-craft were to flank the destroyers' lunge on to the beaches; infiltrators in rubber boats were to enter the lagoon. On the signal, they headed for the shore; and the destroyers grounded.

A searchlight flashed on and machine-guns opened up. The only gun bearing on the grounded destroyers was near the airstrip; its scratch crew of Marines and civilians put 15 shells into the nearer destroyer. As Japanese troops tumbled clear, the ship exploded and broke her back. In the lurid light, the thin groups of defenders could see the Japanese swarming ashore from the other ship and from barges along the beach.

By dawn at least 1,000 Japanese were ashore, fighting amid brush and boulders along the southern leg of Wake Island, overrunning the airfield, but stopping at the perimeter manned by the surviving officers and men of VMF-211 who, in the tradition of their corps, had formed as infantry when the last aircraft was gone. North of the airstrip, Major Devereux had a precarious line across the other leg of the island, but there was no knowing how long this could hold—40 riflemen against hundreds. Now the sun was up, dive-bombers and cruisers hammered the island.

Devereux went to Cunningham. When the answer was negative, Devereux explained the hopelessness of the situation, and Cunningham went to find a dress uniform for the surrender. With a white flag, Devereux marched sadly towards the Japanese.

Lacking radar, with less than half the crews for its guns, with no infantry reserve, Wake was foredoomed when its fighters could no longer contest the sky. That this handful of Marines could hold out more than two weeks, sinking Japanese ships, downing 21 Japanese aircraft, and fighting to the last with rifle and bayonet, gave encouragement and resolution to their countrymen.

At a press conference in 1942, a reporter, contrasting less brilliant performances elsewhere, asked the Major-General Commandant of the Marine Corps how he explained Wake's stout resistance. The reply spoke like a howitzer: 'Just what did you expect of the Marines, anyway?'

AMERICA'S AIR ARM

When the war in the Pacific opened, the American and Allied air forces were tactically and numerically inferior. Their standard fighter aircraft (F-2A Buffalo and the P-40) were totally outclassed by the Japanese Zero. The B-17 Flying Fortress bomber proved a formidable weapon, but for all its toughness and hitting power its value was jeopardised by the lack of Allied fighter protection—and this only time could remedy

Boeing B-17 Flying Fortress served with the U Army Air Force throughout the war, also servin with the RAF. Japanese pilots respected its bristling armament. **Max speed:** 300 mph. **Range:** 1,850 miles. **Armament:** up to 13 ·50 machine-guns; up to 8,000 lbs of bombs

FROM THE JAPANESE ARSENAL

The Japanese army was primarily an infantry force, and consequently its field units were relatively well supplied with artillery. The equipment compared well with that in other armies, being soundly constructed, reliable in action, and with good range and hitting power. All these howitzers had their gun counterparts, but these were less widely used because the terrain made the plunging fire of howitzers and mortars of higher value in the Pacific War

Model 91 (1931) 105-mm howitzer. With the '75' the '105' was the standard field artillery piece of the Japanese army. The field artillery regiment had three battalions— 12 '75s' and 24 '105s'. The '105' was noted for its light weight, and was often horse-drawn. **Total weight in action:** 4,250 lb. **Max range:** 11,050 yards

Curtiss P-40 was the first mass-produced US monoplane fighter, and constituted more than half the US fighter strength at the beginning of the war. It was supplied to the RAF, where it was known as the Tomahawk. **Max speed:** 357 mph. **Max range:** 1,400 miles. **Armament:** two ·30, two ·50 machine-guns

Brewster F2A Buffalo was the US Navy's first monoplane fighter. Official vacillation resulted in its near obsolescence by the beginning of the Pacific War. **Max speed:** 313 mph. **Max range:** 650 miles. **Armament:** two ·50 machine-guns

Model 92 (1932) 70-mm howitzer. Every Japanese infantry battalion had a two-gun, two-platoon company equipped with this infantry support weapon. It was light in weight and manoeuvrable, and fired a projectile of relatively large weight. **Total weight in action:** 468 lb. **Max range:** 3,075 yards

Model 4 (1915) 150-mm howitzer. One of the standard medium artillery weapons; each battalion had three companies with four '150s' apiece. The newer model 96 (1936) could be fired at the unusually high elevation of 75 if a deep loading-pit were dug beneath the breech. **Total weight in action:** 6,100 lb. **Max range:** 10,500 yards

Japanese expansion
to May 1942

SOVIET UNION

MONGOLIA

MANCHURIA
(MANCHUKUO)
Harbin
Vladivostok
Mukden

CHINA

Peking
Tientsin

KOREA
Port Arthur

Seoul

Yellow
Sea

Nanking

Shanghai

Kagoshima

East
China
Sea

Ryukyu Is

Okinawa

Formosa
(Taiwan)

Pescadores Is

Hong Kong

Hainan I.

Indo-China

Bataan
Peninsula
Corregidor
Cavite

Luzon
Manila

Philippine Is.

Guam

Mindanao

TIBET

BHUTAN
NEPAL

Chindwin R

Calcutta

Mandalay
Rangoon

SIAM
Bangkok

Gulf
of
Siam

Saigon

Kota Bharu
Penang

Brunei

Kuala Lumpur
Singapore
Kuching

British North Borneo
Sarawak
Celebes

Borneo

Moluccas

Sumatra

Palembang

Batavia
(Jakarta)

Banjermasin

Java

Makassar

Java Sea

Flores
Sea

Banda
Sea

Dutch
New Guinea

Timor Sea

Darwin

Arafura Sea

JAPAN
Tokyo

Hakodate

Kurile Is

Sakhalin

Amur R.

North Pacific Ocean

Midway I.

Wake I.

Saipan
League of Nations mandate to Japan

Kwajalein

Truk

Marshall Is

Caroline Is

Gilbert Is

Hollandia
New Guinea
Rabaul
New Ireland
New Britain

Papua
Finschhafen
Lae
Port Moresby

Solomon Is
Tulagi

Coral Sea

Ellice Is

South Pacific Ocean

New Hebrides

Fiji Is

New Caledonia

Bering Sea

ALASKA

Attu
Kiska
Aleutian Is

Dutch Harbour

A

B

C

Oahu
Pearl Harbour
Hawaiian Is
Hawaii

Johnston I.

D

Palmyra I.

E

F

G

H9

AUSTRALIA

Cairns

NEW ZEALAND

International
Date
Line

Japanese
Allied to Japan
Japanese expansion to July 1941
Japanese expansion to May 1942
Dutch
American
Portuguese
British
British Commonwealth
Australian
French

200 400 600 ML
400   800 KM

Chungking
Kunming
Lashio
Hanoi
Burma Road
Amoy
Swatow
Canton

South
China
Sea

Marianas Is

Ceylon
Colombo

Indian Ocean

Yangtze R.

Yellow River

Indian Ocean

BLITZKRIEG OF THE RISING SUN

On December 8, 1941, while fires around Ford Island, Pearl Harbor, were still burning, Japanese bombers destroyed 42 US planes on the ground in the Philippines. Far to the west, General Yamashita's 60,000-strong XXV Army, together with 459 Army and 159 Navy aircraft of the 111 Air Group and airborne troops drawn from the battlefields of Manchuria arrived in an armada of transports to establish beach-heads in Thailand and the north of Malaya. Way out in the Pacific, to the north of the Marshall Islands group, Japanese forces opened an attack on Wake Island—an attack that was to

cost them two destroyers and 1,150 men and take until December 23 to complete. The same day, from their bases on the Chinese mainland, Japanese forces began an assault on the British base of Hong Kong lying one mile offshore.

The first round of the 'Oriental Blitzkrieg' had begun, and everywhere the Allies—though fully expecting an enemy offensive—had been caught unprepared.

In the next few days, though, the situation worsened considerably. Guam, an important American base far out on the Pacific rim, was overrun in only 30 minutes on the 10th. The same day, in the Gulf of Siam, a British battleship force

The sinking of Force Z. Below: *Repulse* narrowly dodges bombs

Left: Japan strikes south. Map showing the expansion of Japan to May 1942 – the fruits of the 'Oriental Blitzkrieg'

Above: In Burma, as Japanese infantry charge, a machine-gun covers the advance

Japan's Aerial Élite—Her Long-Range Strike Force

The Japanese Navy and Army Air Forces had a numerous fleet of medium bombers with remarkable ranges, needed to deal with the vast distances of the Pacific theatre. Japanese bombers all suffered to some extent from weak defensive armament— none of them had as many machine-guns as the US B-25 Mitchell, for example. But in the first Japanese sweep through the Pacific—when the Zeros ruled the skies— Japanese bombing-strikes were never effectively challenged; and their weaker army fighters were able to hold their own

Mitsubishi G4M (Betty) was the Japanese navy's principal wartime bomber; but the needs of its strike and support role demanded range, which had to be purchased at the expense of defensive armament. This inevitably meant high losses for the Betty crews. It served as transport, level- and torpedo-bomber, and reconnaissance aircraft. **Max speed:** 276 mph. **Range:** 2,620 miles. **Armament:** up to five 7·7-mm machine-guns. **Bomb load:** 1,765 lbs

Mitsubishi Ki-21 (Sally) was the standard bomber type at the time of Pearl Harbor, and played an important role throughout the war, although it had become obsolescent long before 1945. **Max speed:** 248 mph. **Range:** 1,180 miles. **Armament:** up to five 7·7-mm machine-guns. **Bomb load:** 2,100 lbs

Nakajima Ki-43 (Oscar) had the highest production of any of the Japanese army's fighters. It served in all theatres of the Pacific War, although it was far outclassed by later Japanese fighter designs; and it had the typical manoeuvrability of Japanese fighters. **Max speed:** 308 mph. **Range:** 745 miles. **Armament:** two 7·7-mm machine-guns

America's Challenge – Her Carrier-Borne Aircraft

In the first year of the Pacific War, the US carrier-borne force had no fighter which could match the Japanese Zero in manoeuvrability and hitting-power. But both the Dauntless and Devastator strike aircraft – although obsolescent at the time of Pearl Harbor – served with great distinction, and inflicted heavy damage on the ships of the Japanese navy

Douglas SBD-III Dauntless became the backbone of the US carrier light-bomber force. Not only could it absorb considerable punishment, but it also had the lowest loss figures of any US carrier aircraft. **Max speed:** 275 mph. **Max range:** 875 miles. **Crew:** 2. **Armament:** twin ·50 machine-guns; one 500-lb bomb

Douglas TBD-1 Devastator suffered heavy losses because of its inadequate defensive armament, but it formed the mainstay of the US navy's carrier torpedo-bomber force in the early stages of the Pacific War. **Max speed:** 225 mph. **Max range:** 985 miles. **Crew:** 3. **Armament:** one ·30, one ·50 machine-gun; one 1,000-lb torpedo

Grumman F4F Wildcat was the standard US navy fighter in 1941 and the first five months of 1942. It earned undying battle-honours in its defence of Wake Atoll, and also served with the RAF as the 'Martlet'. **Max speed:** 330 mph. **Max range:** 845 miles. **Armament:** four ·50 machine-guns

Above: Japanese troops cheer the news of the surrender of the Hong Kong garrison

sent north from Singapore to intercept enemy transports supplying the landings in Malaya and Thailand (Force Z), was caught without air cover by a flight of Japanese bombers from Saigon. The capital ships *Prince of Wales* and *Repulse* were both sunk within the hour, and with them the fate of Malaya was sealed and Japanese control of the Pacific and Indian Oceans was confirmed.

This control was to be illustrated later in two actions that virtually eliminated any Allied naval presence east of the Persian Gulf. The first, the Battle of the Java Sea, on February 27, 1942, resulted in the loss of 11 out of 14 Dutch, American, Australian and British ships without loss to the Imperial Navy. The second, off Ceylon on April 1, 1942, set the British Eastern Fleet against the victors of Pearl Harbor – Admiral Nagumo's well-trained and practised naval aviators of the Fast Carrier Striking Force. The outcome was yet another disaster for the Allies, with the loss to bombs and torpedoes of the heavy cruisers *Cornwall* and *Dorsetshire*. But still the essential lessons of air cover for naval forces had not been learned, and on April 9 the same Japanese aviators were able to sink the old British carrier *Hermes*, the destroyer *Vampire*, a corvette, a tanker and a fleet auxiliary in a

Above: Japanese flame-thrower attack on an American blockhouse in the main defence line on the Bataan Peninsula of Luzon
Below: Japanese infantry advance stealthily through a Malayan rail-yard

1941 December 7: The Japanese bomb US naval and air units at Pearl Harbor.
December 8: News of the Japanese attack on Pearl Harbor is received at 0230 hours, but the Japanese still catch the majority of American aircraft in the Philippines on the ground when they attack at 1215 hours. Some 17 B-17s, 56 fighters, and 30 other aircraft are destroyed. First Japanese landing on the island of Batan. Four hours after the Pearl Harbor air-strike, Japanese forces in China begin the attack on the British colony of Hong Kong. From Singapore, Admiral Phillips heads north with *Repulse* and *Prince of Wales* (Force Z) to strike at the Japanese supplies for the beach-heads at Kota Bharu and Singora, which have started the invasion of Malaya and Thailand.
December 8/9: The Japanese seize and retain the initiative in Malaya: the British fall back from Jitra to Alor Star. Force Z abandons its northward sweep, but is sighted and its position reported by a Japanese submarine.
December 10: *Repulse* and *Prince of Wales* are sunk by Japanese air attacks due to the lack of British air cover.
December 10/22: Japanese advance forces land in north and south Luzon, Mindanao, and Jolo, capturing airfields and liquidating local opposition.
December 12: The British begin evacuation from Hong Kong's mainland defences.
December 17: In Malaya, the British withdraw to the Perak river.

JAPAN'S LIGHT TANKS – OUT-DATED BUT UNCHALLENGED

Japanese tanks in 1941 were light—none of their designs were over 22 tons—but in the Pacific theatre this made them easily transportable for attacks on the 'Southern Area', and for later amphibious warfare in the Pacific islands. British troops in the Far East were equipped with obsolete weapons, however, and Japan's armoured attacks in Burma and Malaya faced little positive opposition.

Light Type 95. This Japanese tank saw action both in Malaya and later Pacific campaigns, remaining operational until 1943. **Weight:** 10 tons. **Crew:** 3. **Armour:** 14-mm (max). **Armament:** 1 × 37-mm gun, 2 × 7·7-mm machine-guns. **Speed:** 28 mph. **Range:** 100 miles

Below: Surrender at Singapore. Some of the 130,000 Allies lost with the city

December 18/19: Japanese land large forces on Hong Kong island and establish beach-heads.

December 22: Main Japanese landings at Lingayen Bay and Lamon Bay in the Philippines meet with light resistance. The Japanese now begin to advance on Manila from north and south.

December 23: MacArthur announces a plan for withdrawal to Bataan, leaving Manila as an 'open city'. Japanese receive the surrender of Wake.

December 25: The British garrison of Hong Kong surrenders.

December 26: In Malaya, Japanese forces break the Perak river defences and advance south to Ipoh. Carmen falls, and Japanese gain control of the main road to Manila.

December 29: Japanese aircraft make their first heavy raid on Corregidor.

December 31: Japanese have advanced to within 30 miles of Manila, but their failure to destroy the bridges at Calumpit allows the American and Philippine troops to withdraw and form a defence line between Porac and Guagua.

1942 January 1: The US troops on Corregidor are put on half rations.

January 2: Japanese begin air attacks on Rabaul and Balikpapan—the prelude to invasion of New Britain and Borneo.

January 2/9: American and Philippine troops dig in on Bataan peninsula.

January 7: Japanese break the Slim

river defences: central Malaya is open to them.

January 9/February 28: Savage fighting in the Philippines, the Japanese suffer heavy casualties while forcing back the defenders.

January 10: The Allies in the south-west Pacific set up a combined command—ABDA (American, British, Dutch, and Australian). General Sir Archibald Wavell is appointed Supreme Commander.

January 11: The Japanese begin their campaign in the Dutch East Indies by attacking Tarakan and Manado. Both targets fall within a few days.

January 11: Japanese enter Kuala Lumpur. The Japanese drive down the west coast of Malaya begins.

January 23/February 9: Japanese forces continue their sweep of the Dutch East Indies by taking Balikpapan, Kendari, Ambon, Ulin, and the port of Makassar.

January 30/31: British and Empire forces withdraw to Singapore Island.

February 3: Port Moresby—a major Japanese target—is subjected to its first air raid.

February 7/9: Japanese land large forces on Singapore Island and establish beach-heads.

February 8: A proposal that the Philippines be granted their independence and declared a neutral area is rejected by President Roosevelt.

February 15: Singapore surrenders to the Japanese on 'Black Sunday'.

February 19: Some 135 Japanese aircraft

Above: Japanese troops go ashore in the attack against North Borneo, part of a massive sweep into the 'Southern Area'

further continuation of the same action.

By this time, though, the situation on land had gone from bad to desperate. On Christmas Day, 1941, the British bastion of Hong Kong fell, leaving the uselessly exposed garrison of 12,000 to their fate as Japanese prisoners of war. In Malaya, 80,000 British and Commonwealth troops – inadequately trained and unprepared to meet an attack from the north – fell back disorganised and demoralised in the face of General Yamashita's specially trained and equipped jungle fighters. On January 31 they reeled into Singapore, where – virtually without air cover and defenceless from the landward side – they could offer little resistance to Japanese landings. As a result, on February 15, the island surrendered – 138,708 prisoners and casualties falling to the Japanese who, at a cost of a mere 9,284 casualties, had inflicted one of the most disastrous defeats in British military history.

But there was still more to come. To the north, in the longest retreat in British

Below: A blazing B-17 bomber after a Japanese air-raid on Bandung airfield, Java

Below: Faces of the 'Bataan Death March'

ilitary history, Japanese forces harried the lies through Malaya, Thailand and Burma.
a cost of 4,597 casualties against the lies' 13,463, the Japanese eventually shed the British and Commonwealth oops across the Indian frontier on May , 1942.

Meanwhile, on January 11, 1942, the Japnese began their campaign against the rategically vital, oil and mineral-rich utch East Indies. Within days Tarakan in orneo and Manado in the Celebes had llen. By February 9, Makassar in the Cele-

Nakajima B5N2 'Kate'. This plane was in the forefront of the Pearl Harbor attack, and was later to deliver fatal blows to the carriers *Lexington*, *Yorktown* and *Hornet*. **Max speed:** 235 mph at 11,810 feet. **Max range:** 1237 miles. **Armament:** 1 × 7·7-mm machine-gun plus 1764 lbs of bombs or torpedoes

bes, the island of Ambon, and Balikpapan in Borneo had fallen. Resistance in the ill-defended jungle terrain was virtually impossible, and on March 8 – after the Battle of the Java Sea had destroyed any hope of Allied counter-measures – the Dutch East Indies surrendered unconditionally.

In the Philippines, Japanese landings since December 10 had driven the diseased, demoralised American and Filipino troops – since March 12 without their commander, General Douglas MacArthur, who had repaired on Presidential orders to Australia – onto the Bataan Peninsula and the fortress of Corregidor Island guarding Manila Bay. But there was no escape, and on April 9, 78,000 unfortunate Allied troops surrendered to Japan's General Homma. *En route* to prison camps 65 miles distant, so many of these prisoners were to die that the journey became known as the 'Bataan Death March'.

With the fall of the Dutch East Indies, though, the 'Oriental Blitzkrieg' had achieved its objective, and the first phase of the Pacific War was over. Japan had established an island ring in the Pacific behind which she would consolidate her gains and prepare for the inevitable Allied counter-offensive.

Amid all the optimism born of success, though, the Japanese planners had somewhere lost sight of the reality of the war to which they were now committed. In not destroying those two American carriers at Pearl Harbor or in fleet actions soon after, and in extending their conquests far beyond their ability to resist concentrated attack, they had in fact planted the seeds of their own eventual destruction.

In naval aviation alone, America still had a counter-offensive capability equal to that of Japan, and in the fleet actions that were soon to follow this over-confidence would be dramatically and fatally illustrated.

The 'Oriental Blitzkrieg' was indeed an astonishing military victory, but with its completion the Japanese Empire in the Pacific and South-East Asia had reached its limit.

Below: May 6, 1942. The final surrender of 15,000 Allied troops on Corregidor

bomb and strafe the port of Darwin in northern Australia. In this one raid alone, 240 people are killed and more than 150 wounded.
February 27: Battle of the Java Sea. Allied ships challenge a superior Japanese naval force in an attempt to stop the invasion of Java. But Allied losses are heavy, and the invasion takes place, delayed for only one day by the action.
March 4: Japanese Zeros attack the harbour and airfield at Broome, Australia: 16 flying boats and seven aircraft are destroyed in the 15-minute raid.
March 8: The Dutch East Indies government, after talks with the Japanese C-in-C, decides to surrender unconditionally.
March 12: MacArthur leaves Corregidor – 'I shall return'.
March 17: The first of three US fighter squadrons arrives at Darwin: from now on, Japanese raids on Darwin begin to lose intensity.
March 24: Japanese begin their attack on Bataan, and begin a regular artillery bombardment of Corregidor.
April 8: Japanese receive the last surrenders of Bataan in the Philippines.
April 18: 16 Mitchell B-25 bombers, launched from US aircraft-carriers, carry out the first air raid on Japan.
May 5: The Japanese forces cross to Corregidor island and establish a beach-head.
May 6: Japanese receive the surrender of Corregidor.

Four 14-inch guns   Two 14-inch guns   Eight p

Beam: 103 feet

Draught: 27¾ feet   Overall length: 745 feet   Twin 5.25-inch guns

Two 15-inch guns   Two 15-inch guns   Three 4-inch guns   Eight p

Beam: 90 feet

Draught: 26¾ feet   Overall length: 794¾ feet   One 4-inc

Hangar for four Walrus aircraft   Four 14-inch guns

Prince of Wales represented the ultimate in battleship design for the Royal Navy. She had been laid down in 1939 and completed in 1941; she was a 'KG V' – a battleship of the *King George V* class. The main armament of these battleships was arranged in an entirely novel way: two turrets, each carrying four 14-inch guns, with another two-gun turret above the forward turret. She had originally been intended to have another two-gun turret aft, but this was altered to allow for heavier armour. **Length:** 745 feet overall. **Beam:** 103 feet. **Draught:** 27¾ feet. **Displacement:** 35,000 tons. **Armour:** *Main belt:* 4½/5½-inch to 14/15-inch. *Deck:* 5/6-inch to 12-inch. *Main turrets:* 9/16-inch. **Speed:** 29 knots. **Armament:** ten 14-inch, 16 5·25-inch, 60 2-pounder AA. Four aircraft. **Crew:** 1,612

Twin 5.25-inch guns   One 40-mm Bofors

Catapult   Three 4-inch guns   Two 15-inch guns

Repulse, a veteran of the First World War, was completed in 1916. She was the sister ship of the *Renown*, which was serving with Force H in the Mediterranean; like *Renown* (and the ill-fated *Hood*), her original design as a battle-cruiser meant that she was deficient in the weight of deck armour. This was needed above all else to stand a chance against determined air attack. **Length:** 794¾ feet overall. **Beam:** 90 feet. **Draught:** 26¾ feet. **Displacement:** 26,500 tons. **Speed:** 29 knots. **Armour:** *Main belt:* 3/9-inch. *Deck:* 2½/4-inch. *Main turrets:* 7/11-inch. **Armament:** six 15-inch, 12 4-inch, eight 4-inch AA. Four aircraft. **Crew:** 1,309

Hangar for four Walrus aircraft   Two 4-inch AA

Above and below: Near misses burst alongside the *Shokaku* as it frantically zig-zags to avoid US bombs. Above, centre and right: The loss of the *Lexington*. Listing and on fire from leaking fuel, the carrier is abandoned by its crew after several violent explosions. Below, centre and right: The *Lexington*'s crew is picked up

The outstanding success of the 'Oriental Blitzkrieg' in the first months of the Pacific War left Japan in a commanding strategic position. With the conquest of Burma, Malaya, the Dutch East Indies and the Philippines, the defensible perimeter in the Pacific and Southern Asia that her initial war plans called for had been achieved.

By the early spring of 1942, then, Japan's military planners were faced with choosing between the various conflicting possibilities open to them in their conduct of the second phase of the Pacific War.

First, there was the proposal from the Army for an offensive against the powerful Allied base of Port Moresby in Papua, continuing through the Solomons, New Hebrides, New Caledonia, Fiji and Samoa – an offensive that would effectively isolate Australia and put her out of the war.

Second, the Naval General Staff advocated either an advance against India and Ceylon or a direct thrust at Australia.

Third, Admiral Yamamoto – forever aware of the economic might of the United States and the counter-offensive capacity of her carriers still loose within the Pacific defence perimeter – urged a thrust against Midway and the Aleutian Islands to precipitate a decisive battle with what remained of the US Pacific Fleet.

As a result – in a fatal combination of all but the Indian option – the occupation of Port Moresby was scheduled for the beginning of May, to be followed early in June by operations against Midway and the Western Aleutians. The Port Moresby operation – which would not only leave Australia isolated, but also put the Japanese in control of the Coral Sea area – was planned along simple premises, but its detailed operation involved a tactical complexity and separation of forces that was to prove disastrous.

In overall command of the Japanese force heading for the Coral Sea at the end of April, 1942, was Vice-Admiral Inouye. Under him the main elements of the Japanese force of three carriers, 180 aircraft and six cruisers were split into the Port Moresby Invasion Group, a Covering Group commanded by Rear-Admiral Goto and including the light carrier *Shoho*, and a Striking Force under Vice-Admiral Takagi including Rear-Admiral Hara's carriers *Shokaku* and *Zuikahu* of the

THE CORAL SEA

small map shows the Japanese strategy behind their outflanking against New Guinea. Operations hinged on the vital bastion of Port Moresby; and Admiral Nimitz knew that the Japanese were planning yet another amphibious operation. The Japanese invasion-group, with the carrier Shoho and a cruiser force, was to head straight for Moresby round the tail of New Guinea. The carrier striking-force was to cruise the Coral Sea past the Solomon Islands and ward off any US carrier opposition. The US Navy countermoves (large map, overleaf) resulted in the first of the war's great carrier actions—one which lasted three days. In terms of enemy ships destroyed, the Japanese had the higher score; but they were forced to content themselves with occupying Tulagi and Florida islands in the Solomons. Their attempt to seize Port Moresby had been a definite failure—their first major setback of the war, and a major portent of what was to follow at Midway.

V Carrier Division charged with the task of repelling any US forces that might attempt to interfere.

But interference was just the thing that Admiral Chester W. Nimitz, C-in-C US Pacific Fleet, and General MacArthur, C-in-C SW Pacific Area, had in mind. Unlike the Japanese, who had divided their ships assigned to the operation into six separate forces, Admiral Nimitz boldly concentrated every ship available to meet the Japanese in the Coral Sea, where —because the Americans had cracked the Japanese naval code—he knew he could expect an attack on Port Moresby on or after May 3.

Nimitz's force of two carriers, 121 aircraft and seven cruisers comprised the Yorktown task force under the command of Rear-Admiral Fletcher, the Lexington task force commanded by Rear-Admiral Fitch, and a force under Rear-Admiral Grace (RN) comprising the Australian heavy cruisers Australia and Hobart and the American heavy cruiser Chicago and destroyer Perkins. Called Task Force 17, the fleet was under overall command of Rear-Admiral Fletcher.

By May 3, 1942, the Allied force had assembled in the Coral Sea area. There, on hearing reports of Japanese landings at Tulagi in the Lower Solomons, Fletcher took the Yorktown force north to launch an attack on the 4th. Dauntlesses and Devastators from the carrier took off at 0630 hours and, in a brief action later known as the 'Battle' of Tulagi, despatched an enemy destroyer, three minesweepers and various smaller craft for the loss of three planes.

The following two days, though, were anti-climactic for the Americans who had already tasted blood. Instead of the long-awaited combat, the days were spent refuelling and jockeying for position as reports came in of the movement of the enemy forces into the Coral Sea area, suitably advertised by a bombing attack on Port Moresby on the 5th.

On the evening of the 6th, as news reached the Japanese force of the surrender of the last Allied resistance on Corregidor in the Philippines the Port Moresby Invasion Group was beginning the run up to its objective, covered on its left flank by Rear-Admiral Goto on board the carrier Shoho. Further out to sea, Vice-Admiral Takagi's Strike Force was cruising, preparing to move in and support the Invasion Group.

The next day the battle began in earnest. Accepting Hara's recommendation that a thorough search to the south should be made before he moved to provide cover for the Port Moresby Invasion Group, Takagi accordingly launched reconnaissance aircraft at 0600 hours. As Hara later admitted: 'It did not prove to be a fortunate decision.' At 0736 one of the aircraft reported sighting an aircraft-carrier and a cruiser at the eastern edge of the search sector, and Hara, accepting this evaluation, closed distance and ordered an all-out bombing and torpedo attack. In fact, the vessels which had been sighted were the luckless *Neosho* and *Sims*.

After a single Japanese aircraft had attacked at 0900 hours, 15 high-level bombers appeared half an hour later, but failed to hit their targets. At 1038 the *Sims*, by swinging hard to starboard, avoided nine bombs dropped simultaneously by ten aircraft attacking horizontally. However, about noon, a further attack by 36 dive-bombers sealed the fate of the destroyer. Three 500-pound bombs hit the *Sims*, of which two exploded in her engine room. The ship buckled and sank stern first within a few minutes, with the loss of 379 lives.

Meanwhile, 20 dive-bombers had turned their attention to *Neosho*, scoring seven direct hits and causing blazing gasoline to flow along her decks. Although some hands took the order to 'make preparations to abandon ship and stand by' as a signal to jump over the side, the *Neosho* was in fact to drift in a westerly direction until May 11, when 123 men were taken off by the destroyer *Henley* and the oiler was scuttled. But the sacrifice of these two ships was not

in vain, for if Hara's planes had not been drawn off in this way, the Japanese might have found and attacked Fletcher on the 7th, while he was busy dealing with the *Shoho*.

Fortune indeed smiled on Fletcher that day. At 0645, when a little over 120 miles south of Rossel Island, he ordered Crace's support group to push ahead on a north-westerly course to attack the Port Moresby Invasion Group, while the rest of Task Force 17 turned north. Apparently Fletcher, who expected an air duel with Takagi's aircraft-carriers, wished to prevent the invasion regardless of his own fate but, by detaching Crace, was in fact weakening his own anti-aircraft screen while depriving part of his force of the protection of carrier air cover.

The consequences of this move might have been fatal but, instead, the Japanese were to make another vital error by concentrating their land-based air groups on Crace rather than Fletcher's aircraft-carriers. A Japanese seaplane spotted the support group at 0810, and at 1358, when the ships of Crace's force were south and a little west of Jomard Passage, 11 single-engined bombers launched an unsuccessful attack. Soon afterwards, 12 Sallys (land-based naval bombers) came in low, dropping eight torpedoes. These were

avoided by violent manoeuvres, and five of the bombers were shot down. Then 19 high flying bombers attacked from 15,000 to 20,000 feet, the ships dodging the bombs as they had the torpedoes.

Before the day was out, Crace had survived another attack, this time from American B-26s which mistook his vessels for Japanese. By midnight he had reached a point 120 miles south of the New Guinea tail, later turning back south on hearing that the Port Moresby Invasion Group had retired.

While Takagi's aircraft were dealing with *Neosho* and *Sims*, the *Shoho*, of Goto's Covering Group, had turned south-east into the wind to launch four reconnaissance aircraft and to send up other aircraft to protect the invasion force 30 miles to the south-west. By 0830 Goto knew exactly where Fletcher was, and ordered *Shoho* to prepare for an attack. Other aircraft had meanwhile spotted Crace's ships to the west. The result of these reports was to make Inouye anxious for the security of the Invasion Group, and at 0900 he ordered it to turn away instead of entering Jomard Passage, thus keeping it out of harm's way until Fletcher and Crace had been dealt with. In fact, this was the nearest the transports got to their goal.

Fletcher had launched a search mission early on the 7th, and at 0815 one of *York-town*'s reconnaissance aircraft reported 'two carriers and four heavy cruisers' about 225 miles to the north-west, on the other side of the Louisiades. Assuming that this was Takagi's Striking Force, Fletcher launched a total of 93 aircraft between 0926 and 1030, leaving 47 for combat patrol. By this time Task Force 17 had re-entered the cold front

Douglas TBD-1 Devastator. The backbone of the US Navy's carrier torpedo forces at the outbreak of the Pacific War, the Devastator was already obsolete. With its light armament and slow approach speed, it was easy prey for Japanese Zeros. **Max speed:** 225 mph. **Max range:** 985 miles. **Armament:** 1×·3-inch and 1×·5-inch machine-guns plus 1×1000-lb bomb or 1×21-inch torpedo

Coral Sea: the progress of the battle

Map labels:

NEW GUINEA

PACIFIC OCEAN

New Ireland

Rabaul

New Britain

PORT MORESBY INVASION GROUP

Truk Is.

JAPANESE CARRIER STRIKING FORCE (HARA)
(ZUIKAKU, SHOKAKU)

Lae

Salamaua

Bougainville

S o l o m o n I s.

MAY 3
JAPANESE LAND
ON FLORIDA IS.

P A P U A

SUPPORT GROUP

COVERING GROUP
(SHOHO AND CRUISERS)

Santa Isabel

0815 HRS., MAY 4
FIRST STRIKE BY
FLETCHER'S AIRCRAFT

Port Moresby

0900 HRS., MAY 7
INVASION GROUP
RETIRES

1030 HRS., MAY 6
AUSTRALIAN BASED
B-17's BOMB SHOHO

Savo Is.   Tulagi

MAY 5
BOMBED BY AIRCRAFT
FROM CARRIER FORCE

1135 HRS., MAY 7
SHOHO BOMBED AND
SINKS LATER

Guadalcanal

0930 HRS.,
MAY 6

San Cristobal

Misima

Desboyne Is.

Jomard Passage

Rossel Is.

L O U I S I A D E A R C H O

2400 HRS.,
MAY 7

1630 HRS., MAY
NIGHT AIR ATTACK
FAILS

0630 HRS.,
MAY 4   Rennell

1930 HRS., MAY 5

Santa Cruz

CRACE'S CRUISER
SUPPORT GROUP

1358 HRS.,
MAY 7
UNSUCCESSFUL
AIR ATTACK

FORCE
17

C   O   R   A   L

0645 HRS., MAY 7

S   E   A

0900 HRS.,
MAY 8
JAPANESE
AIR ATTACK
ON FORCE 17

YORKTOWN
(Fletcher)

AUSTRALIA

0900 HRS., MAY 8
AIR ATTACK LAUNCHED
ON SHOKAKU AND
ZUIKAKU

2400 HRS.,
MAY 6

1900 HRS., MAY 6

0816 HRS., MAY 5
YORKTOWN AND LEXINGTON
RENDEZVOUS

Cairns

1127 HRS.,
LEXINGTON HIT

2000 HRS., MAY 8
LEXINGTON SINKS

LEXINGTON
(Fitch)

YORKTOWN

1200 HRS., MAY 7
NEOSHO AND SIMS BOMBED.
SIMS SUNK, NEOSHO DAMAGED
SCUTTLED MAY 11

Japanese naval units
American and Australian naval units

0   100   Miles   300   400

while Goto's force lay in bright sunlight near the reported position of the 'two carriers'. However, no sooner had *Yorktown*'s attack group become airborne than her scouts returned, and it immediately became obvious that the 'two carriers and four heavy cruisers' should have read 'two heavy cruisers and two destroyers' – the error being due to the improper arrangement of the pilot's coding pad. Actually the vessels seen were two light cruisers and two gunboats of Marushige's Support Group. Fletcher, now knowing that he had sent a major strike against a minor target, courageously allowed the strike to proceed, thinking that with the invasion force nearby there must be some profitable targets in the vicinity.

The attack group from *Lexington*, well ahead of the *Yorktown* aircraft, was nearing Misima Island in the Louisiades shortly after 1100, when Lieutenant-Commander Hamilton, leading one of *Lexington*'s Dauntless squadrons, spotted an aircraft-carrier, two or three cruisers, and some destroyers, about 25 miles to the starboard. This was the *Shoho* with the rest of Goto's Covering Group. As the *Shoho* was only 35 miles south-east of the original target location, it was a simple matter to re-direct the attack groups over the carrier. The first attack, led by Commander W. B. Ault, succeeded only in blowing five aircraft over the *Shoho*'s side, but he was closely followed by Hamilton's ten Dauntlesses at 1110, the *Lexington*'s torpedo squadron at 1117, and the *Yorktown*'s attack group at 1125. Under such a concentrated attack, the *Shoho* stood little chance: soon she was on fire and dead in the water – and, smothered by 13 bomb and seven torpedo hits, she sank soon after 1135.

Only six American aircraft were lost in the attack off Misima. Back on the American aircraft-carriers, listeners in the radio rooms heard the jubilant report from Lieutenant-Commander Dixon, leading *Lexington*'s other Dauntless squadron: 'Scratch one flat-top! Dixon to carrier, scratch one flat-top!'

With the air groups safely landed again, Fletcher decided to call off any further strikes against Goto, as he now knew, from inte[r]cepted radio messages, that his own positi[on] was known to Takagi – although he had n[ot] yet located the other Japanese aircra[ft] carriers himself. The worsening weather d[is]suaded him from further searches, and [he] thus set a westerly course during the nig[ht] of May 7/8, thinking that the Japanese i[n]vasion force would come through the Joma[rd] Passage the next morning. He did not y[et] know of Inouye's timid decision to recall th[e] transports.

May 7 had been a day of serious blunde[rs] from the Japanese viewpoint, but Takagi an[d] Hara were determined to try once more [to] destroy the American aircraft-carriers be[-]fore the next day. Selecting the 27 pilots be[st] qualified in night operations, Hara launche[d] a strike from the *Shokaku* and *Zuikaku* jus[t] before 1630, with orders to attack Fletche[r]. Although the Japanese aircraft passed clos[e] to Task Force 17, they failed to locate owin[g]

Below: A Japanese reconnaissance seaplane casts off from its parent warship to the foul weather and poor visibility. The American combat air-patrol, vectored out by radar to intercept, shot down nine of Hara's precious aircraft. An hour later, some of the returning Japanese laid a course for home right over the American carriers, which they mistook for their own. At 1900 three Japanese aircraft were spotted on Yorktown's starboard beam, blinking in Morse code on Aldis lamps. Though recognised, they managed to escape. Twenty minutes later, three more attempted to join the Yorktown's landing circle, and one was shot down. Hara was to lose 11 more aircraft which 'splashed' when attempting night landings on his aircraft-carriers. Only six of the original 27 got back safely.

With the day's operations virtually at an end, the commanders on both sides now toyed with the idea of a surface night action. At 1930 the Lexington's radar showed what appeared to be a Japanese landing circle 30 miles to the east, but Fletcher did not receive the report until 2200, by which time he knew it might be impossible to locate Takagi's new position (at that moment the Japanese carriers were actually 95 miles to the east of Task Force 17). Fletcher rejected the idea of detaching a cruiser/destroyer force for a night attack, as the last-quarter moon would not afford much light, and he urgently needed all the anti-aircraft protection he could get for the next day's operations. In his

own words: 'The best plan seemed to be to keep our force concentrated and prepare for a battle with enemy carriers next morning.'

Inouye, meanwhile, had ordered Goto's cruisers to rendezvous east of Rossel Island and make an attack on the Allied force, though he did not specify whether the target was to be Fletcher or Crace. By midnight he had reconsidered the plan, ordered the invasion to be postponed for two days, and split Got's cruisers up between the invasion transports and Takagi's force. Takagi, too, on receiving his pilot's reports that the American carriers were 50-60 miles away, considered a night action, but his air crews were tired—and he was in any case forestalled by a call for protection from the transports, which it was his basic mission to protect, and which had now lost the cover of the Shoho. Thus the main action was delayed yet again, although both sides expected a decision on the 8th. Everything now depended on locating the enemy as early as possible in the morning.

In the event, reconnaissance aircraft of both sides, launched a little before dawn, located the opposing aircraft-carrier force almost simultaneously, between 0815 and 0838. Fitch, now in tactical command of the American aircraft-carrier operations, had 121 aircraft available, while Hara, his opposite number, had 122. The Japanese had more combat experience and better torpedoes, while the Americans were stronger in bomber aircraft. Thus the two sides began the first ever 'carrier-versus-carrier' battle roughly on equal terms, although by moving south during the night, Fletcher had run out of the bad weather and lay under clear skies, while the Japanese remained under the shelter of clouds and squalls.

The first sighting of the Japanese carriers had been at 0815, by one of Lexington's scouts, the pilot reporting that Takagi was 175 miles to the north-east of Fletcher's position. Later, at 0930, Lieutenant-Commander Dixon sighted the Japanese Striking Force steaming due south in a position 25 miles north-east of the original contact, but about 45 miles north of Takagi's expected position at 0900 as predicted on the strength of that contact.

The discrepancy was to cause trouble for Lexington's attack group, which by this time was airborne. Fitch had begun launching his strike between 0900 and 0925, the Yorktown group of 24 bombers with two fighters, and nine torpedo-bombers with four fighters, departing ten minutes before the Lexington aircraft. The dive-bombers spotted the Japanese first, at 1030, and took cloud cover to await the arrival of the Devastators. While Shokaku was engaged in launching further combat patrols, Zuikaku disappeared into a rain squall. The attack, which began at 1057, thus fell only on the Shokaku. Although the American's pilots co-ordinated their attack well, only moderate success was achieved. The slow American torpedoes were either avoided or failed to explode, and only two bomb hits were scored on the Shokaku, one damaging the flight-deck well forward on the starboard bow and setting fire to fuel, while the other destroyed a repair compartment aft. The Shokaku, now burning, could still recover aircraft, but could no longer launch any.

Of the Lexington group, ten minutes behind, the 22 dive-bombers failed to locate the target, leaving only 11 Devastators and four reconnaissance-bombers for the attack. Once again the torpedoes were ineffective, but the bombers scored a third hit on the Japanese aircraft-carrier. Although 108 of the vessel's crew had been killed, she had not been holed below the waterline, and her fires were soon brought under control. Most of her aircraft were transferred to the Zuikaku before Takagi detached Shokaku at 1300, with orders to proceed to Truk. Although in poor shape, she was not 'settling fast', as the American pilots had reported.

Captain Sherman, in the Lexington, had

Aichi D3A2 'Val'. This rugged carrier-borne dive-bomber sank more Allied fighting ships than any other Axis aircraft type. **Max speed:** 267 mph at 9845 feet. **Max range:** 840 miles. **Armament:** 3 × 7·7-mm machine-guns, 1 × 550-lb bomb plus 2 × 132-lb bombs estimated that the Japanese attack on Task Force 17 would begin at about 1100, basing his deduction on Japanese radio traffic. In fact, the *Yorktown* and *Lexington* were to come under attack in the interval between the strikes of their respective air groups on the Japanese aircraft-carriers. The Japanese

had begun launching at about the same time as the Americans, but their attack group of 18 torpedo-bombers, 33 bombers, and 18 fighters was larger, better balanced, and more accurately directed to the target. Although the American radar picked them up 70 miles away, Fitch had far too few fighters to intercept successfully, and was forced to

Below: Coral Sea, an aerial view

Bibliothek für Zeitgeschichte

rely mainly on his AA gunners for protection.

At 1118 hours the battle 'busted out', as one American sailor described it. The *Yorktown*, with a smaller turning circle than the *Lexington*, successfully avoided eight torpedoes launched on her port quarter. Five minutes later she came under dive-bomber attack but, skilfully handled by Captain Buckmaster, escaped unscathed until 1127, when she received her only hit – from an 800-pound bomb which penetrated to the fourth deck, but did not impair flight operations. During this time, the evasive manoeuvres gradually drew the American aircraft-carriers apart and, although the screening vessels divided fairly evenly between them, the breaking of their defensive circle contributed to Japanese success.

The *Lexington*, larger than the *Yorktown*, had a turning circle of 1,500 to 2,000 yards in diameter, compared with the 1,000-yard tactical diameter of her consort. Moreover, she had the misfortune to suffer an 'anvil' attack from the Japanese torpedo-bombers, which came in on both bows at 1118 to launch their missiles at altitudes of about 50 to 200

feet, and about half a mile from the *'Lady Lex'*. Despite valiant manoeuvres by Sherman, she received one torpedo hit on the port side forward at 1120, quickly followed by a second opposite the bridge. At the same time a dive-bombing attack commenced from 17,000 feet, the *Lexington* receiving two hits from small bombs. One exploded in a ready-ammunition box on the port side, while the other hit the smokestack structure. To add to the din of battle, the ship's siren jammed as a result of an explosion and shrieked weirdly throughout most of the attack.

Some 19 minutes later, the aircraft-carrier battle was, to all intents and purposes, at an end. At this point, honours were more or less equal – but for the Americans the real tragedy was still to come. At first it appeared that the doughty *Lexington* had survived to fight another day. A list of 7 degrees caused by the torpedo hits was corrected by shifting oil ballast, while her engines remained unharmed. To her returning pilots she did not appear to be seriously damaged, and the recovery of the air group went ahead. At about 1240 hours, Commander H. R. 'Pop'

186

Healy, the damage control officer, reported to Captain Sherman: 'We've got the torpedo damage temporarily shored up, the fires out, and soon will have the ship back on an even keel. But I would suggest, sir, that if you have to take any more torpedoes, you take 'em on the starboard side.'

Minutes later, at 1247, a tremendous internal explosion, caused by the ignition of fuel vapours by a motor generator which had been left running, shook the whole ship. Although the *Lexington* continued landing her planes, a series of further violent explosions seriously disrupted internal communications. Yet another major detonation occurred at 1445, and the fires soon passed beyond control. Despite the fact that the destroyer *Morris* came alongside to help fight the blaze, while *Yorktown* recovered all aircraft still airborne, the need for evacuation became increasingly apparent.

At 1630 hours the *Lexington* had come to a dead stop, and all hands prepared to abandon ship. At 1710 Fitch called to Sherman to 'get the men off', the *Minneapolis, Hammann, Morris,* and *Anderson* assisting with the rescue operations. Evacuation was orderly — even the ship's dog being rescued — and Sherman was the last to leave the aircraft-carrier, sliding down a line over the stern. At 1956 the destroyer *Phelps* was ordered to deliver the 'coup de grace' with five torpedoes, and the *Lexington* sank at 2000, a final explosion occurring as she slipped beneath the waves.

The Battle of the Coral Sea was now over. The Japanese pilots had reported sinking both American aircraft-carriers, and Hara's acceptance of this evaluation influenced Takagi's decision to detach the *Shokaku* for repairs, as well as Inouye's order that the Striking Force should be withdrawn. Even though he thought that both American aircraft-carriers had been destroyed, the cautious Inouye still deemed it necessary to postpone the invasion, apparently because he felt unable to protect the landing units against Allied land-based aircraft. Yamamoto did not agree with this decision and, at 2400 hours, countermanded the order, detailing Takagi to locate and annihilate the remaining American ships. But, by the time Takagi made his search to the south and east, Fletcher had gone.

Tactically, the battle had been a victory for the Japanese. Although they had lost 43 aircraft on May 8 (as against 33 lost by the Americans), and Hara had been left with only nine operational aircraft after the *Zuikaku* had proved unable to take on all *Shokaku*'s aircraft, their air strikes had achieved greater results. The sinking of the *Lexington, Neosho,* and *Sims* far outweighed the loss of the *Shoho*.

Strategically, however, Coral Sea was an American victory: the whole object of the Japanese operation — the capture of Port Moresby — had been thwarted. Despite the occupation of Tulagi, later won back by the US Marines at a heavy price, the Japanese had gained very little of their initial objectives. Moreover, the damage to the *Shokaku*, and the need to re-form the battered air groups of the *Zuikaku*, was to keep both these carriers out of the Midway battle, where they might have been decisive.

Though the Coral Sea engagement was full of errors by the commanders on both sides, the Americans did take its lessons to heart. The ratio of fighters to bombers and torpedo-bombers was increased, and improvements were made in the organisation of attacks in the weeks that remained before the next great naval clash. But the really significant feature of the Coral Sea battle was that it opened a new chapter in the annals of naval warfare: it was the first ever 'carrier-against-carrier' action in which all losses were inflicted by air action, and no ship on either side made visual surface contact with the enemy.

The stage for Midway was now set.

Douglas SBD Dauntless dive-bomber. Approaching obsolescence by 1941, this aircraft still outperformed its successor, the Helldiver, at Coral Sea, Midway and the Philippine Sea. **Max speed:** 255 mph at 14,000 feet. **Max range:** 773 miles. **Armament:** 2×·5-inch machine-guns and 1×500-lb bomb

THE BATTLE OF MIDWAY

The Battle of Midway, 4th-5th June 1942

Ⓐ 1022 *Kaga, Akagi* crippled
Ⓑ 1025 *Soryu* crippled
Ⓒ 1435 *Yorktown* crippled
Ⓓ 1705 *Hiryu* crippled

Task-Force 17
Fletcher
Task-Force 16
Spruance

Main Body
Yamamoto

I Carrier Striking Force
Nagumo

II Fleet **Kondo**
Destroyer Squadron **Tanaka**

Cruiser Division **Kurita**

400 miles   300   200   100

Midway I.

Midway I.

Above: Midway, the course of the battle. Below: *Yorktown* struck by a torpedo

Above: The *Yorktown*, listing and doomed

...TURNING POINT OF WW2

Japan's naval strategists had long prepared for a 'decisive fleet action' with the Americans in the Pacific. At Midway in early June, 1942, they hoped to destroy the surviving vessels of the US Pacific Fleet in just such an encounter.

Admiral Yamamoto, C-in-C of the Japanese Combined Fleet, was rightly convinced that a threat to Midway Island – the westernmost outpost of the Hawaiian island chain – would compel the weaker enemy fleet to challenge overwhelming Japanese forces . . . under whose guns and bombs, he imagined, it could not hope to survive.

At the Battle of the Coral Sea the month before, though, there had been several important indications that should have suggested to Yamamoto that his confidence at the outcome of a fleet action in the Pacific was perhaps misplaced.

Although roughly equal shipping losses had been sustained – the Americans had lost the carrier *Lexington* and 81 aircraft, the Japanese the carrier *Shoho* and 105 aircraft – every advantage had actually fallen with the Americans. Not only had the Japanese attack on Port Moresby been countermanded, but the carriers *Shokaku* and *Zuikaku* had also been withdrawn from service as a result of the action.

Most· importantly, though, the US carrier force in the Pacific had lived to fight another day . . . despite all the efforts of a clearly superior enemy force. This had only been made possible because the Japanese tactics of dividing their ships into small, relatively ineffective units operating separately within an overall operational plan had proved indecisive in practice despite their foolproof appearance on paper.

Arrogant and over-confident, unaware of the lessons to be learned from Coral Sea, Japan's naval planners were now about to fall into the same tactical trap once again. The Battle of Midway – when seven Japanese battleships, six carriers, 13 cruisers, 50 destroyers and 325 aircraft lined up against Admiral Nimitz's three carriers, eight cruisers, 14 destroyers and 348 land- and sea-based aircraft – was to prove one of the truly decisive battles of history . . . the turning-point of the Second World War, and the beginning of the end for the ill-starred fortunes of the Rising Sun.

Below: Devastators prepare to leave the *Enterprise*. Only four returned, but the *Yorktown* and *Hornet*'s losses were even heavier

L to R: Spruance, Task Force 17, evaded the trap. Nimitz, who foresaw the enemy moves. Yamamoto, whose plan was too complex. Kondo, of the Support Group. Fletcher, who lost his flagship, *Yorktown*. Nagumo, whose vacillation proved to be fatal

USS Hornet
Commissioned in 1941, the *Hornet* had a displacement of 19,800 tons and a crew of 2919. Doolittle's historic raid on Tokyo was launched from her deck, and at the Battle of Midway her Avengers helped shatter two Japanese carriers, the *Akagi* and the *Soryu*. However, she was herself severely damaged, and was finally sunk during the Battle of Santa Cruz after being hit by two torpedoes, six bombs and two Kamikaze planes on October 26, 1942

Pearl Harbor was a scene of intense activity during the last week of May 1942: a feeling of great impending events pervaded the atmosphere. On the 26th the aircraft-carriers *Enterprise* and *Hornet* of Task Force (TF) 16 had steamed in and moored, to set about in haste the various operations of refuelling and replenishing after a vain race across the Pacific to try to go to the aid of Rear-Admiral Frank Fletcher's Task Force 17 in the Battle of the Coral Sea. On the next day the surviving carriers of TF 17, the *Yorktown*'s blackened sides and twisted decks providing visible signs of the damage sustained in the battle, berthed in the dry dock of the naval base where an army of workmen swarmed aboard to begin repairs.

Under normal circumstances, weeks of work lay ahead of them, but now word had reached the dockyard that emergency repairs in the utmost haste were required. Work was to go on, night and day, without ceasing, until the ship was at least temporarily battle-worthy. For at the headquarters of the C-in-C Pacific, Admiral Chester Nimitz,

it was known from patient analysis and deciphering of enemy signals that the Japanese fleet was moving out to throw down a challenge which, in spite of local American inferiority, had to be accepted.

So on May 28, Task Force 16 sailed again, the *Enterprise* flying the flag of Rear-Admiral Raymond Spruance, and vanished into the wide wastes of the Pacific. Six cruisers and nine destroyers formed its screen; two replenishment tankers accompanied it. The following day the dockyard gave Nimitz the scarcely credible news that the *Yorktown* was once again battle-worthy. Early on the 30th she, too, left harbour and, having gathered in her air groups, headed north-westward to rendezvous with Task Force 16 at 'Point Luck', 350 miles northeast of the island of Midway. Forming the remainder of Task Force 17 were two cruisers and five destroyers.

The main objective of the Japanese was the assault and occupation of the little atoll of Midway, 1,100 miles west-north-west of Oahu, and forming the western extremity of

the Hawaiian island chain. Together wit the occupation of the Aleutian Islands, th capture of Midway would extend Japan eastern sea frontier so that sufficient warr ing might be obtained of any threatene naval air attack on the homeland – Pea Harbor in reverse. The plan had been give added impetus on April 18 by the raid o Tokyo mounted by Colonel Doolittle's arm bombers taking off from the *Hornet*.

Doubts on the wisdom of the Japanes plan had been voiced in various quarter but Yamamoto, the dynamic C-in-C of th Combined Fleet, had fiercely advocated for reasons of his own. He had always bee certain that only by destroying the America fleet could Japan gain the breathing spac required to consolidate her conquests an negotiate satisfactory peace terms – a beli which had inspired the attack on Pea Harbor. Yamamoto rightly believed tha an attack on Midway was a challenge tha Nimitz could not ignore. It would bring th US Pacific Fleet out where Yamamoto, i overwhelming strength, would be waiting bring it at last to a final, decisive action.

The Japanese plan was an intricate one, as their naval strategic plans customarily were, calling for exact timing for a junction at the crucial moment of several disparate forces; and it involved – also typically – the offering of a decoy or diversion to lure the enemy into dividing his force or expending his strength on a minor objective.

Between May 25/27, Northern Force would sail from Ominato, at the northern tip of Honshu, for the attack on the Aleutians. The II Carrier Striking Force, under Rear-Admiral Kakuta – comprising the small aircraft-carriers *Ryujo* and *Junyo*, two cruisers, and three destroyers – would be the first to sail, its task being to deliver a surprise air attack on Dutch Harbor on June 3. This, it was expected, might induce Nimitz to send at least part of his fleet racing north, in which case it would find waiting to intercept it a Guard Force, of four battleships, two cruisers, and 12 destroyers. Kakuta's force would be followed two days later by the remainder of the Aleutians force – two small transport units with cruiser and destroyer escorts for the invasion of Attu and Kiska on June 5. Meanwhile, from Hashirajima Anchorage in the Inland Sea, the four big aircraft-carriers of Vice-

experienced aircrews that replacements could not be trained in time.

Yamamoto's battle-squadron

In support of the Transport Group, four heavy cruisers under Vice-Admiral Kurita would also sail from Guam. Finally, three powerful forces would sail in company from the Inland Sea during May 28:
• The Main Body, comprising Yamamoto's splendid new flagship *Yamato*, the biggest battleship in the world, mounting nine 18-inch guns, the 16-inch battleships *Nagato* and *Mutsu*, with attendant destroyers;
• The Main Support Force for the Midway invasion force – two battleships, four heavy cruisers, and attendant destroyers – under Vice-Admiral Kondo;
• The Guard Force (mentioned above).

Parting company with Yamamoto's force after getting to sea, Kondo was to head for a supporting position to the south-west of Midway, while the Guard Force would proceed to station itself near the route from Pearl Harbor to the Aleutians. Yamamoto himself, with the Main Body, was to take up a central position from which he could proceed to annihilate whatever enemy force Nimitz sent out. To ensure that the dispatch of any such American force should not go

had passed in favour of the aircraft-carrier which could deliver its blows at a range 30 times greater than that of the biggest guns. The role of the battleship was now as close escort to the vulnerable aircraft-carriers, supplying the defensive anti-aircraft gunpower the latter lacked. Nagumo's force was supported only by two battleships and three cruisers. Had Yamamoto's Main Body kept company with it, the events that were to follow might have been different.

Far more fatal to Yamamoto's plan, however, was his assumption that it was shrouded from the enemy, and that only when news reached Nimitz that Midway was being assaulted would the Pacific Fleet leave Pearl Harbor. Thus long before the scheduled flying-boat reconnaissance – which in the event failed to take place because French Frigate Shoal was found to be in American hands – and before the scouting submarines had reached their stations, Spruance and Fletcher, all unknown to the Japanese, were beyond the patrol lines and poised waiting for the enemy's approach. Details of this approach as well as the broad lines of Yamamoto's plan were known to Nimitz. Beyond sending a small force of five cruisers and ten destroyers to the Aleutians to harass

Admiral Nagumo's I Carrier Striking Force – *Akagi, Kaga, Hiryu,* and *Soryu* – would sail for the vicinity of Midway. There, at dawn on the 4th, their bombers and fighters would take off for the softening-up bombardment of the island prior to the assault landing two days later by troops carried in the Transport Group.

The original plan had called for the inclusion of the *Zuikaku* and *Shokaku* in Nagumo's force. But, like the *Yorktown,* the *Shokaku* had suffered damage in the Coral Sea battle and could not be repaired in time to take part in the Midway operation, while both carriers had lost so many

undetected, Pearl Harbor was to be reconnoitred between May 31 and June 3 by two Japanese flying-boats via French Frigate Shoal (500 miles north-west of Hawaii), where a submarine was to deliver them petrol. As a further precaution, two cordons of submarines were to be stationed to the north-west and west of Hawaii by June 2, with a third cordon farther north towards the Aleutians.

Yamamoto's plan was ingenious, if over-intricate: but it had two fatal defects. For all his enthusiasm for naval aviation, he had not yet appreciated that the day of the monstrous capital ship as the queen of battles

the invasion force, he concentrated all his available force – TF 16 and 17 – in the area.

He had also a squadron of battleships under his command, to be sure; but he had no illusions that, with their insufficient speed to keep up with the aircraft-carriers, their great guns could play any useful part in the events to follow. They were therefore relegated to defensive duties on the American west coast.

For the next few days the Japanese Combined Fleet advanced eastwards according to schedule in its wide-spread, multi-pronged formation. Everywhere a buoyant feeling of confidence showed itself, generated by the memories of the unbroken succession of Japanese victories since the beginning of the war. In the I Carrier Striking Force, so recently returned home after its meteoric career of destruction–from Pearl Harbor through the East Indies, and on to Ceylon without the loss of a ship–the 'Victory Disease' as it was subsequently to be called by the Japanese themselves, was particularly prevalent. Only the admiral–or so Nagumo was subsequently to say–felt doubts of the quality of the many replacements who had come to make up the wastage in experienced aircrews inevitable even in victorious operations.

Spruance and Fletcher had meanwhile made rendezvous during June 2, and Fletcher had assumed command of the two task forces, though they continued to manoeuvre as separate units. The sea was calm under a blue sky split up by towering cumulus clouds. The scouting aircraft, flown off during the following day in perfect visibility, sighted nothing, and Fletcher was able to feel confident that the approaching enemy was all unaware of his presence to the north-east of Midway. Indeed, neither Yamamoto nor Nagumo, pressing forward blindly through rain and fog, gave serious thought to such an apparently remote possibility.

Far to the north on June 3, dawn broke grey and misty over Kikuta's two aircraft-carriers from which, soon after 0300 hours, the first of two strike waves took off to wreak destruction among the installations and fuel tanks of Dutch Harbor. A further attack was delivered the following day, and during the next few days American and Japanese forces sought each other vainly among the swirling fogs, while the virtually unprotected Kiska and Attu were occupied by the Japanese. But as Nimitz refused to let any of his forces be drawn into the skirmish, this part of Yamamoto's plan failed to have much impact on the great drama being enacted farther south.

Setting the scene
The opening scenes of this drama were enacted early on June 3 when a scouting Catalina flying boat some 700 miles west of Midway sighted a large body of ships, steaming in two long lines with a numerous screen in arrowhead formation, which was taken to be the Japanese main fleet. The sighting report brought nine army B-17 bombers from Midway, which delivered

Mitsubishi A6M2 Zero fighter first saw service in 1940 over China. During the period of runaway Japanese victories in the Pacific this model performed outstandingly. **Max speed:** 331 mph at 16,000 feet. **Max range:** 1160 miles. **Armament:** 2×20-mm cannon; 2×7·7-mm machine-guns

three high-level bombing attacks and claimed to have hit two battleships or heavy cruisers and two transports. But the enemy was in reality the Midway Occupation Force of transports and tankers, and no hits were scored on them until four amphibious Catalinas from Midway discovered them again in bright moonlight in the early hours of June 4 and succeeded in torpedoing a tanker. Damage was slight, however, and the tanker remained in formation.

More than 800 miles away to the east, Fletcher intercepted the reports of these encounters but from his detailed knowledge of the enemy's plan was able to identify the Occupation Force. Nagumo's carriers, he knew, were much closer, some 400 miles to the west of him, approaching their flying-off position from the north-west. During the night, therefore, Task Forces 16 and 17 steamed south-west for a position 200 miles

Brewster F2A Buffalo fighter. Small and underpowered this aircraft was long outclassed by 1942. Nonetheless, it performed heroically at Midway. **Max speed:** 313 mph at 13,500 feet. **Max range:** 650 miles. **Armament:** 2×·5-inch machine-guns

orth of Midway which would place them at awn within scouting range of the unsuspecting enemy. The scene was now set for vhat was to be one of the great decisive attles of history.

Deadly game of hide-and-seek

he last hour of darkness before sunrise n June 4 saw the familiar activity in both he carrier forces of ranging-up aircraft on he flight-deck for dawn operations. Aboard he *Yorktown*, whose turn it was to mount the rst scouting flight of the day, there were Dauntless scout dive-bombers, ten of which vere launched at 0430 hours for a search to depth of 100 miles between west and east hrough north, a precaution against being aken by surprise while waiting for news rom the scouting flying boats from Midway.

Reconnaissance aircraft were dispatched t the same moment from Nagumo's force. One each from the *Akagi* and *Kaga*, and wo seaplanes each from the cruisers *Tone* and *Chikuma* were to search to a depth of 00 miles to the east and south. The seaplane carried in the battleship *Haruna*, being of an older type, was restricted to 150 niles. The main activity in Nagumo's carriers, however, was the preparation of the triking force to attack Midway – 36 'Kate' orpedo-bombers each carrying a 1,770-ound bomb, 36 'Val' dive-bombers each vith a single 550-pound bomb, and 36 Zero fighters as escort. Led by Lieutenant loichi Tomonaga, this formidable force also ook off at 0430.

By 0445 all these aircraft were on their vay – with one notable exception. In the ruiser *Tone*, one of the catapults had given rouble, and it was not until 0500 that her econd seaplane got away. This apparently ninor dislocation of the schedule was to ave vital consequences. Meanwhile, the arrier lifts were already hoisting up on leck an equally powerful second wave; but under the bellies of the 'Kates' were slung orpedoes, for these aircraft were to be eady to attack any enemy naval force which night be discovered by the scouts.

The lull in proceedings which followed the lawn fly-off from both carrier forces was proken with dramatic suddenness. At 0520, aboard Nagumo's flagship *Akagi*, the alarm vas sounded. An enemy flying boat on reconnaissance had been sighted. Zeros roared off the deck in pursuit. A deadly game of hide-and-seek among the clouds developed, but the American naval fliers evaded their hunters. At 0534 Fletcher's radio office received the message 'Enemy carriers in sight', followed by another reporting many enemy aircraft heading for Midway; finally, at 0603, details were received of the position and composition of Nagumo's force, 200

miles west-south-west of the *Yorktown*. The time for action had arrived.

The *Yorktown*'s scouting aircraft were at once recalled and while she waited to gather them in, Fletcher ordered Spruance to proceed with his Task Force 16 'south-westerly and attack enemy carriers when definitely located'. *Enterprise* and *Hornet* with their screening cruisers and destroyers turned away, increasing to 25 knots, while hooters blared for 'General Quarters' and aircrews manned their planes to warm-up ready for take-off. Meanwhile, 240 miles to the south, Midway was preparing to meet the impending attack.

Radar had picked up the approaching aerial swarm at 0553 and seven minutes later every available aircraft on the island had taken off. Bombers and flying-boats were ordered to keep clear, but Marine Corps fighters in two groups clawed their way upwards, and at 0616 swooped in to the attack. But of the 26 planes, all but six were obsolescent Brewster Buffaloes, hopelessly outclassed by the highly manoeuvrable Zeros. Though they took their toll of Japanese bombers, they were in turn overwhelmed, 17 being shot down and seven others damaged beyond repair. The survivors of the Japanese squadrons pressed on to drop their bombs on power-plants, seaplane hangars, and oil tanks.

At the same time as the Marine fighters, ten torpedo-bombers had also taken off from Midway – six of the new Grumman Avengers (which were soon to supersede the unsatisfactory Devastator torpedo-bombers in American aircraft-carriers) and four Army Marauders. At 0710 they located and attacked the Japanese carriers; but with no fighter protection against the many Zeros sent up against them, half of them were shot down before they could reach a launching position. Those which broke through, armed with the slow and unreliable torpedoes which had earned Japanese contempt in the Coral Sea battle, failed to score any hits; greeted with a storm of gunfire, only one Avenger and two Marauders escaped to crash-land on Midway.

Unsuccessful as these attacks were, they had important consequences. From over Midway, Lieutenant Tomonaga, surveying the result of his attack, at 0700 signalled that a further strike was necessary to knock out the island's defences. The torpedo attacks seemed to Nagumo to bear this out, and, as no inkling of any enemy surface forces in the vicinity had yet come to him, he made the first of a train of fatal decisions. At 0715 he ordered the second wave of aircraft to stand by to attack Midway. The 'Kate' bombers, concentrated in the *Akagi* and *Kaga*, had to be struck down into the hangars to have

their torpedoes replaced by bombs. Ground crews swarmed round to move them one by one to the lifts which took them below where mechanics set feverishly to work to make the exchange. It could not be a quick operation, however, and it had not been half completed when, at 0728, came a message which threw Nagumo into an agony of indecision.

The reconnaissance seaplane from the *Tone* – the one which had been launched 30 minutes behind schedule – was fated to be the one in whose search sector the American fleet was to be found; and now it sent back the signal – 'Have sighted ten ships, apparently enemy, bearing 010 degrees, 240 miles away from Midway: Course 150 degrees, speed more than 20 knots.' For the next quarter of an hour Nagumo waited with mounting impatience for a further signal giving the composition of the enemy force.

Only if it included carriers was it any immediate menace at its range of 200 miles – but in that case it was vital to get a strike launched against it at once. At 0745 Nagumo ordered the re-arming of the 'Kates' to be suspended and all aircraft to prepare for an attack on ships, and two minutes later he signalled to the search plane: 'Ascertain ship types and maintain contact.' The response was a signal of 0758 reporting only a change of the enemy's course; but 12 minutes later came the report: 'Enemy ships are five cruisers and five destroyers.'

Nagumo's hopes crushed

This message was received with heartfelt relief by Nagumo and his staff; for at this moment his force came under attack first by 16 Marine Corps dive-bombers from Midway, followed by 15 Flying Fortresses, bombing from 20,000 feet, and finally 11 Marine Corps Vindicator scout-bombers. Every available Zero was sent aloft to deal with them, and not a single hit was scored by the bombers. But now, should Nagumo decide to launch an air strike, it would lack escort

Below: The doomed Japanese carrier *Akagi* evades US bombs at Midway

193

fighters until the Zeros had been recovered, refuelled, and re-armed. While the air attacks were in progress, further alarms occupied the attention of the battleship and cruiser screen when the US submarine *Nautilus* – one of 12 covering Midway – fired a torpedo at a battleship at 0825. But neither this nor the massive depth-charge attacks in retaliation were effective; and in the midst of the noise and confusion of the air attacks – at 0820 – Nagumo received the message he dreaded to hear: 'Enemy force accompanied by what appears to be a carrier.'

The luckless Japanese admiral's dilemma, however, had been disastrously resolved for him by the return of the survivors of Tomonaga's Midway strike at 0830. With some damaged and all short of fuel, their recovery was urgent; and rejecting the advice of his subordinate carrier squadron commander – Rear-Admiral Yamaguchi, in the *Hiryu* – to launch his strike force, Nagumo issued the order to strike below all aircraft on deck and land the returning aircraft. By the time this was completed, it was 0918.

Refuelling, re-arming, and ranging-up a striking-force in all four carriers began at once, the force consisting of 36 'Val' dive-bombers and 54 'Kates', now again armed with torpedoes, with an escort of as many Zeros as could be spared from defensive patrol over the carriers. Thus it was at a carrier force's most vulnerable moment that – from his screening ships to the south – Nagumo received the report of an approaching swarm of aircraft. The earlier catapult defect in the *Tone*; the inefficient scouting of its aircraft's crew; Nagumo's own vacillation (perhaps induced by the confusion caused by the otherwise ineffective air attacks from Midway); but above all the fatal assumption that the Midway attack would be over long before any enemy aircraft-carriers could arrive in the area – all had combined to plunge Nagumo into a catastrophic situation. The pride and vainglory of the victorious carrier force had just one more hour to run.

When Task Force 16 had turned to the south-west, leaving the *Yorktown* to recover her reconnaissance aircraft, Nagumo's carriers were still too far away for Spruance's aircraft to reach him and return; and if the Japanese continued to steer towards Midway, it would be nearly 0900 before Spruance could launch his strike. When calculations showed that Nagumo would probably be occupied recovering his aircraft at about that time, however, Spruance had decided to accept the consequences of an earlier launching in order to catch him off balance. Every serviceable aircraft in his two carriers, with the exception of the fighters required for defensive patrol, was to be included, involving a double launching, taking a full hour to complete, during which the first aircraft off would have to orbit and wait, eating up precious fuel.

It was just 0702 when the first of the 67 Dauntless dive-bombers, 29 Devastator torpedo-bombers, and 20 Wildcat fighters, which formed Task Force 16's striking force, flew off. The torpedo squadrons had not yet taken the air when the sight of the *Tone*'s float plane, circling warily on the horizon, told Spruance that he could not afford to wait for his striking force to form up before dispatching them. The *Enterprise*'s dive-bombers led by Lieutenant-Commander Mc-Clusky, which had been the first to take off, were ordered to lead on without waiting for the torpedo-bombers or for the fighter escort whose primary task must be to protect the slow, lumbering Devastators. At 0752, McClusky took departure, steering to intercept Nagumo's force which was assumed to be steering south-east towards Midway. The remainder of the air groups followed at intervals, the dive-bombers and fighters at 19,000 feet, the torpedo-bombers skimming low over the sea.

This distance between them, in which layers of broken cloud made maintenance of contact difficult, had calamitous consequences. The fighters from the *Enterprise* led by Lieutenant Gray, took station above but did not make contact with Lieutenant Commander Waldron's torpedo squadron from the *Hornet*, leaving the *Enterprise* torpedo squadron, led by Lieutenant-Commander Lindsey, unescorted. *Hornet*'s fighters never achieved contact with Waldron and flew instead in company with their dive-bombers. Thus Task Force 16's air strike advanced in four separate, independent groups – McClusky's dive-bombers, the *Hornet*'s dive-bombers and fighters, and the two torpedo squadrons.

All steered initially for the estimated position of Nagumo, assuming he had maintained his south-easterly course for Midway. In fact, at 0918, having recovered Tomonaga's Midway striking force, he had altered course to north-east to close the distance between him and the enemy while his projected strike was being ranged up on deck. When the four air groups from TF 16 found nothing at the expected point of interception, therefore, they had various courses of action to choose between. The *Hornet*'s dive-bombers decided to search south-easterly where, of course, they found nothing. As fuel ran low, some of the bombers returned to the carrier, others made for Midway to refuel. The fighters were not so lucky: one by one they were forced to ditch as their engines spluttered and died.

The two torpedo squadrons, on the other hand, low down over the water, sighted smoke on the northern horizon and, turning towards it, were rewarded with the sight of the Japanese carriers shortly after 0930. Though bereft of fighter protection, both promptly headed in to the attack. Neither Waldron nor Lindsey had any doubts of the suicidal nature of the task ahead of them. The former, in his last message to his squadron had written: 'My greatest hope is that we encounter a favourable tactical situation, but if we don't, and the worst comes to the worst, I want each of us to do his utmost to destroy our enemies. If there is only one plane left to make a final run in, I want that man to go in and get a hit. May God be with us all.'

His hopes for a favourable tactical situation were doomed. Fifty or more Zeros concentrated on his formation long before they reached a launching position. High overhead, Lieutenant Gray, leading the Enterprise's fighter squadron, waited for a call for help as arranged with Lindsey, thinking that Waldron's planes were the torpedo squadron from his own ship—a call which never came. From the cruisers and destroyers of the screen came a withering fire. One by one the torpedo-bombers were shot down. A few managed to get their torpedoes away before crashing, but none hit

the enemy. Only one of the pilots, Ensign George H. Gay, survived the massacre, clinging to a rubber seat cushion which floated away from his smashed aircraft, until dusk when he could inflate his life-raft without attracting strafing Zeros.

Five minutes later it was the turn of Lindsey's 14 Devastators from the Enterprise. Purely by chance, as he was making his attack on the starboard side of the Kaga, the torpedo squadron from the Yorktown came sweeping in from the other side, aiming to attack the Soryu, and drawing off some of the fighter opposition.

The Yorktown's strike group of 17 dive-bombers led by Lieutenant-Commander Maxwell F. Leslie, with 12 torpedo-bombers of Lieutenant-Commander Lance E. Massey's squadron and an escort of six Wildcats, had taken departure from their carrier an hour and a quarter after the strike groups of Task Force 16. A more accurate assessment of probabilities by Leslie, however, had brought the whole of this force simultaneously over the enemy to deliver

the co-ordinated, massed attack which alone could hope to swamp and break through the defences. In addition, at this same moment, McClusky's dive-bombers also arrived overhead. McClusky, after reaching the expected point of interception, had continued for a time on his south-westerly course and had then made a cast to the north-west. There he had sighted a destroyer steering north-east at high speed. This was the Arashi, which had been left behind to depth-charge the Nautilus. Turning to follow her, McClusky was led straight to his objective.

The simultaneous attack by the two torpedo squadrons brought no result of itself. Scores of Zeros swarmed about them, brushing aside the puny force of six Wildcats. The massacre of the clumsy Devastators was re-enacted. Lindsey and ten others of his force were shot down. Of Massey's squadron, only two survived. The few torpedoes launched were easily evaded.

The sacrifice of the torpedo-bombers had not been in vain, nevertheless. For, while every Japanese fighter plane was milling about low over the water, enjoying the easy prey offered to them there, high overhead there were gathering, all unseen and unmolested, the dive-bombers—McClusky's 18, and Leslie's 17. And now, like hawks swooping to their prey, they came plummeting down out of the sky.

Vought-Sikorsky SB2U-1 Vindicator. Known as 'Vibrators' by their Marine crews, the SB2 was one of the US Navy's first monoplane types. Some were still in service at Midway. **Max speed:** 257 mph at 11,000 feet. **Max range:** 700 miles. **Armament:** 5 machine-guns and 1500-lb bombload

In the four Japanese carriers the refuelling and re-arming of the strike force had been almost completed. The decks were crowded with aircraft ranged for take-off. Nagumo had given the order to launch and ships were turning into wind. Aboard the Akagi, all eyes were directed downwards at the flight-deck.

Suddenly, over the rumbling roar of engines, the high-pitched rising scream of dive-bombers was heard. Even as faces swivelled upwards at the sound, the black dots which were 1,000-pound bombs were seen leaving three 'Hell-Divers' as they pulled out from their near-vertical dive. Fascinated eyes watched the bombs grow in size as they fell inexorably towards that most vulnerable of targets, a full deck load of armed and fuelled aircraft. One bomb struck the Akagi squarely amidships, opposite the bridge and just behind the aircraft lift, plunged down into the hangar and there exploded, detonating stored torpedoes, tearing up the flight deck, and destroying the lift. A second exploded in the midst of the 'Kates' on the after part of the deck, starting a tremendous conflagration to add to that in the hangar. In a matter of seconds Nagumo's proud flagship had been reduced to a blazing shambles. From time to time she was further shaken by internal explosions as the flames touched off petrol tanks, bombs, and torpedoes. Within a few minutes Captain Aoki knew that the damage and fires were beyond control. He persuaded the reluctant Nagumo that it was necessary to transfer his flag to a ship with radio communication intact. Admiral and staff picked their way through the flames to reach the forecastle whence they lowered themselves down ropes to a boat which took them to the light cruiser *Nagara* of the screen.

Carnage in the Japanese carriers

Only three dive-bombers from the *Enterprise* had attacked the flagship. The remainder of the air group, 34 dive-bombers, all concentrated on the *Kaga*. Of four bombs which scored direct hits, the first burst just forward of the superstructure, blowing up a petrol truck which stood there, and the sheet of flame which swept the bridge killed everyone on it, including the captain. The other three bombs falling among the massed aircraft on the flight deck set the ship ablaze and started the same fatal train of fires and explosions as in the *Akagi*. Within a few minutes, the situation was so beyond control that the senior surviving officer ordered the transfer of the Emperor's portrait to an attendant destroyer – the custom obligatory when a ship was known to be doomed, and conducted with strict naval ceremony. The *Kaga* was to survive for several hours, nevertheless.

Simultaneously, with the *Akagi* and *Kaga*, the *Soryu* had also been reeling under a devastating attack. Leslie of the *Yorktown* was leading veterans of the Coral Sea battle, probably the most battle-experienced aviators in the American navy at that time. With deadly efficiency they dived in three waves in quick succession from the starboard bow, the starboard quarter, and the port quarter, released their bombs and climbed away without a single casualty. Out of the shower of 1,000-pound bombs, three hit. The first penetrated to the hangar deck and the explosion lifted the steel platform of the lift, folding it back against the bridge. The others landed among the massed aircraft, causing the whole ship to be engulfed in flames. It took Captain Ryusaku Yanaginoto only 20 minutes to decide to order 'Abandon Ship' to save his crew from being burnt alive, though the *Soryu*, like her sisters, was to survive for some hours yet.

Thus, in five brief, searing minutes, half of Japan's entire fleet carrier force, her naval *corps d'élite*, had been shattered. For the time being the *Hiryu*, some miles away, remained untouched. She was to avenge her sisters in some measure before the day was over; but before going on to tell of her part in the battle let us follow the remainder to their deaths in the blue Pacific waters.

On board the *Akagi*, though the bomb damage was confined at first to her flight and hangar decks and her machinery spaces remained intact, the fires fed by aviation petrol from aircraft and from fuel lines were beyond the capacity of the Japanese crew to master. They fought them for seven hours

but by 1715 Captain Aoki had decided there was no hope of saving his ship. The Emperor's portrait was transferred to a destroyer and the ship was abandoned. Permission was asked of the C-in-C to hasten her end but it was not until nearly dawn on the following day – when Yamamoto at last fully understood the fullness of the Japanese defeat – that he gave his approval and the *Akagi* was sent to the bottom by torpedoes from a destroyer.

Petrol-fed fires similarly swept the *Kaga* and defeated all efforts to save her. Lying stopped and burning she became the target for three torpedoes from the *Nautilus* which, after her earlier adventure, had surfaced and chased after the Japanese carriers. Even the stationary target, however, was too much for the unreliable torpedoes with which the Americans were at that time equipped. Of three fired, two missed, and the third struck but failed to explode. At 1640 orders were given to abandon the *Kaga*, and at 1925 two great explosions tore her asunder and sent her to the bottom.

The *Soryu's* story was a similar one, of intermittent internal explosions from within the great mass of flame and smoke which she had become. When Captain Yanaginoto gave the order 'Abandon Ship', he determined to immolate himself, dying in the flames or going down with her. A party of his men returning on board with the intention of persuading him or, if necessary, of forcing him to save himself, fell back

abashed at the heroic, determined figure of their captain, standing sword in hand, facing forward, awaiting his end. They left him to his chosen fate. As they did so they heard him singing the Japanese national anthem. Yanaginoto's resolution held fast till 1913 hours when at last the *Soryu* and the bodies of 718 of her crew slid beneath the surface.

Much had taken place in the meantime before Nagumo's three aircraft-carriers suffered their death throes. The first survivors of the American strike groups to land back on their ships made it clear that one Japanese carrier had not yet been located. This was the *Hiryu* which, at the time of the attack, had become separated from the remainder. Admiral Fletcher therefore launched a ten-plane search from the *Yorktown*, and sent up a defensive patrol of a dozen Wildcats. It was none too soon. A few minutes before noon, the *Yorktown's* radar gave the warning of enemy planes coming in from the west.

These were the *Hiryu's* attack group of 18 dive-bombers and six fighters, led by Lieutenant Michio Kobayashi, a veteran leader who had taken part in every operation of the Nagumo force. As soon as they had flown off, a further strike of ten torpedo bombers and six Zeros, to be led by the redoubtable Tomonaga, was ranged up. Kobayashi's force had followed some of the *Yorktown's* attack planes back and now concentrated on Fletcher's flagship. Wildcats – for once outnumbering the escorting

Above: The major US casualty at Midway, the *Yorktown*, lies dead in the water

Below: A crippling collision with another heavy cruiser, US bombs and engine-room

196

t was later sunk by an enemy submarine

Zeros—broke through to get at the 'Vals', shooting down ten of them, including the leader. Of the eight which remained, two were knocked down by anti-aircraft fire from the cruiser screen.

The six survivors, however, showed that they had lost none of their skill as they creamed down on the carrier. One 'Val' broke up under anti-aircraft fire, but its bomb sped on to burst on the flight-deck, killing many men, and starting a hangar fire below. A second bomb plunged through the side of the funnel and burst inside, starting more fires. With three boiler uptakes smashed and the furnaces of five or six boilers extinguished, the carrier's speed fell away until, 20 minutes later, she came to a stop. A third bomb penetrated to the fourth deck where for a time a fire threatened the forward petrol tanks and magazines.

His flagship immobilised, her radio and radar knocked out, Admiral Fletcher transferred his flag to the cruiser *Astoria*, and ordered the *Portland* to take the aircraft-carrier in tow. The damage-control organization worked wonders, however. Before the towline had been passed, the *Yorktown* was under way again and working up to 20 knots, and the refuelling of the fighters was in progress. Prospects seemed bright. Then a cruiser's radar picked up Tomonaga's air group, 40 miles away and coming in fast. There was just time to launch eight of the refuelling Wildcats to join the four already in the air, but they were unable to get

explosions sank the *Mikuma* at Midway

through the screen of fighters to get at the 'Kates'—though they shot down three of the 'Zeros'. A tremendous screen of bursting shells spread itself in front of the attackers, while the cruisers raised a barrage of splashes with their main armament, a wall of water columns through which it seemed impossible that the skimming 'Kates' could fly.

Yorktown fatally damaged

Five 'Kates' were shot down, but the remainder, coming in from four different angles, displayed all their deadly skill, boring doggedly in to drop their torpedoes at the point-blank range of 500 yards. It was impossible for the carrier to avoid them all. Two hit on her port side, tearing open the double-bottom fuel tanks and causing flooding which soon had her listing at 26 degrees. All power was lost, so that counter-flooding was impossible. It seemed that the *Yorktown* was about to capsize. At 1500, Captain Buckmaster ordered 'Abandon Ship'.

Meanwhile, however, the dive-bombers from Spruance's Task Force 16, operating some 40 miles to the north-east of the *Yorktown*, had wreaked vengeance on the *Hiryu*. Twenty-four Dauntlesses, of which ten had been transferred from the *Yorktown*, arrived overhead undetected soon after the few survivors of *Hiryu*'s attack had been recovered. The aircraft carrier circled and swerved to avoid the bombs from the plummeting dive-bombers, but in vain. Four of them hit, one of which blew the forward lift bodily on to the bridge. The others started the inevitable fires and explosions, and the same prolonged death agonies as the *Hiryu*'s sisters were still suffering. By 2123 she had come to a stop. Desperate efforts to subdue the flames went on through the night; but at 0230 the following morning she was abandoned to be torpedoed by her attendant destroyers.

When the night of June 4 closed over the four smoking Japanese carriers and over the crippled *Yorktown*, the battle of Midway was, in the main, over. Neither of the opposing commanders yet knew it, however, and manoeuvres and skirmishes were to continue for two more days. The Japanese commanders, except Nagumo, were slow to realise that the shattering of their four fleet carriers signified defeat and the end of the Midway operation. Admiral Kondo, with his two fast battleships, four heavy cruisers, and the light carrier *Zuiho* had set off to the help of Nagumo at midday on June 4, and soon afterwards Yamamoto was signalling to all his scattered forces to concentrate and attack the enemy. He himself, with the main body of his fleet, was coming up fast from the west bringing the 18-inch guns of the giant *Yamato* and the 16-inch ones of the *Nagato* and *Mutsu* to throw in their weight. Still underestimating his opponent, he was dreaming of a night encounter in which his immensely powerful fleet would overwhelm the American task force and avenge the losses of the previous day. The great 'fleet action' with battleships in stately line hurling huge shells at each other was still his hope and aim.

Such a concept had been forcibly removed from American naval strategy by the shambles of Pearl Harbor. Raymond Spruance, one of the greatest admirals to come to the fore during the war, was not to be lured within range of Yamamoto's battleships, above all at night, when his carriers, at this time untrained for night-flying, would be at a tremendous disadvantage. At sunset he turned away eastwards, aiming to take up a position on the following day from which he could either 'follow up retreating enemy forces or break up a landing attack on Midway'.

The Japanese C-in-C refused to credit the completeness of the disaster that had overtaken his fleet and the Midway plan until early on June 5 when, at 0255, he ordered a general retirement. Thus, when Spruance, after prudently steering eastwards to keep his distance from the still overwhelmingly superior Japanese surface fleet, and reversing course at midnight so as to be within supporting distance of Midway at daylight, sent a strike of 58 dive-bombers from his two ships during the afternoon of the 5th to seek out Yamamoto's Main Body, his airmen encountered nothing but a lone destroyer sent to search for the *Hiryu*.

Two final incidents remain to be briefly recounted. When Yamamoto ordered his general retirement, the squadron of four heavy cruisers of Admiral Kurita's Support Force, the *Kumano*, *Suzuya*, *Mikuma*, and *Mogami*, was to the westward of Midway, steering through the night to deliver a bombardment at dawn. They now swung round to reverse course full in view of the American submarine *Tambor*. As they steadied on their retirement course, from the flagship the *Tambor* was sighted in the moonlight ahead. The signal for an emergency turn to port was flashed down the line but was not taken in by the rear ship, *Mogami*. Failing to turn with the remainder she collided with the *Mikuma*, suffering serious damage which reduced her speed to 12 knots. Leaving the *Mikuma* and two destroyers to escort the cripple, Kurita hurried on with the remainder.

News of this attractive target soon reached Midway. Twelve army Flying Fortresses took off but were unable to locate it; but 12 Marine Corps dive-bombers sighted the long oil slick being trailed by the *Mikuma*, followed it up—and at 0805 dived to the attack. Their bombs failed to achieve direct hits, but the plane of Captain Richard E. Fleming crashed on the after turret of the *Mikuma*. Petrol fumes were sucked down into the cruiser's starboard engine-room and exploded, killing the whole engine-room crew.

The two cruisers nevertheless continued to limp slowly away, until the following day when Spruance, having abandoned hope of delivering another blow on Yamamoto's Main Fleet, was able to direct his dive-bombers on to them. The *Mikuma* was smothered and sunk, but the *Mogami* miraculously survived, heavily damaged, to reach the Japanese base at Truk.

While these events were taking place, far to the east the abandoned *Yorktown* had drifted crewless through the night of June 4/5. She was still afloat at noon the next day and it became clear she had been prematurely abandoned. A salvage party boarded her and she was taken in tow. Hopes of getting her to port were high until the Japanese submarine *I-168*, sent by Yamamoto for the purpose, found her, penetrated her anti-submarine screen, and put two torpedoes into her. At 0600 on June 7 the *Yorktown* sank at last.

At sundown on the previous day Spruance had turned his force back eastwards to meet his supply tankers. That the Battle of Midway was over was finally clear to all.

Japan's later warplanes

Japan's air forces went to war largely relying on the navy's Zero fighter, Kate torpedo-bomber, and Nell and Betty long-range bombers, and on the army's Oscar fighter and Sally bomber. Production of these machines was kept up to speed the 'Runaway Victory', and the newer designs were shelved. But after 18 months of the Pacific War the back of Japan's carrier fleet had been broken at Midway and her outermost conquests had already fallen to Allied 'island-hopping' offensives. Now the Japanese needed aircraft capable of operating more from shore bases than from aircraft-carriers, and the new aircraft were rushed ahead. The Zero was supplemented by the Jack, the Kate by the Jill and the Judy. For the army, the new single-engined Tony and the twin-engined Nick began to replace the ageing Oscar. A new long-range bomber—the Helen—was intended to replace the Sally, Nell, and Betty, but never did. Yet none of these aircraft, old or new, could halt the swelling flood of Lightnings, Thunderbolts, and Fortresses.

1. JUDY: Yokosuka D4Y-2 *Susei*
A navy carrier bomber, the Judy first saw service as a reconnaissance plane at Midway, was later used extensively, and finally—like most Japanese types—saw service as a Kamikaze. *Max speed:* 335 mph. *Range:* 1,320 miles. *Crew:* two. *Armament:* three 7·7-mm machine-guns; 1,100 lb of bombs

2. JACK: Mitsubishi J2M-3 *Raiden*
Designed as a single-seat shore-based interceptor fighter at the same time as the Zero, the Jack had so many teething troubles that it only entered service in small numbers. *Max speed:* 371 mph. *Range:* 650 miles. *Armament:* two 20-mm cannon, and two 7·1-mm machine-guns

5

6

7

8

3. MAVIS: Kawanishi H6K4-L Flying-boat
This was one of the more elderly Japanese long-range navy patrol bombers; it was an unarmed type, and the lessons learned from it resulted in the 'Emily', which was given five cannon and four MGs. Mavis was then relegated to transport duties. *Max speed:* 237 mph. *Range:* 4,000 miles. *Crew:* nine (plus 18 passengers)

4. IRVING: Nakajima JINI-S Gekko
Designed first as a fighter, then used by the navy in reconnaissance, then converted to a night fighter. It had a unique armament of two pairs of 20-mm cannon above and below the fuselage at an angle of 30°. *Max speed:* 315 mph. *Range:* 1,360 miles. *Crew:* two. *Armament:* four 20-mm cannon

5. TONY: Kawasaki Ki-61 Hien
When allied pilots first met Tony in action in 1943, it was thought to be a version of the German Me-109. Well armed and well protected, Tony was a formidable opponent; but its engine gave considerable trouble in service. *Max speed:* 348 mph. *Range:* 1,185 miles. *Armament:* two 20-mm cannon, and two 12·7-mm machine-guns

6. HELEN: Nakajima Ki-49 Donryu
Helen was an army heavy bomber, designed for use in the event of Japan going to war with Russia, but was first used in action in a raid on Darwin in 1943. It was never produced in great numbers. *Max speed:* 306 mph. *Range:* 1,490 miles. *Crew:* eight. *Armament:* one 20-mm cannon, five 7·7-mm machine-guns

7. JILL: Nakajima B6N-2 Tenzan
The Jill was the direct replacement for the Kate torpedo-bomber, and its first major action was the Battle of the Philippine Sea in June 1944. *Max speed:* 299 mph. *Range:* 1,600 miles. *Armament:* one 13-mm, one 7·9-mm machine-gun; one 1,764-lb torpedo OR six 220-lb bombs

8. NICK: Kawasaki Ki-45 Toryu
The Nick was the first twin-engined fighter to enter service with the Japanese army air force; the Allies first met it in action over New Guinea in 1943, and it was also used in home defence duties. *Max speed:* 340 mph. *Range:* 932 miles. *Crew:* two. *Armament:* varied, but a typical combination was: one 37-mm, two 20-mm cannon, and one 7·7-mm machine-gun

GUADALCANAL:
JAPAN'S FIRST LAND DEFEAT

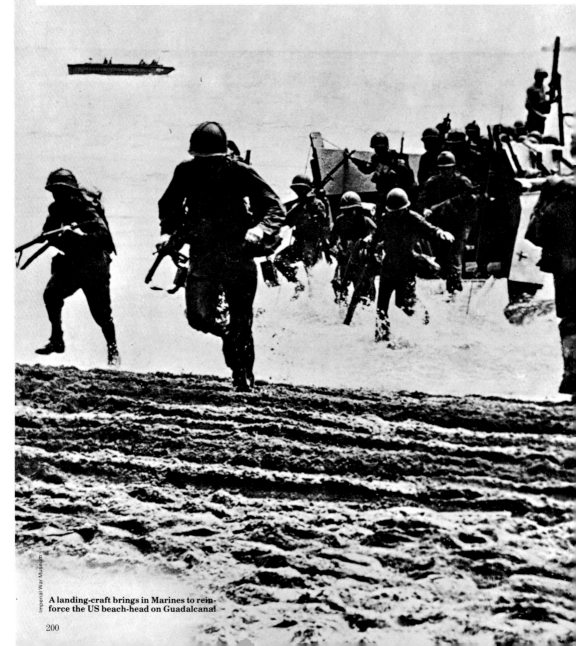

A landing-craft brings in Marines to reinforce the US beach-head on Guadalcanal

Imperial War Museum

At 0641 on the morning of August 7, 1942 – eight months to the day after Pearl Harbor – the order to 'land the Marines' passed around the armada of transports and landing-craft gathered off the beaches of Guadalcanal. US land forces were, for the first time in the Pacific War, taking the offensive against the all-conquering might of the Rising Sun.

The object of the exercise, Guadalcanal, was a small, humid, hilly island in the Solomons group of the South Pacific, sitting astride the north-eastern approaches to Australia. Fever-ridden and almost uninhabitable, it was, nonetheless, a priceless possession for whichever side could hold it. And in early May, 1942, units of the Japanese army had occupied both Guadalcanal and the smaller neighbouring island of Tulagi, a fine anchorage from which to dominate the area. It was only in June, however, that coast-watchers reported up to 3,000 Japanese soldiers had moved from their base on Tulagi to begin building an airstrip on Guadalcanal.

Occupying one of the few patches of flat ground in the whole of the Solomons group, this airstrip at Henderson Field immediately presented a major strategic threat to the Allies. From there, enemy air forces would be able to dominate the skies on the approaches to Australia from America, thus isolating that continent as a base for future Allied operations in the Pacific. Clearly this situation could not long be tolerated, but Admiral King – the newly-appointed US naval chief – stressed that to merely destroy enemy installations and retire was not enough. Instead, he convinced Washington, the Solomons must be *denied* to the Japanese.

As a result, the 1st US Marine Division, reinforced by Marine Raider units and paratroop units, was chosen to do the job. Although nominally up to war strength, this Division was, in fact, made-up of thousands of raw recruits and a small core of seasoned veterans. Under its commander, Major-General Vandegrift, the Division left its North Carolina training base in late May, 1942; and it wasn't until June 25 that Vandegrift was actually informed that his men were destined

for combat on August 1. By that time half his Division had not even arrived at its assembly-point in New Zealand.

Things were no better at sea. The cruiser force comprised the Australian ships *Hobart*, *Canberra* and *Australia*, and the US ships *Chicago* and *San Juan* backed up by nine destroyers under the command of Britain's Rear-Admiral Crutchley. Also present were Vice-Admiral Fletcher's US carriers *Saratoga*, *Wasp* and *Enterprise*, screened by the battleship *North Carolina*. These ships and Rear-Admiral Turner's South Pacific Amphibious Force of grey transports had never before worked together . . . and had no experience of amphibious landings.

Nonetheless, after postponements of D-Day first to the 4th and then the 7th, rehearsals of the assault went ahead off Koro in Fiji for four days from July 26. Bombing, bombardment, disembarkation, air-support, ship-to-shore and air-to-ground practices . . . all were chaotic. The whole rehearsal was described by senior officers as 'a fiasco'.

But there was no more time. On the morning of August 7, the Australian coastwatchers in their hill-top hide-outs saw the sea off Guadalcanal filled with the most powerful amphibious attack force at that time ever assembled. In 36-man boat teams, thousands of Marines arrived on the beaches in regulated waves.

Japanese resistance, amazingly, was non-existent. The invaders had achieved complete tactical surprise. Had they in fact met opposition in any force, the outcome of this first, hastily-planned Allied amphibious assault of the Pacific War might have been disastrously different.

Instead, by the evening of the 7th, troops had been landed, supplies had been piled high in chaotic heaps on the beaches, transport sections had moved off blindly into the jungle, and soldiers – exhausted by the tropic heat and often separated from their units – wandered around dazed and confused. The bitter, six-month struggle for Guadalcanal had begun amid a god-sent but ominous calm.

While there was no fighting on Guadalcanal in the first 24 hours, it was a different story on the neighbouring islands. On the larger island General Vandegrift had, as events had shown, picked as his point of disembarkation a spot where there were no Japanese and his men could go in unopposed. On the smaller islands he could expect no such bonus and it was therefore against these that he threw his more seasoned units led by officers with previous combat experience.

Colonel Merritt Edson, of 1st Marine Raiders, who was to seize Tulagi, ordered his men to strip down to minimum combat equipment – 'Don't worry about food,' he told them, 'Japs eat it too. All you have to do is get it.' Although their swift landing tactics got them established on the island before noon, stiff Japanese resistance made it impossible to capture the whole island before nightfall, and during the night the Japanese, liberally equipped with light mortars, grenade throwers, and heavy and light machine-guns, counterattacked. Four times they threw themselves against the Raiders and four times they were thrown back. Although most of the Japanese garrison died in these night attacks, it took the Raiders most of August 8 to eliminate the survivors.

The fighting was even tougher on the islet of Gavutu. The islet had been bombed from the air and shelled by ships' guns, but as the paratroops moved inshore, it became clear that the bombardment had had no effect on the defending Japanese in their reinforced dugouts and caves. The paratroops were met by a hail of fire. Their commanders asked for covering gunfire from the warships offshore, but because the waters around Gavutu were uncharted, none of the warships could move in close enough to give pin-point cover. Only after heavy losses did the paratroops secure a foothold.

On the neighbouring islet of Tanambogo, connected to Gavutu by a causeway, the story was grimmer still; the assault troops and their boats were shot to pieces by the defending Japanese before they touched land. Reinforcements were asked for and arrived on the morning of August 8. The Japanese were blasted and blown out of the caves and dugouts on Gavutu but there remained the problem of Tanambogo. Before crossing over from Gavutu, the American commander asked for two preliminary air-strikes to soften up Tanambogo's defenders, but neither air-strike made any impression. The heaviest casualties were suffered by the American assault troops poised on Gavutu, by bombs that fell short of their target. In despair their commander called on the US destroyer *Buchanan* to open fire on the Japanese in their caves and let go with everything she had. The bombardment was devastating and within minutes assault parties had captured Tanambogo.

On Guadalcanal the Americans had still encountered no Japanese but progress towards the airfield continued to be slow. Only as a result of General Vandegrift's unrelenting drive did the first American patrols eventually reach the airfield late in the afternoon of August 8. The Japanese construction teams and their Naval Landing Force protectors had fled into the jungle after the bombardment in the early hours of August 7. The Japanese had obviously been taken completely by surprise, for there were signs of panic everywhere – uniforms, shirts, caps, chopsticks, helmets, mosquito netting, rifles, teacups, and rice bowls, their contents half-consumed, littered the ground.

It had taken the Americans much longer to reach the airfield than General Vandegrift had hoped, and the speed and control of unloading at the main disembarkation point had shown up serious shortcomings. Moreover, the heavy casualties the Americans had suffered on Tulagi, Gavutu, and Tanambogo – in some cases higher than 20% – showed what tough and resourceful fighters the Japanese were in defence even when outmanned and outgunned.

Still the airfield on Guadalcanal and the islands in the immediate vicinity of the part of the coast of Guadalcanal where the airfield was situated, were in American hands. Despite delays, deficiencies, and mistakes the operation had achieved its objective of denying the Japanese a base from which to cut Allied supply lines and isolate Australia. There was immense relief in Australia, Washington, and London. But the feeling was not to last long. For, on the night of August 8/9, a Japanese cruiser force shattered the Allied naval forces under Admiral Crutchley, and the transports were forced to withdraw.

By the late afternoon of August 9, the last of Admiral Turner's ships had disappeared. The Marines were on their own.

Could the Marines hold out?

The position facing General Vandegrift after Admiral Turner's departure was unenviable. He and his 1st Marine Division held an enclave consisting of a partially completed airfield surrounded by a few acres, on an island covered with dense, inhospitable jungle, in which lurked the remnants of the original Japanese construction and occupation forces. The waters around Guadalcanal were dominated by the Japanese navy. Indeed, in the days that followed, Japanese warships usually patrolled just off his enclave outside the range of his guns. On one occasion a Japanese submarine surfaced and in a leisurely fashion shelled the Marines' position on the beach and on another a Japanese cruiser landed a 200-

Below: The six-month battle for Guadalcanal has since become a Marine legend

Camera Press

strong advance echelon and supplies along the coast in broad daylight. Moreover, constant Japanese bombing attacks on 'Henderson' (as the airfield came to be known) and the American-held area around it, never allowed General Vandegrift and his men to forget for long who was in control of the skies above Guadalcanal. Above all, the general knew that the Japanese were bound to try and annihilate his division sooner or later.

His main concern, therefore, was to build up his defences against assault both from the sea and from inland, and to complete the airfield so that it could be used by American aircraft to give him his own air cover. His difficulties in pursuing both these aims were immense, largely because so much essential equipment had sailed away in the holds of Admiral Turner's transports – only 18 spools of barbed wire had been landed; there were no anti-tank or anti-personnel mines, and no tools like axes, saws, shovels, machetes, or picks. Fortunately the equipment left behind by the Japanese – which included four heavy-duty tractors, six road-rollers, 12 trucks, and two petrol locomotives with hopper cars – made good these deficiences to some extent and within days the airfield was completed and work was begun on two subsidiary strips. On August 20 the first American aircraft – 19 Wildcat fighters and 12 Dauntless dive-bombers launched from an aircraft-carrier well to the south of Guadalcanal – landed on Henderson Field. A few hours later, shortly after midnight, before the aircraft could go into action, the Japanese attacked from the east.

Radio Tokyo had made no secret of its answer to the question of what fate had in store for the Marines on Guadalcanal. Admiral Mikawa (the area commander), it announced in triumph, had routed 'the remnants of Anglo-American naval strength in the Pacific and isolated Australia'. The Marines were like 'summer insects which have dropped into the fire by themselves'.

Such exaggerated claims may be excusable in propagandists intent on bolstering the morale of their own side and striking fear into the heart of the enemy. But what was astonishing in this instance was that these claims reflected the attitude of many senior Japanese staff officers. Men trained to assess every given situation coolly and without passion and then to lay their plans with care and attention to detail, refused to take the Marines on Guadalcanal seriously. It could, in their view, be no more than a reconnaissance in force, a manoeuvre to distract and annoy, and as such it was an insolent affront to the honour of Japanese arms which had to be washed away in blood without delay. No attempt was made to obtain an accurate picture of American strength and dispositions. Lieutenant-General Hyakutake, in command of XVII Army in the South Pacific area, was ordered to 'eliminate' the Americans, and he allocated the XXXV Infantry Brigade under Major-General Kawaguchi for the purpose but since the brigade had still to be assembled, it was decided to send in at once, in two echelons, the only units immediately available – Colonel Ichiki's regiment and a special naval landing force.

Colonel Ichiki landed with the first echelon on August 18. He was a distinguished officer who had fought in China in the 1930s, with

Imperial War Museum

Above: Marines embark for the beaches

LCI(L): landing-craft (infantry, large). With or without opening bows, these ocean-going craft were developed for use in the vast spaces of the Pacific. **Capacity:** 6 officers and 182 troops *or* 75 tons of cargo. **Range:** 4000 miles at 12 knots. **Armament:** 1 × 40-mm, 4 × 20-mm guns. **Displacement:** 280 tons (loaded)

The six-month battle for Guadalcanal

1942 **August 7:** US Marines land on Guadalcanal, meeting no opposition. But there is savage fighting on the neighbouring islands of Tulagi, Gavutu, and Tanambogo, before they are occupied.
August 8: American forces reach Henderson Field, to find that the Japanese have fled.
August 8/9: The Battle of Savo is fought at sea off Guadalcanal. Admiral Turner's transports are forced to retire, taking much of the Marines' equipment.
August 18: First Japanese reinforcements, Colonel Ichiki's regiment lands.
August 20: Henderson Field receives its first aircraft – 19 Wildcats and 12 Dauntlesses.
August 21/22: *Battle of the Tenaru:* Japanese forces attack across the Ilu and Tenaru rivers. They are driven back with heavy losses but continue to harass the

Marines. General Vandegrift sends his reserve battalion around behind them, and the Japanese force is driven into the sea. Colonel Ichiki commits hara-kiri.
August 23/24: The Battle of the Eastern Solomons is fought at sea off Guadalcanal.
September 7: US Marine Raiders land at Taivu, capturing stores and equipment, and gaining intelligence about an impending Japanese attack.
September 12: Japanese bombers attack Henderson Field and the southern perimeter of the defences.
September 13: Japanese launch further heavy attacks, but they are driven back after losing 1,200 men.
September/October: Japanese II Division and the headquarters of XVII Army HQ are transferred to Guadalcanal. Meanwhile the

US 7th Marines, the 164th Infantry Regiment, and other units reinforce the American forces.
October 9: The Battle of Cape Esperance is fought at sea off Guadalcanal.
October 23/24: Two major Japanese assaults are launched on the south of Henderson Field but lack of communication means that they are uncoordinated, and the Americans defeat them piecemeal. Battle of Santa Cruz is fought off Guadalcanal.
December 1/15: US 1st Marine Division is relieved by the 14th Army Corps.
December 31: Apalled by their mounting losses the Japanese begin to plan the withdrawal of XVII Army.

1943 **February 1/9:** The 'Tokyo Express' takes the remnant of the once-proud Japanese XVII Army.

Behind the Allied victory

Even in the early days of the Pacific War, when the Japanese had the numerical advantage, they tended to split their forces and thus fall prey to the compact and well-deployed American task forces. But the American victory in the Pacific was due as much to her transports and replenishment craft as to the main arm of her sea power, her mighty aircraft-carriers. It was also due in no small measure to the spectacular losses inflicted by US submarines and surface raiders on Japanese transports, replenishment craft, and merchant shipping in general. Here we show two typical support ships—a transport and an oiler—an *Essex* class carrier, a chart showing the Allied success against Japanese tonnage, and a plan view of a typical task group (a component of a task force). It was these four elements—carrier superiority, huge logistic support, destruction of enemy shipping, and superior tactics—which helped to give the Americans the upper hand in the Pacific

A typical US task group, protected by a screen of destroyers and an inner ring of cruisers, contained at its heart its main striking force: the aircraft of the carriers, and the guns of the battleships

Heavy carrier
Light carrier
Battleship
Light cruiser
AA Light cruiser
Destroyer

Type C2-5-B1 Attack Cargo Ship. The attack cargo ship, essential for amphibious operations, could carry troops, their inshore landing craft, plus follow-up supplies, ammunition, spare parts, and so on. For operations in the Pacific, the US Navy had some 95 to 100 of these craft. *Length (overall):* 459 feet. *Beam:* 63 feet. *Armament:* one 5-inch gun, and eight 40-mm AA guns. *Crew (plus troops):* 404. *Displacement:* 6,556 tons

US Fleet Oiler T3-S2-A1. The huge distances involved in the Pacific War made some method of refuelling the fleet at sea indispensable. It also meant that the oiler, full, became an extremely important ship, and a much-prized target for submarine captains. *Length (overall):* 553 feet. *Beam:* 75 feet. *Armament:* four 5-inch guns, eight 40-mm guns. *Crew:* 304. *Displacement:* 7,356 tons.

The *Essex* class (the *Wasp* is shown here) became the standard US fleet carrier of the war and made up the core of the fast carrier forces. It introduced the outboard elevator on the port side. *Length:* 820 feet (waterline), 872 (overall). *Max Beam:* 147 feet. *Max Speed:* 32 knots. *Armament:* 12 5-inch guns, 44 to 68 40-mm AA guns, and 100 aircraft *Crew:* 3,500. *Displacement:* 27,100 tons

The Diminishing Asset: At the outbreak of war the Japanese had afloat some 6,000,000 tons of shipping, but by 1945 this had declined to 1,500,000 tons. With much Japanese shipping devoted to the hopeless task of maintaining their isolated island garrisons, the rate of sinkings by the Allies rose sharply to coincide with each major campaign. The result was a crescendo of destruction at a time when the Japanese could least afford it

TOTAL JAPANESE TONNAGE AFLOAT (million tons)

JAPANESE TONNAGE LOSSES (Ships over 500 tons)

Thousand tons

6·0 5·8 4·9 2·7 1·5

1941 1942 1943 1944 1945

D J F M A M J J A S O N D J F M A M J J A S O N D J F M A M J J A S O N D J F M A M J J A S O N D J F M A M J J

GUADALCANAL & NEW GUINEA CAMPAIGNS

SOLOMONS & GILBERTS CAMPAIGNS

MARSHALLS CAMPAIGN: TRUK & PALAU CARRIER RAIDS

MARIANAS CAMPAIGN

PHILIPPINES CAMPAIGN

OKINAWA CAMPAIGN

This cross-section view of an *Essex* class carrier, taken from the lift looking aft, shows many of the features of the improved design of this class. Two of them are the reinforced armour at and below the waterline, and the oil storage tanks well isolated from vulnerable spots

1 Lift
2 20- & 40-mm AA guns
3 Two stacked lifeboats
4 Fan motors
5 Airframe workshop
6 Workshop deck & lift machinery
7 Ammo & aircraft stores
8 Air-conditioning plants
9 Main hangar (aft)
10 AA guns
11 AA guns
12 Servicing hangar
13 Aero engine stores
14 Engine servicing shop
15 Port ammunition stores
16 Emergency lighting plant
17 Engine-cooling motor
18 Steam pipes to turbines
19 Turbines
20 Fireproof coffer-dam
21 Aviation spirit tank
22 Oil fuel tanks

Above: Japanese troops in the Shortland Islands embark to reinforce Guadalcanal

years of experience as a battalion and regimental commander, but on this occasion he disregarded all he had learned. Japanese Intelligence had told him that the Marines were no more than 2,000 strong and that their morale was low. In any case Colonel Ichiki was one of many Japanese officers who believed firmly that man for man the Japanese were infinitely superior to the Americans who were only effective when they had superior equipment. He therefore decided that he had no cause to wait even for his second echelon; he could wipe out this 'jungle beach-head' at one stroke.

In the early hours of August 21, after a brief preparatory mortar bombardment of the American positions on General Vandegrift's eastern perimeter, Colonel Ichiki's men who had waded across the Ilu and Tenaru rivers, threw themselves at the Marines in a bayonet charge. They were met and stopped by a deadly wall of fire from carefully sited positions, but somehow Ichiki managed to rally his men and launch a second bayonet charge, only to be stopped again. This time he decided to withdraw across the Ilu.

Only a crack formation like Ichiki's could have survived such a mauling without disintegrating, but the accurate and often telling fire to which the Marines were subjected from across the river on the following morning, told them that they were still facing a fighting unit that had to be reckoned with. General Vandegrift, who had had reports

that further Japanese reinforcements were on the way, decided that Ichiki's men constituted too great a danger to be left where they were. He ordered one of his reserve battalions to cross the river and swing north in an enveloping movement.

By early afternoon Ichiki's men were encircled, and the final phase of what came to be known among the Marines as the 'Battle of the Tenaru' began. Bombed and strafed by the American aircraft that had landed at Henderson Field on the previous day, and bombarded at short range by artillery, the Japanese were pushed back slowly towards the sea from three sides. Finally, the few light tanks which had been landed with Vandegrift's division moved in, their steel treads mangling and crushing the living, the dying, and the dead. But still the Japanese refused to surrender. 'The rear of the tanks,' General Vandegrift wrote in his report, 'looked like meat grinders.' Even after organised fighting had ceased, the Japanese survivors did not allow themselves to be taken prisoner. 'The wounded will wait until men come up to examine them,' Vandegrift wrote, 'and blow themselves and the other fellow to pieces with a hand grenade.' At 'the Tenaru' the Marines learned what the Japanese meant by total resistance, resistance to the last breath of the last man.

Only a handful of men, led by Colonel Ichiki, got away to Taivu further along the

coast to the east. There the Colonel ceremoniously tore up his regiment's colour and committed *hara-kiri*.

The victory at the Tenaru lives on in the history of the US Marine Corps, but General Vandegrift knew that it did not answer the question of whether the Marines could hold out. It was merely the prelude to other stronger attempts by the Japanese. In fact in the last ten days of August, a far more menacing force consisting of the late Colonel Ichiki's second echelon and General Kawaguchi's XXXV Brigade were waiting to be taken to Guadalcanal to finish the job. The main problem was how to get them there. Rear-Admiral Tanaka, who had been made commander of the Reinforcement Force with his base in the Shortlands to the north-west of Guadalcanal, understood the difficulties. The second echelon of Ichiki's detachment, which he had been ordered to take to Guadalcanal in transports screened by a light cruiser and destroyers, had been spotted by aircraft from Henderson Field, bombed, and had had to turn back.

The arrival of the aircraft on Henderson Field had drastically altered the situation, the Japanese, Tanaka pointed out to General Kawaguchi, could only use the waters around Guadalcanal safely between dusk and dawn, and he therefore planned to move the Japanese army to Guadalcanal in a series of what were aptly named 'Rat runs' using fast destroyers as transports at night. Kawaguchi at first insisted on slower and more cumbersome barges being used as transport, and one barge 'run' that was organised against Tanaka's advice, ended in disaster. In the end Tanaka had his way and by the end of August, the 'Rat runs' were dashing back and forth with the precision of express trains, while the Marine positions were regularly bombarded from the sea.

General Vandegrift was aware of the gradual Japanese build-up to the east and west of his position. He brought Colonel Edson's crack Marine Raiders and the paratroops over from Tulagi and after dark on September 7 sent the Raiders by sea on a reconnaissance in force to Taivu, one of the main Japanese bases. Their foray was a complete success: they found only communications and headquarters personnel at the base who promptly fled into the jungle. They also found valuable stores and provisions which they brought back with

Type 99-1 7·7-mm Heavy Machine-Gun. This standard Japanese weapon was developed from the French Hotchkiss design. **Action:** gas-operated. **Coolant:** air. **Length:** 42·4 inches. **Ammunition:** 30-round clips. **Rate of fire:** 550 rpm

Browning ·50-inch M-2 Machine-Gun. This US infantry support weapon was also used in an AA role. **Action:** recoil. **Coolant:** air. **Weight:** 82 lb. **Length:** 65 inches. **Ammunition:** metal link belt, 100-round units. **Rate of fire:** 450 rpm

them. But the most valuable thing they brought back was information about the strength of the forces they would soon have to face and the news that General Kawaguchi had already moved off into the jungle with the bulk of his force. The second Japanese attack could not be long delayed, and General Vandegrift calculated that the main assault would be launched against the ridge to the south of Henderson Field. It was to this ridge that Vandegrift moved the Raiders and the paratroops, with his reserve – a Marine battalion – immediately behind them. He had no other uncommitted troops.

The Battle of Bloody Ridge

At noon on September 12, when Japanese bombers heavily bombed not Henderson Field, but the ridge south of the airfield, Vandegrift knew that his calculations about Japanese intentions had been correct. Shortly after darkness a Japanese cruiser and three destroyers started shelling the ridge, and when their gunfire ceased, Kawaguchi's troops began their probing. They cut off one Raider platoon but it fought back into the American lines.

When daylight came the Americans assumed that the Japanese had only been testing. They would have been heartened if they had known that Kawaguchi had intended his attack of the previous night to be decisive. His plan had been to attack the

ridge with three battalions while his other units pinned down the Americans on the western and eastern flanks of his perimeter. But his long and arduous march had exhausted his troops, cut his communications with other units of his command, and deprived him of effective control. Despite these handicaps, however, he plunged ahead as recklessly as Ichiki had done before him and rigidly stuck to the order to attack on September 12.

At 2100 hours on September 13, Kawaguchi renewed his assault. As his two battalions – almost 2,000 men – rushed up the slopes of the ridge, Marine mortars sited in defilade poured shells into the assault waves as fast as loaders could slide them down the hot tubes. Marine artillery just to the rear of the Raiders pumped round after round into the attackers while seven Japanese destroyers shelled Henderson Field, which was illuminated by Japanese flares. On the ridge the Raiders' defences were bent but not broken, and eventually the Japanese fell back. Before long they returned in an assault as fierce as the first. Again the defences were dented but not broken; and again the Japanese fell back.

Two hours later, after a preparatory mortar bombardment which cut the Raiders' communications with Vandegrift and supporting artillery, the Japanese swept forward to within 1,000 yards of Henderson

Field, only to be beaten back after some of the most ferocious fighting on Guadalcanal. They launched two more attacks before daybreak noticeably weaker than the first three, and when cannon-firing fighters from Henderson Field strafed the fringes of the jungle below the ridge, Kawaguchi decided to withdraw. He had over 1,200 officers and men killed, missing, and wounded. Hungry and plagued by disease the disorganised remnants of the XXXV Brigade, carrying only their rifles, clawed their way through the jungle for eight grim days to Point Cruz, west of Henderson Field.

The Raiders and the paratroops, too, had suffered heavily. Of slightly over 750 men who had landed on August 7, the Raiders had lost 234 casualties, and of 377 paratroops, 212 had been killed or wounded. But as far as the Marines were concerned, the question whether they could hold Guadalcanal, had been answered in the affirmative.

Imperial General Headquarters in Tokyo did not share the Marines' view. The XXXVIII Division, veterans of Hong Kong, Java, and Sumatra, were ordered to proceed to the South Pacific to join Lieutenant-General Hyakutake's XVII Army. In the meantime, the II Division under Lieutenant-General Maruyama, which was already in the area, was to be transported to Guadalcanal. Operations on

Below: A US Stuart light tank in action

Below: Fighting in the jungles of Guadalcanal was necessarily at close quarters

Keystone

207

Above: By November, fatigue and strain were showing on the faces of the US Marines. Below: The object of the bloody exercise – Henderson Field airstrip

Below: Wary of enemy snipers, a Marine patrol advances beyond the defence zone

New Guinea against Port Moresby were to be suspended so that all naval, air, and military resources could be concentrated on recapturing Guadalcanal, and General Hyakutake transferred XVII Army HQ to the island, to control a total force of some 20,000 men – including a regiment and three batteries of heavy artillery, a mortar battalion, and a tank company. In the next six weeks Admiral Tanaka's 'Rat run' or 'Tokyo Night Express' was busier than ever, and the Marines were bombarded every night from the sea.

Fortunately General Vandegrift, too, received reinforcements: the 7th Marines, an artillery battalion, motor transport companies, communications personnel, and later 164th Infantry Regiment, US Army – more than 6,000 men altogether, bringing his total strength to over 23,000. And equally vital the air force on Henderson Field was strengthened considerably. On paper Vandegrift's force looked impressive, in practice, it was less so. Although battle casualties had not yet reached 1,000, large numbers of Marines suffered from malnutrition, dysentery, virulent fungus infections, exposure, and plain exhaustion. Elsewhere, in fact, over a third of the men would have been unfit for combat.

On October 23 the Japanese II Division – consisting of some eight battalions totalling 5,600 troops, attacked the eastern perimeter in force with tanks across the Matanikau river. Concentrated artillery fire brought their advance to a bloody halt. Then, 24 hours later, General Maruyama attacked with the main force of more than 7,000 men from the south. For two days the Japanese flung themselves against the ridges to the south of Henderson Field – at one stage there was a Japanese enclave inside the perimeter – and then, like Kawaguchi's brigade, they sank back into the jungle, decimated and exhausted, having lost 3,500 men.

What had happened was that Japanese communications had broken down once again. Maruyama's approach march through the jungle – which had begun on October 16 – had been slower and more arduous than he had expected, and the artillery and mortars had had to be abandoned. Twice Maruyama had to postpone his offensive, and the second time, news of the postponement did not reach the Japanese commander on the Matanikau. Instead of being simultaneous, the two assaults took place

24 hours apart and General Vandegrift operating on interior lines, was able to defeat each in turn.

General Vandegrift had now defeated three attempts by the Japanese to dislodge him, and both the Americans and th Japanese had to face the problem of what to do next. For Vandegrift and Admiral Halsey, who had recently replaced Admiral Ghormley as Area Commander, there wa no doubt about the answer: it was time to go over to the offensive and drive wha remained of the XVII Army out of Guadal canal. It was equally obvious to both officer that the 1st Marine Division, after all it ha been through, was not the ideal instrumen for a long, harsh, and bitter offensive Fresher and bigger units were required. An so after spending November in extendin the perimeter and reducing threatenin Japanese outposts around it in preparatio for future offensive action, General Vande grift and the 1st Marine Division were re lieved at the beginning of December, an their place taken by the 25th Infantry Divi sion, US Army, the 2nd Marine Division and the America Division – all combine as 14th Corps under General Patch.

For the Japanese the problem was whethe to go on trying to wrest Henderson Field an the shattered coconut groves around it fron the Americans. Imperial General Head quarters refused to accept defeat; fres divisions and brigades from distant part of the Empire were allocated to XVII Arm and Lieutenant-General Sano's XXVI Division was ordered to Guadalcanal, i preparation for a fourth determined attemp to drive out the Americans to be launche about the middle of January 1943. But i mid-November 1942 a US naval squadro despite crippling losses, stopped a Japanes squadron from bombarding Henderson Field and neutralising its air force, and th Henderson Field aircraft, saved by thi gallant action, pounced on a convoy of 1 transports in which the bulk of Genera Sano's division was being taken to Guadal canal. Six transports were sunk, one wa crippled, and four had to be beached. Onl 2,000 men, most of them without equip ment, reached Guadalcanal. The drain i men and resources, Imperial General Head quarters decided reluctantly after muc argument, was too great to sustain an longer. Since August 7, the Japanese ha lost 65 combat ships and more than 80 aircraft. On December 31, 1942, the Empero gave his approval to the withdrawal of th XVII Army from Guadalcanal.

General Hyakutake accepted the orde reluctantly. As he withdrew to the east 14th Corps learned how tough and re sourceful even starving and ill-equippe Japanese troops could be in defensive jungl warfare. At no time during January an early February were the Americans able t upset the pace and timing of the withdrawa and between February 1 and 9 the des troyers of the 'Tokyo Night Express' too off what remained of the XVII Army – 11,00 men, only a fraction of those who had arrive to drive the Americans into the sea but sti a fighting force destined to return to d battle another day.

For the Americans and their allies th successful seizure and defence of Guadal canal brought immense advantages. Austra lia and New Zealand were safe, and Allie forces now stood on the flank of the Palau Truk/Marshalls line, the outer cordon of th Japanese empire.

GUADALCANAL:
THE SEA BATTLES

The struggle of the Marines on Guadalcanal was accompanied by an
equally bloody campaign at sea to intercept the 'Tokyo Express'
and secure control of the approaches. In one disastrous action
alone—the Battle of Savo Island—the Allied naval force was
shattered; at the Battle of Santa Cruz on October 23/24 the large
carriers on both sides were temporarily eliminated; and in a series
of battles in November, Japanese ships scored notable victories over
American cruisers and destroyers. In the end both sides lost 24
warships of roughly equal tonnage off Guadalcanal—but the
Americans were able to accept such attrition far
more easily than the Japanese . . .

A Japanese dive-bomber swoops on USS
Hornet while a torpedo plane circles—
Battle of Santa Cruz

1. SAVO ISLAND – August 8/9, 1942

A Japanese cruiser force under Vice-Admiral Mikawa advances down 'The Slot' to attack the American transports unloading off Guadalcanal. An Allied cruiser force under Rear-Admiral Crutchley RN, divided into three squadrons, patrols the approaches around Savo Island. 0100 hours: The Japanese cruisers slip past the destroyers *Blue* and *Ralph Talbot*. 0138 hours: The cruisers *Canberra* and *Chicago* are sighted and disabled with accurate gunfire. When the *Vincennes*, *Quincy*, and *Astoria* intervene they too are disabled. The Japanese then retire damaging the *Ralph Talbot* as they go.

2. EASTERN SOLOMONS – August 23, 1942

An attempt to run supplies to the Japanese troops on Guadalcanal is supported by the aircraft-carriers *Shokaku*, *Zuikaku*, and *Ryujo*. Vice-Admiral Fletcher's Task Force 61, patrolling to the east of the Solomon Islands, sights the Japanese fleet. The Japanese reverse course, and avoid the American strike aircraft.

August 24: *Ryujo*, sailing ahead of the main Japanese fleet, is sighted by an American flying boat. An armed reconnaissance is flown off from *Enterprise*, and followed, at 1345 hours, by a strike force from *Saratoga*. *Ryujo* launches her aircraft to attack Henderson Field. Just as the American strike flies off, another reconnaissance aircraft sights *Shokaku* and *Zuikaku*, who have launched a massive striking force. An attempt to divert the US aircraft to the new target fails, but the *Ryujo* is sunk. *Enterprise* is hit three times by dive-bombers, but is able to continue recovering her aircraft.

3. CAPE ESPERANCE – October 11/12, 1942

American supply convoy sails for Guadalcanal. It is escorted by a cruiser squadron commanded by Rear-Admiral Scott, which is also to ambush any Japanese forces moving down the Slot.

October 11/12: A Japanese convoy, covered by Rear-Admiral Goto's cruiser squadron, moves down the Slot. Scott receives information of its approach, and steers to intercept it. 2325 hours: The cruiser *Helena*'s radar detects the Japanese at a range of 14 miles but she fails to inform Scott. At 2333 hours he decides to reverse course, but in the confusion the cohesion of his force is broken. Scott then learns of the enemy's approach. The destroyer *Duncan* attacks independently, and the *Helena* opens fire, followed by the other cruisers. An order to cease fire does not take effect until the *Aoba* and *Furutaka* have been severely damaged. The Japanese turn and retreat, and during the pursuit they damage the *Boise* and lose the destroyer *Fubuki*.

4. SANTA CRUZ – October 24/26, 1942

The Japanese Combined Fleet moves to the north of Guadalcanal, ready to fly aircraft in to Henderson Field as soon as it is captured.
October 24: US Task Force 16 *(Enterprise)* rejoins Task Force 17 *(Hornet)*, and is ordered to sweep in a wide circle around the Santa Cruz Islands to intercept any Japanese forces approaching Guadalcanal.
October 25: At noon an American flying boat sights two Japanese aircraft-carriers, but an American strike fails to make contact.

Grumman TBF-1 Avenger. With the defensive and strike capabilities of a twin-engined aircraft, the Avenger had the handling of a carrier aircraft and could carry bombs, depth charges or torpedoes. **Max speed:** 259 mph at 11,200 feet. **Max range:** 1000 miles loaded. **Armament:** 2 × 5-inch, 1 × 3-inch and 1 × ·5-inch machine-guns; 1 × 22-inch torpedo or 2000-lb bombload

October 26: The Japanese fleet is again sighted and the *Enterprise* launches 16 dive-bombers to make an armed reconnaissance. At 0658 hours the Japanese aircraft-carriers *(Shokaku, Zuikaku,* and *Zuiho)* launch a first striking force. As a second force is being ranged up, two of the *Enterprise*'s dive-bombers attack *Zuiho* and put her out of action. 0730/0815 hours: *Enterprise* and *Hornet* launch three small strike forces. 0822 hours: *Shokaku* and *Zuikaku* launch their second strike. The main Japanese attack falls on *Hornet*, which is struck by two torpedoes and six bombs. Meanwhile *Shokaku* is seriously damaged by American dive-bombers. The second Japanese strike concentrates on the *Enterprise*: her forward lift is put permanently out of action, but her speed and manoeuvrability are unaffected. A third Japanese strike fails to achieve any results. The American forces then withdraw. *Hornet* is sunk by the Japanese when they find her burning hulk.

Below: Santa Cruz. A Japanese Kate makes a torpedo run on the *South Dakota*

Below: Santa Cruz. The Japanese cruiser *Chikuma* evades an American attack

US Navy

1. BATTLE OF SAVO ISLAND	
Cruisers Vincennes, Quincy, Astoria and Canberra	
2. BATTLE OF EASTERN SOLOMONS	
	Aircraft-carrier Ryujo
	Destroyer Mutsuki
3. BATTLE OF CAPE ESPERANCE	
Destroyer Duncan	Destroyer Fubuki
	Cruiser Furutaka
4. BATTLE OF SANTA CRUZ	
Aircraft-carrier Hornet	

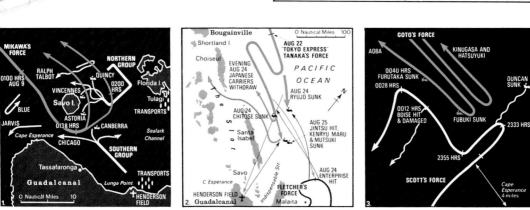

Below: The end of the US carrier *Wasp*, torpedoed by the Japanese submarine *I-19* while escorting a transport convoy

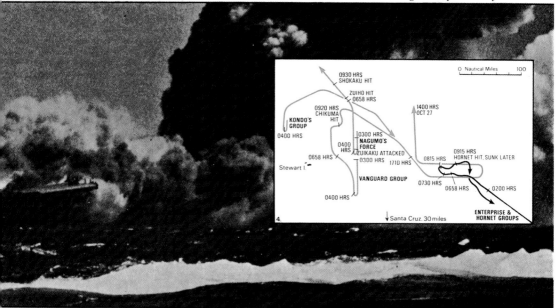

211

CRUISERS: KEY WARSHIPS IN THE

When the battle for Guadalcanal began in August 1942, the sea approaches to that vitally important island were dominated during the daylight hours by air power. And since two-thirds of the Japanese carrier fleet had been shattered at the Battle of Midway, and the Americans held the only air base in the Solomon Islands, air power was largely in American hands. No Japanese surface forces dared operate by day in those waters, but as darkness fell, the surface forces of both sides – particularly the cruisers and destroyers – moved in and clashed in savage combat in the narrow straits between the islands. In these skirmishes the Japanese showed themselves initially the masters. The Americans had radar, but the Japanese crews were trained to the highest pitch of night-fighting efficiency, and they had the superb 'Long Lance' torpedo – better than any torpedo in the American armoury. But the Americans had enormous reserves of ships and men to throw into the fight, whereas the Japanese ships and their crack crews, exhausted by battle after battle, were irreplaceable.

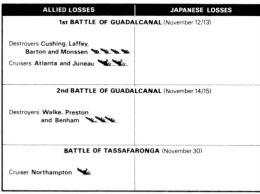

ALLIED LOSSES	JAPANESE LOSSES
1st BATTLE OF GUADALCANAL (November 12/13)	
Destroyers Cushing, Laffey, Barton and Monssen	
Cruisers Atlanta and Juneau	
2nd BATTLE OF GUADALCANAL (November 14/15)	
Destroyers Walke, Preston and Benham	
BATTLE OF TASSAFARONGA (November 30)	
Cruiser Northampton	

△ Naval balance sheet for the last battles for Guadalcanal

△ '1st Guadalcanal', November 12/13. Callaghan's line of destroyers and cruisers was surprised by the Japanese, who smashed four destroyers and threw the US force into confusion – but *Hiei* was lost after US air attacks the following afternoon

GUADALCANAL BATTLES

BOISE

'2nd Guadalcanal', November 14/15. Again the Japanese were able to exploit their mastery of night combat; but the superior gun-power of the US battleships recouped the initial losses and sank the battleship *Kirishima*

**Map labels:**
KONDO'S FORCE
HASHIMOTO'S FORCE
2210 HRS JAPANESE SIGHT US SHIPS
KIRISHIMA ATAGO TAKAO & 2 DESTROYERS
NAGARA & 4 DESTROYERS
AYANAMI & URANAMI
SENDAI & DESTROYER SHADOW ENEMY
KIRISHIMA
NAGARA RETIRES
Savo Island
LEE'S FORCE
AYANAMI
2400 HRS WASHINGTON FIRES ON KIRISHIMA
SOUTH DAKOTA WASHINGTON GWIN PRESTON BENHAM WALKE
SOUTH DAKOTA DAMAGED
WALKE SUNK
PRESTON SUNK
2316 HRS BATTLESHIPS OPEN FIRE
2252 HRS
GWIN & BENHAM RETIRE DAMAGED
2322 HRS WALKE FIRES ON AYANAMI
2300 HRS WASHINGTON'S RADAR LOCATES SENDAI
Guadalcanal
0 Nautical Miles 10

USS BOISE

Boise belonged to the *Brooklyn* class of light cruisers, which had been started in the mid-1930s. In this class, the hull design placed the seaplane catapult in the stern, and the main armament was mounted in triple turrets. *Boise* received heavy damage in the Battle of Cape Esperance on October 9, where she was part of Admiral Scott's squadron. **Length:** 608½ feet (overall). **Beam:** 61¾ feet. **Draught:** 19½ feet. **Max speed:** 34 knots. **Range:** 14,500 miles at 15 knots. **Armament:** 15 6-inch, eight 5-inch, four 3-pounder; multiple 20-mm AA guns. Four aircraft. **Complement:** 868

CHOKAI (far left)

Chokai belonged to the *Takao* class, which was launched in 1927/28, and which represented the 'second generation' of Japan's 10,000-ton cruisers. Main distinguishing features were the massive bridge structure and the high elevation of the main battery (up to 70° for AA use). *Chokai* was Admiral Mikawa's flagship in the Battle of Savo Island on the night of August 8/9, 1942. **Length:** 650 feet (overall). **Beam:** 62½ feet. **Draught:** 16⅝ feet. **Max speed:** 33 knots. **Range:** 14,000 miles at 15 knots. **Armament:** ten 8-inch guns, four 4·7-inch guns; eight 24-inch torpedo tubes. **Complement:** 692

BATTLESHIPS CLASH AT GUADALCANAL

The later naval battles off Guadalcanal saw the first direct clashes between battleships of the American and Japanese fleets — clashes that were disastrous for the Japanese battle fleet. In two successive battles, the Japanese lost first the *Hiei* and then the *Kirishima*; serious damage was caused to the USS *South Dakota*, but neither of the two American battleships in the actions was lost. Ship for ship, the Americans had all the advantages: superior manoeuvrability, superior hitting-power, and vastly superior protection; against these advantages, the Japanese superiority in speed proved of little value. But in the crews the story was different: the Japanese crews were the product of long training and were able to get the very best out of their ships. The Americans had only just managed to produce another Pacific battle fleet out of new crews and new ships.

South Dakota and *Washington* represented the first two classes of the US Navy's new fast battleships; they featured shorter length to improve manoeuvrability, a massive armour-belt, and 16-inch guns.
Specifications for *South Dakota*. *Length:* 680 feet. *Beam:* 108 feet. *Draught:* 29 feet. *Speed:* 28 knots. *Max armour belt thickness:* 18 inches. *Armament:* nine 16-inch, 16 5-inch, 56 40-mm. AA. Three aircraft. *Complement:* 2,500

△ 'Battle of Tassafaronga', November 30. This was the last major clash before the Japanese pulled out of Guadalcanal. Tanaka repeated all the successful Japanese tactics, sinking one US cruiser and crippling four others which were towed back to Tulagi for repairs

Kirishima and her sister-ship **Hiei** were both *Kongo*-class battleships. These ships had been classed as battle-cruisers when completed during the First World War, but were reclassed as fast battleships during the 1930s.
Specifications for Kirishima. *Length:* 730 feet. *Beam:* 101 feet. *Draught:* 32 feet. *Speed:* 30 knots. *Max armour belt thickness:* 8 inches. *Armament:* eight 14-inch, 14 6-inch, eight 5-inch AA, 20 25-mm AA. Three aircraft. *Complement:* 1,437

THE ROAD TO VICTORY....

In the early months of 1943, with renewed confidence following the six-month ordeal of Guadalcanal, American forces in the Pacific took the initiative. Using newly-developed techniques of amphibious warfare and the strategy of island-hopping to establish an overlapping system of controlled air-space, the bitterly-fought US offensive in New Georgia developed into a relentless advance through the Solomons towards Japan's massive strategic base of Rabaul in New Britain.

Meanwhile, in late 1942, Australian troops in New Guinea had shown that as a jungle fighter the Japanese soldier was not unbeatable. After months of bitter struggle along the Kokoda Trail a major enemy assault on Port Moresby – key to Australia and naval control of the South Pacific – had finally been crushed.

And then, in April, 1943, US fighters ambushed and shot down a plane carrying Admiral Yamamoto, undoubtedly Japan's outstanding naval strategist of the century. Everywhere the fortunes of the Rising Sun were waning. For the Allies, though, victories in the Solomons and New Guinea were just the beginning of a long, bloody campaign . . . one that would take them, island by island in the face of heroic enemy resistance, all the way to Okinawa.

Above: American soldiers struggle through Solomons swamps

Above: Australian troops in New Guinea numbered 54,000

Buffalo. This armoured amphibious carrier was able to carry assault troops to the heart of enemy beach defences and proved invaluable during the Pacific War: **Speed:** 27 mph (land), 5·7 knots (sea). **Range:** 140 miles (land), 80 miles (sea). **Load:** 4·5 tons or 40 troops

GUADALCANAL TO OKINAWA

American and Australian forces bound towards Japan, island-hopping from Guadalcanal to Okinawa

CHI HA Type 97. This 1937-model Japanese medium tank was used extensively in Burma, China and on Guadalcanal. **Weight:** 15 tons. **Length:** 18 feet. **Armour:** 25-mm (max). **Crew:** 4. **Armament:** 1×57-mm gun; 2×7·7-mm machine-guns. **Speed:** 25 mph. **Range:** 120 miles

By December 1943, the situation in the Pacific was tense. In New Guinea, the Australian and American divisions under General MacArthur were closing in on the Huon Peninsular which was to fall that month. Further east, Admiral Nimitz's forces, with the Solomon Islands safely secured, had taken Tarawa Atoll in the Gilbert Islands in late November after a bitterly contested landing and were preparing for the next amphibious attack on the Marshall Islands in the central Pacific. As the two prongs of the Allied advance — MacArthur in New Guinea and Nimitz in the Solomons — had struggled forward in the summer of 1943, it had been thought necessary to capture Rabaul, the big Japanese naval airbase in New Britain. But as American air power began to overwhelm the Japanese, it was decided to bypass Rabaul and let it wither away through lack of supplies. During 1944 Nimitz's amphibious forces were to advance to the Marshalls, within bombing range of the great Japanese base at Truk which would be bypassed, and thence to Ponape in the Caroline Islands. Meanwhile MacArthur, supported by the 7th Fleet, was to work westward along the New Guinea coast, capturing Manus and its fine harbour in the Admiralty Islands en route. Thus by the end of 1944, the two prongs of the advance would meet for an attack on the Philippines which MacArthur was determined should be the next objective. But since Admiral King preferred that Nimitz's forces should swing north to the Marianas Islands and Formosa, no decision was taken at the time, and the argument eventually continued for many months.

THE MARSHALLS

On 1st February 1944, the 4th Marine Division landed on Kwajalein Atoll. The lesson of Tarawa had been well learned. Area bombardment which had failed to neutralize Japanese resistance there was replaced by close-range gunfire at selected targets. Small islands were captured to provide flank artillery support. Amphibious DUKWs were introduced for the first time in the Pacific. The results were good: the northern islands of Roi and Namur were taken on 2nd February by the marines and Kwajalein itself on 4th February by the army. Six weeks ahead of programme, Eniwetok Island was assaulted by the reserve which had not been required at Kwajalein and its capture was complete by the 23rd February.

THE MARIANAS

The next objective was now the Marianas Islands from which B-29 bombers would be able to reach the Japanese homeland. Saipan was to be attacked first on 15th June, followed by Tinian and Guam as soon as conditions allowed. Two vast assault forces, the northern comprising 71,000 troops for Saipan and Tinian and the southern of 56,000 men for Guam, were formed and the preliminary pounding from the air was allotted Task Force 58 of Admiral Spruance's 5th Fleet. This task force now contained no less than four separate aircraft-carrier groups and each had its own escort of battleships or cruisers

Above: Out of a 4836-man garrison, 4690 Japanese died in the battle for Tarawa. The two above committed *hara-kiri* in their bunker rather than surrender

Below: A Japanese dive-bomber crashes over the US Saipan invasion fleet

and destroyers and carried about 250 aircraft. On 11th June, the air attack started, the first targets being Guam, Saipan, and Tinian, with a diversion by two of the groups to neutralize Chichi Jima and Iwo Jima on the 12th. By 13th June, air supremacy was complete and on 15th June the first Americans landed in Saipan, supported by a bombarding group from Task Force 58.

THE PHILIPPINE SEA

But the Japanese had suspected that the Marianas or Palau in the western Carolines would be the next target and had prepared an elaborate plan to lure the American fleet within range of shore-based aircraft after which carrier aircraft from the Japanese main fleet would deliver the coup de grâce. The result was the Battle of the Philippine Sea on 19-20th June — the greatest carrier battle of history. Neither fleet sighted the other but during the action American air-strikes virtually destroyed remaining Japanese air strength at small loss. Although only two of the eight Japanese carriers were sunk (three were seriously damaged), there can be little doubt that the battle dealt the Japanese navy a blow from which it never recovered. The subsequent assaults were severe and long drawn out, but the issue was never in doubt. Saipan was secured by 9th July, Tinian by 1st August, and Guam by 15th August.

NEW BRITAIN

Attention must now turn to the left-hand prong. In the last weeks of December 1943, the 7th and 1st Marine Divisions, the latter a veteran of Guadalcanal which had been resting and re-training in Australia, landed on Cape Gloucester at the western end of New Britain and quickly established themselves ashore. Despite appalling terrain — the intelligence reports had been too optimistic — and bitter Japanese resistance, the airfield was captured on 1st January 1944, and thereafter the marines pushed steadily eastwards against a skilful and determined enemy retiring through easily defended jungle. The 5th Marine Division landed on

Villaumez Peninsula on 6th March, and the airfield at Talasea was quickly taken; the western part of the island was now secure and the straits between New Britain and New Guinea were safe. By the end of April an army division, the 45th, arrived to replace the marines who were released for further amphibious attacks. Meanwhile, on 29th February, units from the 1st Cavalry Division had made a reconnaissance in force on Los Negros Island in the Admiralties. MacArthur himself came ashore on the first day to assess the strength of the defences and it was soon evident that more forces would be needed. During the next two weeks, units from the 5th, 8th, and 12th Cavalry Divisions landed, both at Los Negros and on Manus Island itself near the airfield at Lorengau. By the end of March, the main resistance had ended, though sporadic fighting continued during May. A fine natural harbour was now available – it was used later by the British Pacific Fleet – and two large airfields were quickly constructed. The defence, as always, had been determined to the point of suicide and no Japanese prisoners were taken. A comparison of the American casualties – 329 killed and 1,189 wounded – with those of the Japanese – 3,280 killed – reflects the tenacity of the Japanese and the skill and weapon superiority of the Americans.

Concurrently, on 20th March, an unopposed landing by the 4th Marine Division on Emirau in the St Matthias Islands led to the speedy construction of a fine airfield. A glance at the map will show that both Rabaul and Kavieng, another Japanese base on New Ireland, were now surrounded by airfields at Manus, Emirau, Talasea, and Green Island, and the usefulness of the Japanese garrisons was rapidly nullified. Amphibious attacks were now unnecessary and both bases were 'mopped up' in 1945.

THE STRATEGIES

There were three important strategic possibilities – the first to defer the dispatch of the British fleet to join Nimitz in the central Pacific and to concentrate all available Commonwealth forces in South-East Asia with an object of completing the conquest of Burma, Sumatra, Malaya, and possibly Indo-China; the second to reduce the effort in South-East Asia and to form a British Commonwealth Task Force of all arms in the south-west Pacific under MacArthur. In this case, the British fleet could be detached to join Nimitz in the central Pacific if this was found desirable. The third possibility was to send the British fleet to the Pacific as soon as possible and to adopt a modified effort in S-E Asia.

Eventually it was decided at the Octagon Conference at Quebec in September 1944 to adopt the third course, with the addition of a bomber force of forty squadrons of Lancasters to join in the air attack on Japan when Germany had been defeated. President Roosevelt accepted this course in the face of a reluctant Admiral King, who would have preferred to finish off Japan unaided, and in the event, the coming of the Kamikaze suicide attacks made the contribution of the British fleet most welcome.

We must now return to the Pacific in the autumn of 1944. Admiral Halsey, with his

Above: A painting by T. Ishikawa shows American and Japanese carrier-borne aircraft duelling over the South Pacific, an ocean where the skies ruled supreme

3rd Fleet (the Fleet was called the 3rd under Halsey and the 5th under Spruance; the ships were the same but the staff and command changed) was attacking the Philippines with his aircraft in mid-September, when, finding opposition unexpectedly light, he suggested that the invasion of Leyte Gulf be brought forward two months and that the operations against Yap, Palau, and Mindanao be abandoned. This was at once agreed by the Joint Chiefs of Staff, then meeting at Quebec, and so the shape of future strategy was decided. MacArthur's 'Philippines first' concept had won.

LEYTE GULF

The operations which then centred on Leyte Gulf involved the greatest number of warships ever engaged in battle at sea, while the land and air force units which took part were also very powerful. Again, the Japanese navy had planned to lure away the main American fleet, leaving the amphibious forces to be destroyed by two powerful surface forces attacking from the west. The plan at first succeeded admirably and on 24th October, Halsey with the whole of the 3rd Fleet, was drawn northwards by the Japanese aircraft carrier force under Ozawa. Ozawa had few aircraft in his carriers and his mission was suicidal; he lost all four carriers, but the beachhead in the Leyte Gulf was left very lightly defend-

ed – by a few escort-carriers and destroyers. However, the main Japanese surface force under Kurita, which had lost a battleship and two cruisers from air and submarine attacks en route, hesitated, and so reached the beachhead via the San Bernardino Straits too late. By then the second surface force under Nishima had already been destroyed in the Surigao Straits by Admiral Ollendorf's battleships, cruisers, and destroyers, and Kurita's nerve seemed to fail. He mistook the escort carriers and

Model 97 81-mm Mortar. A particularly useful weapon, this heavy Japanese mortar could fire delayed-action shells. **Weight:** 145 lbs. **Length:** 49·5 inches. **Range:** 3100 yards. **Weight of projectile:** 6·93 lbs

Above left: On Luzon, the horrifying effects of an American flame-thrower attack. Above centre: US Marines inching their

destroyers at the beachhead, which fought very bravely, for a 'gigantic task force', and after a short engagement he turned back, so losing a perfect opportunity of causing extensive damage to the assault forces. The Japanese navy had failed, and so ended its last great battle of the war for it never succeeded in getting into action again.

Ashore, the fighting was hard and there were delays in setting up the airfields, but after heavy losses Leyte Island was secured by 25th December.

LUZON & IWO JIMA

The next step was the invasion of Luzon which started on 9th January 1945. Again, the fighting was bitter and involved the largest scale land operations of the Pacific War. Admiral Kreuger's 6th army contained over 200,000 men, and the Japanese defenders over 250,000 men. The approach to Lingayan Gulf was made most disagreeable by the first *Kamikaze* air attacks, which succeeded in hitting several Ameri-

can and Australian ships, but the landing itself was unopposed and the serious fighting started well away from the beachhead. Corregidor, MacArthur's former headquarters, was taken on 21st February and Manila was secured by the end of March; after this the operation became that of 'mopping up' a desperate and fanatical enemy, but by April the main battle was over the the key points captured.

Almost at once, Nimitz took over the headlines by the attack on Iwo Jima, which was needed as an airbase for fighter planes to escort the bombers over Japan, and as a refuge for damaged aircraft. After several weeks of aerial bombardment from the Marianas and several days battering by ships, the 4th and 5th Marine Division landed on 19th February 1945. The 3rd Marine Division was in reserve, but was soon committed to the fight. Spruance's 5th Fleet was in support and made sure that no reinforcements reached Iwo Jima. The island was small—only eight square miles

—but it had three airfield sites and the volcanic hills had been made into defensive warrens with many disguised weapon sites. Serious fortification did not start till December 1944, and the full plan was not completed by the day of the landing but the garrison had been reinforced to a total of 21,000 men. The initial landing was not strongly opposed and the Americans were first attacked when about 200 yards from the beach, when they met a murderous fire from the island's caves, pillboxes, and blockhouses. But they had been able to land much engineering equipment as well as tanks and guns and were well prepared for a tough battle. Co-operation with the bombarding ships and aircraft was excellent and gradually the most important defence positions were destroyed, but the honeycombs were difficult to subdue and the island was not declared secure until 18th March, while fighting continued spasmodically until 26th March. Even so, the first damaged B-29 landed safely on

Yamato
Displacement: 64,170 tons. **Dimensions:** 863 × 127 × 35 feet. **Armour:** *Main belt* 16 inches; *Deck* 7¾ inches; *Turrets* 20-25 inches. **Armament:** 9 × 18-inch, 12 × 6·1-inch AA, 24 × 25-mm AA, 4 × 13-mm guns, plus 6 aircraft. **Crew:** 3332. **Speed:** 27 knots

way up the beach on Iwo Jima. Above right: The scene on Okinawa beach in the early days after the massive US landings

4th March (the first of 850 emergency landings in three months) and on 7th April the first fighters left to escort a daylight bombing raid on Tokyo. The Americans lost about 7,000 marines and sailors.

OKINAWA

The next main operations quickly followed with the invasion of Okinawa by Buckner's 10th Army, which included three marine divisions for the intial landings. At this point the Royal Navy came into action in the Pacific with the task of neutralizing the airfields on the Sakishima Islands, through which the Japanese hoped to fly reinforcements to Okinawa.

After a bombardment of Palembang in Sumatra, the British fleet had arrived in Australia on 4th February 1945. By April, when Okinawa was attacked, its main elements were four aircraft-carriers, two battleships, four cruisers, eleven destroyers, and a large 'fleet train' of supply ships which enabled operations to continue

for many weeks without putting in to harbour. Admiral Fraser was in overall command. Admiral Rawlings the commander at sea, and Admiral Vian in charge of the carriers. It is enough to say that the British force acquitted itself well and in particular that its armoured deck aircraft-carriers were able to survive the *Kamikaze* attacks whereas the lighter decked Americans had to retire when struck.

The attack on Okinawa was on an enormous scale. During the campaign, which lasted eighty-two days, over half a million Allied troops took part and the initial assault was carried out by 183,000 soldiers and marines. The ships at sea suffered severely from the *Kamikaze* attacks and many were sunk or damaged during their long ordeal. Again, the troops landed without opposition, but soon came up against a fanatical defence. The campaign was long and bitter but the island was finally secure by 21st June, by which time the Japanese had lost 110,000 men, while the Americans

had suffered nearly 8,000 killed and the ships afloat nearly 5,000 – the latter almost all victims of *Kamikaze* attacks.

Although it was not known at the time, the last great operation of the Pacific War was over, though in July and August Halsey's 3rd Fleet, of which the British contingent formed part, cruised freely off Honshu, attacking the enemy with aircraft and bombarding him.

INSIDE JAPAN

It is now time to consider the internal situation in Japan. By the middle of 1944, a number of thoughtful politicians and serving officers had come to the conclusion that defeat was inevitable and that it was in the interest of the country to negotiate a settlement of the war as soon as possible. Otherwise, it was argued, Communism would follow the inevitable chaos.

After the fall of Saipan in July 1944, the government of General Tojo, who had been Prime Minister since 1941, fell and a

DEATH OF A BEHEMOTH

The *Yamato*, the greatest battleship ever built, had also the shortest active career of any capital ship in the Second World War. Intended originally to be the first of a 'super' battle fleet, she was the foundation of Japanese naval hopes of defeating the Americans at sea. She was believed to be absolutely superior in guns, speed, and armour to any other capital ship, as indeed she was – but without air cover these great assets were of no avail. The pointless loss of this ship in a 'special' attack on the Okinawa landings emphasises the straits to which the Japanese navy was reduced.

coalition took over with a mandate to continue to prosecute the war. Tojo had accumulated much power over the years and he ended up as his own Chief of the Army General Staff as well as being Prime Minister. He refused to consider the possibility of defeat and believed, like many of the Japanese generals, that honour demanded the destruction of the whole Japanese people rather than voluntary submission. By early 1945, the Emperor was extremely worried and he consulted many elder statesmen, most of whom advised the continuation of the war. Prince Konoye, a former Prime Minister, declared roundly, however, that the war had been lost and that peace must be made as soon as possible. The loss of Iwo Jima in April 1945 brought the fall of the coalition government: almost simultaneously the Russians announced that they would not renew the neutrality pact with Japan which was due to expire in April 1946. After much discussion, an elderly Admiral, Suzuki, was nominated as Prime Minister with a clear mandate to bring the war to an end as soon as possible. The shipping situation was disastrous, heavy air-raids were destroying Japanese cities one by one, and production of war materials was coming to an end. Suzuki's task was not easy — most of the generals were fanatically determined on resistance to the bitter end and the Japanese people had relapsed into fatalistic despair. After the end of the war in Europe, it was decided to ask the Russians for mediation and talks were held with the Russian ambassador to Japan Jacob Malik. But the Russians did not answer and it was not until 12th July that the Japanese ambassador in Moscow was ordered by cable to approach the Russian government. On 21st July he made a formal request for Soviet mediation to bring the war to an end. The Potsdam Conference was then in session, and Stalin informed Roosevelt and Churchill of this approach (of which the Americans were already aware through their reading of the Japanese cyphers), but nothing was done because the Japanese had not yet agreed to surrender unconditionally. Behind all these discussions loomed the atomic bomb, which was successfully tested during the conference. The first bomb was dropped on 6th August, and the second on 9th August, on the same day as the Russian invasion of Manchuria. On 15th August

the Emperor broadcast his rescript which ended the war.

The Russian invasion was swift and successful and the whole of Manchuria and north Korea was in their hands by the end of August. Elsewhere, Hong Kong was reoccupied by British naval forces in early September, and in many Pacific islands surrenders were being arranged. On 2nd September a formal surrender ceremony was held aboard the American battleship *Missouri* in Tokyo Bay. General MacArthur signed as Supreme Commander of the Allied Powers, and he was followed by representatives of all the powers which had taken part in the war against Japan.

Thus, happily, the great invasion of the Japanese homeland, which had been planned during the summer of 1945, was unnecessary. 'Operation Olympic' against Kyusho was due to take place on 1st November, and the main operations against Honshu in March or April of 1946 ('Operation Coronet'). Both invasions would have been on an enormous scale. A British Commonwealth force of two or three divisions was planned to join Coronet and by then British bombers would also have been taking part in the air attack on Japan. While there can be no doubt as to the eventual outcome, the operations would have been tough and losses high. The Japanese armies were still intact and they had good supplies of ammunition, while the remaining aircraft would have been used in suicide attacks which could cause great damage. The American High Command was divided on the problem of whether the invasion would be ultimately necessary and some high officers believed that capitulation would come through the air and sea blockade alone. Historians are similarly divided, though the full knowledge of the underground work of the peace party in the summer of 1945 has only been widely known comparatively recently, and thus the evidence against invasion has been somewhat strengthened. It is too soon for a certain judgement to be made — the issue is still fogged by inter-service rivalry. Whatever the decision of history, however, nothing can alter the superb achievements of the American forces nor of the industry which worked miracles of production to support them. Nor can the story of the fanatical bravery and skill — however misguided — of the Japanese fighting men ever be diminished.

Above: A Japanese suicide plane *(Kamikaze)* approaches an American warship, explodes in a ball of fire, and leaves in its wake a serious danger to the ship and crew. Left: A small section of a fire-bombed Japanese city.

National Archives

Artwork Index